Macroeconomic Modeling

Macroeconomic Modeling

The Cowles Commission Approach

Ray C. Fair

The MIT Press
Cambridge, Massachusetts
London, England

The MIT Press would like to thank the anonymous peer reviewers who provided comments on drafts of this book. The generous work of academic experts is essential for establishing the authority and quality of our publications. We acknowledge with gratitude the contributions of these otherwise uncredited readers.

This book was set in Stone Serif and Stone Sans by Westchester Publishing Services. Printed and bound in the United States of America.

Library of Congress Cataloging-in-Publication Data

Names: Fair, Ray C., author.
Title: Macroeconomic modeling : the Cowles Commission approach / Ray C. Fair.
Description: Cambridge, Massachusetts : The MIT Press, [2024] | Includes bibliographical references and index.
Identifiers: LCCN 2024017169 (print) | LCCN 2024017170 (ebook) | ISBN 9780262549844 (paperback) | ISBN 9780262380904 (pdf) | ISBN 9780262380911 (epub)
Subjects: LCSH: Econometric models. | Macroeconomics—Mathematical models.
Classification: LCC HB141 .F339 2024 (print) | LCC HB141 (ebook) | DDC 330.01/5195—dc23/eng/20240418
LC record available at https://lccn.loc.gov/2024017169
LC ebook record available at https://lccn.loc.gov/2024017170

10 9 8 7 6 5 4 3 2 1

Contents

I Introduction

1 Why This Book?

I was an economics graduate student at MIT, starting in 1964. This was a period when large-scale macroeconometric models were beginning to be developed. This research had a strong empirical focus. At that time, the data were not very good, and considerable effort was needed to understand the data, both their strengths and weaknesses. The data sharply restricted what could be estimated. There was a pragmatic aspect to this research. The aim was to estimate aggregate relationships and possibly use these estimated relationships to predict the future course of the economy. This research was not always elegant, did not always use consistent estimation techniques, sometimes overreached, possibly at times confused correlation with causation, and possibly data mined. But there was a serious attempt to explain the data, to estimate structural equations that fit well.

The specification of the structural equations to be estimated was constrained by economic theory, but fairly loosely. Theory was used to specify the left-hand side (LHS) and right-hand side (RHS) variables in an equation to be estimated. Usually, these equations were thought of as a decision equation of a representative agent, like a consumption equation of a household. The LHS variable was the decision variable, and the RHS variables were what the theory said affected the decision variable. The choices could, for example, be guided by a utility maximizing model or, for firms, a profit maximizing model. There was much back and forth movement between empirical results and theory. If some RHS variable was not statistically significant, another variable might be tried. Lagged dependent variables were used freely, and they generally greatly improved the fit of the equations. The use of lagged dependent variables could be justified either as picking up partial adjustment effects or as reflecting adaptive expectations, and there was usually little attempt to distinguish between the two reasons. There was no attempt to impose the restriction that expectations are rational. Expectations were meant to be proxied by lagged values of variables. This style of research is sometimes called the "Cowles Commission" (CC) approach. Although it was used by some researchers at the Cowles Commission beginning in the 1950s, it goes back further. An important early example is the work of Tinbergen (1939). Here are two quotes from Tinbergen (1939) that give a flavor of the approach. The first concerns the choice of lags in an estimated equation, and the second concerns the macroeconomic nature of the analysis.

> The method essentially starts with *a priori* considerations about what explanatory variables are to be included. This choice must be based on economic theory or common sense. If *a priori* knowledge regarding the lags to be taken is available, these may be specified also. In many cases, for example, reactions are so quick that only lags of zero length are acceptable. If no such *a priori* knowledge is available, lags may be tried according to the same principle as coefficients—i.e., by finding what lags give the highest correlation. (p. 10)
>
> It goes without saying that any regression coefficient found for a market or a group of markets represents only an average for all individuals included, and cannot be applied to problems concerning one individual. (p. 12)

There was what one might consider a "complete model" feature to this research. Given that the aim was to explain and possibly predict the macroeconomy, many important variables had to be explained. On the aggregate demand side, for example, there are various categories of consumption and of investment, as well as imports, exports, and government spending. Government spending variables and tax rates were usually taken to be exogenous, and exports many times were, but the general aim was not to take as exogenous some variable that seemed clearly endogenous. This obviously led to large models. Disaggregation was also taken seriously. If, for example, expenditures on consumer services behave differently than expenditures on consumer durables, which is obvious from both theory and the data, separate equations would need to be estimated and generally were. Also, residential investment, nonresidential fixed investment, and inventory investment behave much differently, and separate equations were generally estimated for each.

In this book, I will call this procedure the "Cowles Commission approach," although this is somewhat misleading. Heckman (2000) points out that the approach outlined in Haavelmo (1944) is much narrower, being in the tradition of classical statistical inference. There is no back and forth between empirical results and specifications. Heckman also points out that Haavelmo's approach is almost never followed in practice. It is much too rigid. Also, not everyone at the Cowles Commission followed this approach. But for want of a better alternative, I will use this phrase.

Beginning in the 1970s, this style of research fell out of favor among academics. Some of the model-building work became commercial. This led to subjective adjustments of forecasts to try to make them more accurate. Because the models were not taken that seriously, there was less concern about testing and about using consistent estimation techniques. Ordinary least squares (OLS) was generally used for the commercial models even when not appropriate. Some of the models became very large, requiring teams of researchers. Coordination became difficult, and the models became difficult to follow.

In the academic literature, the use of lagged variables to pick up partial adjustment and expectational effects was called into question. If this use is not a good approximation to reality, the model will be misspecified and may have misleading properties. The true structural parameters will not be estimated, and so the reduced-form equations will not be right. This problem is discussed in Marschak's (1953) classic paper. Lucas (1976) stressed possible errors in specifying how expectations are formed. In particular, if expectations are rational and if a policy rule is changed, then agents will know this and adjust their expectations accordingly. Under adaptive expectations, expectations only adjust over time as the actual values of variables change. Later, it became possible using the CC approach to add the constraint of model consistent expectations of future values of variables,[1] but not at this time.

The backlash against this work led to smaller models with rational expectations and with much tighter theoretical restrictions. It eventually led to dynamic, stochastic, general equilibrium (DSGE) models. A widely cited and analyzed model is that of Smets and Wouters (2007). Models of this type are still being used today. (I will use "DSGE" to refer to this general body of work even though not all of it is strictly a DSGE model.)

So why this book? One cost of the backlash has been the loss of complete models. DSGE models are "general equilibrium" within the context of the model, but they generally leave out variables that may be important in complete macro models. For example, consumption of services, nondurables, and durables behave quite differently, and it is problematic to not treat them separately. The same is true for nonresidential fixed investment, residential investment, and inventory investment. The level of imports is likely to be important in a complete model, and in many cases, it is not a variable in the model. The models are also less influenced by the data in that a number of parameters are usually calibrated.

My view is that the backlash has gone too far. The CC approach is virtually excluded from the academic literature. There should be room for alternative methodologies. At the least, the CC approach can provide a check on the new macro. Given that the CC approach is more empirically based, if some result is contrary to results using the CC approach, this may be a cause of concern. There is also need for complete models, which the CC approach is better at than the DSGE approach.

Other than what has just been said, this book is not meant to be a criticism or evaluation of DSGE models. It is meant to be constructive in simply presenting a more empirical-based methodology. Since this methodology is not generally taught in graduate macro courses anymore, I have tried to write the book assuming that I am starting from scratch; therefore, I explain more than I would if I were writing a professional journal article.

The approach is explained using a particular model, my US macroeconometric model, called the "US model." The specification and estimation of the stochastic equations of the model are discussed in chapter 4. This is by far the longest chapter in the book since the core of a model is the set of estimated equations. Part III uses the model to analyze various macro questions and events. As will be explained, some of these results are contrary to those in the current literature.

I have tried to be completely forthright regarding the strengths and weaknesses of the CC approach. In the development of the US model, using this approach I have indicated where the estimates and results may be unreliable. Sometimes, an estimated equation is retained even though the estimates may be weak for lack of a better alternative. But the data always rule. There is no calibration, and I don't impose any coefficient restrictions without testing them.

2 Macro Data

Related to the second quote of Tinbergen in chapter 1, macro data are aggregate. The two main sources of data in the United States are the national income and product accounts (NIPA) from the Department of Commerce and the flow of funds accounts (FFA) from the Board of Governors of the Federal Reserve System. Given these data, one is forced to use a representative agent model. Some recent work in macro stresses heterogeneity, which clearly exists in the economy, but this work is useful in the construction of complete macro models only if it provides insights into how to specify a representative agent's decision equation. There are, for example, data on the total consumption of services from the NIPA, but not consumption by different types of households. One can obviously use survey and other data to ask macro questions, but when it comes to building a complete macro model, one is back to the NIPA and FFA data.

There are, however, sectors in the aggregate data, so one can talk about a representative agent per sector. For the US model, there are six sectors: household, firm, financial, foreign, federal government, and state and local government. There can be a number of decision variables per agent. For example, each category of consumption can be taken as a decision variable of a household. Similarly, nonresidential fixed investment and inventory investment can be taken as separate decision variables of a firm.

There are a variety of financial constraints in the data. Each sector's total financial saving in a period is equal to its total income minus its total expenses. The sum of financial saving across all the sectors is zero since once sector's income is some other sector's expense. There are also equations linking stocks and flows. The change in a sector's net financial assets in a period is equal to its financial saving plus any capital gains or losses on its net financial assets during the period. These definitions can be constructed by linking the NIPA and FFA data.

Many macro variables are "smooth" in the sense that they are serially correlated. An equation with only the constant term and the lagged dependent variable (LDV) on the RHS in many cases fits well. The data used for the US model are quarterly, beginning in 1952.1 and ending in 2023.2, 286 observations. While this may seem like a large number of observations, there are only two high-inflation periods in the data—the 1970s and the very recent period. The period of very high interest rates occurs only under Volcker (late 1970s and early 1980s). The period of large stock-price and housing-price fluctuations began only in about 1995. Excluding various extreme periods from the estimation can result in quite different estimates because of reduced variance of the explanatory variables. The estimates may mostly be just picking up the serial correlation. More will be said about this later.

Another aim of this book is to stress the importance of being careful with the data, something that I mentioned in chapter 1 was true when I came to MIT in 1964. Care with the data has not been a strong point of the new macro. As noted in chapter 1, the Smets and Wouters (2007) model has been widely used in the literature, including the data in the model. Many of the variables in the model, however, are mismeasured. First, real consumption is taken to be nominal consumption divided by the GDP deflator, not the consumption deflator. This results in large errors in measuring real consumption. The same is true for real investment, which is taken to be nominal investment divided by the GDP deflator.

Second, hours worked is taken to be average weekly hours of all persons in the nonfarm business sector multiplied by total civilian employment. This implicitly assumes that government workers have the same average weekly hours as workers in the nonfarm business sector, which is not the case. But more important, civilian employment from the household survey is used instead of jobs from the establishment survey. Some people have two jobs, and so civilian employment underestimates the number of jobs in the economy. This is not just a level difference because the number of people with two jobs is a cyclical variable. The correct data are simply not being used.[1]

An interesting aside about the macro profession is that business economists, who generally don't have the prestige of academic economists, would never be caught confusing household survey data with establishment survey data (or using the wrong deflators). On the Friday morning of each month in which the two surveys are simultaneously released, business economists are glued to their computers waiting for the announcements. The data from both surveys are analyzed immediately.

The appendix lists all the data in the US model. Table A.5 lists the "raw data" variables, which are variables obtained directly from a data source. Table A.7 lists how each variable in the model is computed from the raw data variables. In principle, it would be possible to duplicate this work. The appendix discusses some adjustments that were made to the raw data variables. Chapter 6 explains the construction of some of the variables in the model and chapter 7 plots some of the key exogenous variables in the model.

establishment survey data by using the wrong deflators. On the [illegible]

3 The Econometrics

3.1 The General Model and Nonlinear Two-Stage Least Squares

In general, models in the CC tradition are dynamic, nonlinear, simultaneous, and can have errors that are serially correlated. Serial correlation of the errors if it exists likely comes about because of omitted variables. If a variable is excluded from an equation when it should not be and if the variable is serially correlated, this will lead to the error term being serially correlated.

Nonlinear two-stage least squares (NL2SLS) can deal with these problems and is easy to use. I will use this estimator throughout this book. The econometrics needed for the CC approach is thus fairly simple: it just requires learning one estimator!

The general model can be written:

$$f_i(y_t, y_{t-1}, \ldots, y_{t-p}, x_t, \alpha_i) = u_{it}, \quad i = 1, \ldots, n, \quad t = 1, \ldots, T, \tag{3.1}$$

where y_t is an n–dimensional vector of endogenous variables, x_t is a vector of exogenous variables, and α_i is a k_i–dimensional vector of coefficients in equation i. The first m equations are assumed to be stochastic, with the remaining equations identities (zero error terms). The vector of error terms, $u_t = (u_{1t}, \ldots, u_{mt})'$, is assumed to be *iid*. The function f_i may be nonlinear in variables and coefficients. u_i will be used to denote the T–dimensional vector $(u_{i1}, \ldots, u_{iT})'$. Finally, let G_i' denote the $k_i \times T$ matrix whose ith column is $\partial f_i(\ldots)/\partial \alpha_i$. The exogenous and lagged endogenous variables will be called "predetermined" variables.

This specification is fairly general. It includes as a special case the VAR model. It also incorporates autoregressive errors. If the original error term in equation i follows an rth-order autoregressive process, say $w_{it} = \rho_{1i} w_{it-1} + \cdots + \rho_{ri} w_{it-r} + u_{it}$, then equation i in the model in (3.1) can be assumed to have been transformed into one with u_{it} on the RHS. The autoregressive coefficients $\rho_{1i}, \ldots, \rho_{ri}$ are incorporated into the α_i coefficient vector, and additional lagged variable values are introduced. This transformation makes the equation nonlinear in coefficients if it were not otherwise, but this adds no further complications because the model is already allowed to be nonlinear. The assumption that u_t is *iid* is thus not as restrictive as it would be if the model were required to be linear in coefficients.

There can also be a priori restrictions on the coefficients in α_i. For a single-equation estimator like NL2SLS, however, there cannot be restrictions across the α_is.

The NL2SLS estimate of α_i (denoted $\hat{\alpha}_i$) is obtained by minimizing

$$S_i = u_i' Z_i (Z_i' Z_i)^{-1} Z_i' u_i = u_i' D_i u_i \tag{3.2}$$

with respect to α_i, where Z_i is a $T \times K_i$ matrix of first-stage regressors and K_i can differ from equation to equation. The first-stage regressors are assumed to be correlated with the RHS endogenous variables in the equation but not with the error term. An estimate of the covariance matrix of $\hat{\alpha}_i$ (denoted $\hat{V}_i$) is

$$\hat{V}_i = \hat{\sigma}_i^2 (\hat{G}_i' D_i \hat{G}_i)^{-1}, \tag{3.3}$$

where $\hat{G}_i'$ is G_i' evaluated at $\hat{\alpha}_i$ and $\hat{\sigma}_i^2 = T^{-1} \sum_{t=1}^{T} \hat{u}_{it}^2$, $\hat{u}_{it} = f_i(y_t, y_{t-1}, \ldots, y_{t-p}, x_t, \hat{\alpha}_i)$.

This minimization is computationally trivial. If the equation is linear in coefficients with non-serially correlated errors, there is a closed-form solution. Otherwise, a numerical nonlinear optimization algorithm like the DFP algorithm can be used.

It may help to consider the linear-in-coefficients case. Write equation i in (3.1) as

$$y_i = X_i \alpha_i + u_i, \tag{3.4}$$

where y_i is the T–dimensional vector $(y_{i1}, \ldots, y_{iT})'$ and X_i is a $T \times k_i$ matrix of observations on the explanatory variables in the equation. X_i includes both endogenous and predetermined variables. Both y_i and the variables in X_i can be nonlinear functions of other variables, and thus (3.4) is more general than the standard linear model. All that is required is that the equation be linear in α_i. Substituting $u_i = y_i - X_i \alpha_i$ into (3.2), differentiating with respect to α_i, and setting the derivatives equal to zero yields the following formula for $\hat{\alpha}_i$:

$$\hat{\alpha}_i = (X_i' D_i X_i)^{-1} X_i' D_i y_i = (\hat{X}_i' X_i)^{-1} \hat{X}_i' y_i, \tag{3.5}$$

where $\hat{X}_i = D_i X_i$ is the matrix of predicted values of the regression of X_i on Z_i. Since $D_i' = D_i$ and $D_i D_i = D_i$, $\hat{X}_i'\hat{X}_i = X_i' D_i D_i X_i = \hat{X}_i' D_i X_i = \hat{X}_i' X_i$, and thus (3.5) can be written as

$$\hat{\alpha}_i = (\hat{X}_i'\hat{X}_i)^{-1} \hat{X}_i' y_i, \tag{3.6}$$

which is the standard 2SLS formula in the linear-in-coefficients case. In this case, G_i' is simply X_i', and the formula (3.3) for $\hat{V}_i$ reduces to

$$\hat{V}_i = \hat{\sigma}_i^2 (\hat{X}_i'\hat{X}_i)^{-1}. \tag{3.7}$$

In the discussion of the estimated equations in chapter 4, a coefficient estimate will be said to be "significant" if its t-value is greater or equal to 1.96 in absolute value, a 95 percent confidence level.

3.2 Choosing First-Stage Regressors

In a linear model where analytic expressions for the reduced-form equations are available, the first-stage regressors (FSRs) are all the predetermined variables in the reduced-form equations. For nonlinear models, however, analytic expressions for the reduced-form equations are not generally available. In either case, there may be more predetermined variables than observations, in which case a subset has to be used. An advantage of the NL2SLS estimator is that consistent estimates of the reduced-form equations are not needed. All that is required is that the FSRs be uncorrelated with the error terms in the structural equations. Also, there can be different sets of FSRs for each structural equation.

There is no rigorous procedure for choosing FSRs; however, there are a few rules of thumb. Consider estimating an equation with y_{2t} and y_{3t} as RHS endogenous variables. The predetermined variables in the equations determining these two variables are candidates. Also, say that y_{4t} is a RHS endogenous in one of these equations, then the predetermined variables in the structural equation for y_{4t} are candidates. One can continue this procedure through further layers as desired.[1]

In the choice of FSRs for the US model, government spending variables are always lagged one quarter before being used as FSRs. This is to insure that even though these variables are assumed to be exogenous, there is no correlation between the error term in the equation and the FSRs. Also, as discussed in section 7.2, a wealth variable is lagged two quarters before being used as an FSR.

The list of FSRs for each equation is presented in the table for the equation, tables A1–A30. Although not shown in the tables, when a test requires adding a variable, the variable is added as an FSR if it is exogenous. If it is endogenous, its one-quarter-lagged value is added as an FSR.

3.3 Expectations of Agents

The predicted values from the FSRs that are used as explanatory variables in the second-stage regressions can, if desired, be interpreted as expectations of the agents. For example, the predicted value of income used in a consumer expenditure equation can be interpreted as a household's (actually, the household sector's) expectation of its income for the current period. These are not rational expectations, but just expectations based on predictions from the FSRs.

3.4 Robustness Tests for the Estimated Equations

Some single-equation tests are simply of the form of adding a variable or a set of variables to an equation and testing whether the addition is statistically significant. Let S_i^{**} denote the value of the minimand before the addition, let S_i^* denote the value after the addition, and let $\hat{\sigma}_{ii}$ denote the estimated variance of the error term after the addition. Under fairly general conditions, as discussed in Andrews and Fair (1988), $(S_i^{**} - S_i^*)/\hat{\sigma}_{ii}$ is distributed as χ^2 with k degrees of freedom, where k is the number of variables added. For the NL2SLS estimator, the minimand is defined in equation (3.2). If only one variable is added, the χ^2 test is simply the t-test. The following sections discuss some of the robustness tests done for the equations of the US model.

When discussing the robustness tests in chapter 4, adding a variable or variables will be said to be "significant" if the p-value is less than 0.05, a 95 percent confidence level. If the addition is significant, this is evidence of a lack of robustness.

3.4.1 Testing for Serial Correlation of the Error Term (RHO test)

As noted in section 3.1, if the error term in an equation follows an autoregressive process, the equation can be transformed and the coefficients of the autoregressive process can be estimated along with the structural coefficients. The NL2SLS estimates provide *t*-statistics for the estimates of the autoregressive coefficients along with the estimates of the structural coefficients. The significance of an autoregressive coefficient estimate is thus just a *t*-test. This is a better test than the Durbin–Watson test, which is biased if there is an LDV.

In some of the equations in the US model, significant autoregressive coefficients have been found, and these have been retained. For those equations where no autoregressive coefficient is used, it is informative to test whether one should be. One test, therefore, which will be called the "RHO" test, is to assume a first-order autoregressive process, estimate the first-order serial correlation coefficient, and test its significance.

3.4.2 Time Trend Test (*t* test)

Long before unit roots and cointegration became popular, model builders worried about picking up spurious correlation from common trending variables. One check on whether the correlation might be spurious is to add the time trend to an equation. If adding the time trend to an equation substantially changes some of the coefficient estimates, this is cause for concern. A simple test is thus to add the time trend to the equation and test if this addition is significant.

3.4.3 Testing the Dynamic Specification (Lags test)

Many macroeconomic equations include the LDV and other lagged endogenous variables among the explanatory variables. A test of the dynamic specification of a particular equation is to add *further* lagged values to the equation and see if they are significant. If, for example, in equation 1 y_{1t} is explained by y_{1t-1}, y_{2t-1}, and x_{1t-2}, then the variables added are y_{1t-2}, y_{2t-2}, and x_{1t-3}. Hendry, Pagan, and Sargan (1984) show that adding these lagged values is quite general in that it encompasses many different types of dynamic specifications. Therefore, adding the lagged values and testing for their significance is a test against a fairly general dynamic specification.

3.4.4 Testing Coefficient Restrictions

Sometimes, there is a coefficient restriction that has been imposed in the estimation. A test is simply to relax the restriction and see if there is a significant increase in fit. This is done for the US model for a few equations.

3.5 Time-Varying Coefficients

It may be that some of the coefficients in the stochastic equations vary over time. It is hard to deal with this case when using macro data because the variation in the data is generally modest. Postulating time-varying coefficients introduces more coefficients to estimate per equation, and the estimates may lack precision. This section describes a method that I have used for a few equations in the US model that allows for a particular type of time variation.

A common assumption in the time-varying literature is that coefficients follow random walks.[2] This assumption may not be realistic in macro work since it does not seem likely that macroeconomic relationships change randomly. It's more likely that they change in slower, perhaps trend-like ways. Also, it seems unlikely that changes take place over the entire sample period. If there is a change, it may begin after the beginning of the sample period and end before the end of the sample period. The method described here postulates no change for a while, then linear trend change for a while, and then no change after that. The assumption can be applied to any number of coefficients in an equation, although it is probably not practical with macro data to deal with more than one or two coefficients per equation. The method can be applied to equations estimated by NL2SLS.

For simplicity, the following notation departs from the notation for the general model in (3.1). Assume that the equation to be estimated is

$$y_t = \beta_t + X_t\alpha + u_t, \qquad t = 1, \ldots, T, \tag{3.8}$$

where y_t is the value of variable y at time t, β_t is a time-varying scalar, α is a vector, and the vector X_t can include endogenous and lagged endogenous variables. Define T_1 to be $\pi_1 T$ and T_2 to be $\pi_2 T$, where $0 < \pi_1 < \pi_2 < 1$. It is assumed that

$$\beta_t = \begin{cases} \gamma & : \ 1 \le t < T_1 \\ \gamma + \frac{\delta}{T_2 - T_1}(t - T_1) & : \ T_1 \le t \le T_2 \\ \gamma + \delta & : \ t > T_2 \end{cases} \tag{3.9}$$

where $\delta/(T_2 - T_1)$ is the amount that β_t changes per period between T_1 and T_2. Before T_1, β_t is constant and equal to γ, and after T_2, it is constant and equal to $\gamma + \delta$. The parameters to estimate are α, γ, δ, π_1, and π_2. There are thus two parameters to estimate per changing coefficient, γ and δ, plus π_1 and π_2. This specification is flexible in that it allows the point at which β_t begins to change and the point at which it ceases to change to be estimated. One could do this for any of the coefficients in α, at a cost of one additional parameter estimated per coefficient and assuming that π_1 and π_2 are the same for all coefficients.

Assume that equation (3.8) is to be estimated by NL2SLS using a $T \times K$ matrix Z as FSRs, where K is the number of FSRs. Given values of α, γ, δ, π_1, and π_2, u_t can be computed given data on y_t and X_t, $t = 1, \ldots, T$. The minimand is

$$S = u'Z(Z'Z)^{-1}Z'u, \tag{3.10}$$

where $u = (u_1, \ldots, u_T)'$. The problem can thus be turned over to a non-linear minimization algorithm like DFP. The estimated covariance matrix of the coefficient estimates (including the estimates of π_1 and π_2) is the standard matrix for NL2SLS—equation (3.3) in the notation of the general model.

To simplify the computations, one can scan over T_1 and T_2. Given values of T_1 and T_2, the estimation is simple. Substituting (3.9) into (3.8), γ in the resulting equation is the coefficient of the constant term (the vector of ones) and δ is the coefficient of

$$C_{2t} = D_{2t}\frac{t - T_1}{T_2 - T_1} + D_{3t}, \tag{3.11}$$

where D_{2t} is 1 between T_1 and T_2 and zero otherwise and D_{3t} is 1 after T_2 and 0 otherwise. For each pair of values, one can compute S in (3.10) and then scan over various pairs to find the minimum value of S.

Note that if β_t is changing over the whole sample period in the manner specified above, this is handled by simply adding the constant term and t as explanatory variables to the equation.

3.6 Age-Distribution Effects

A striking feature of postwar US society has been the baby boom of the late 1940s and throughout the 1950s and the subsequent falling off of the birth rate in the 1960s. The number of births in the United States rose from 2.5

million in 1945 to 4.2 million in 1961 and then fell back to 3.1 million in 1974. This birth pattern implies large changes in the percentage of prime age (25–54) people in the working age (16+) population. In 1952, this percentage was 57.9, whereas by 1977, it had fallen to 49.5. After 1980, the percentage of prime-aged workers rose sharply as the baby boomers began to pass the age of 25.

It may be that the changing age distribution affects aggregate relationships, like between aggregate consumption and aggregate income. To test for this, age-distribution variables have been added as explanatory variables to some of the household equations in the US model.[3] The age-distribution data are from the US Census Bureau's monthly population estimates. Population estimates are available monthly for ages 0 through 100+, from which quarterly estimates were calculated. Eighty-five age groups can be considered: ages $16, 17, \ldots, 100+$. From these data, 85 p_{jt} variables ($j = 1, \ldots, 85$) can be calculated, where p_{jt} is the fraction of people in age group j in the total population 16+ in period t. The 85 variables sum to one for a given t.

The p_{jt} variables could in principle be used to test whether the constant term in an aggregate equation differs by age. Add the 85 variables, constrain the coefficients of the variables to sum to zero, and estimate the equation (84 extra estimates). If the aggregate relationship differs by age, the coefficient estimates of the p_{jt} variables should be significant.

84 extra coefficients is, however, not sensible, and some constraints have to be imposed on the coefficients. For the subsequent estimation, the population 16+ was divided into four groups (16–25, 26–55, 56–65, and 66+), and it was assumed that the coefficients are the same within each group. Given the constraint that the coefficients sum to zero, this leaves three unconstrained coefficients to estimate. Let $P1625$ denote the percent of the 16+ population aged 16–25, and similarly for $P2655$, $P5665$, and $P66+$. Let γ_0 denote the coefficient of $P1625$ in the estimated equation, γ_1 the coefficient of $P2655$, γ_2 the coefficient of $P5665$, and γ_3 the coefficient of $P66+$, where $\gamma_0 + \gamma_1 + \gamma_2 + \gamma_3 = 0$. The summation constraint can be imposed by entering three variables in the estimated equation:

$$AG1 = P2655 - P1625$$
$$AG2 = P5665 - P1625$$
$$AG3 = (P66+) - P1625$$

where $AG1$, $AG2$, and $AG3$ are variables in the US model. The coefficient of $AG1$ in an equation is $\gamma_1 - \gamma_0$, the coefficient of $AG2$ is $\gamma_2 - \gamma_0$, and the coefficient of $AG3$ is $\gamma_3 - \gamma_0$. From the estimated coefficients for $AG1$, $AG2$, and $AG3$ and the summation constraint, one can calculate the four γ coefficients.

3.7 Full Information Estimation Methods (optional)

Full information estimation methods use information in the covariance matrix of the error terms across equations and can handle coefficient restrictions across coefficients in different equations. The two main candidates are nonlinear three-stage least squares (3SLS) and full information maximum likelihood (FIML). These methods are rarely used in practice. The setup can be tedious and the computations difficult. These methods are not used in this book, although for sake of completeness, the function that 3SLS minimizes and that FIML maximizes will be presented. More details are in chapter 6 in Fair (1984).

More notation is needed. Let $k = \sum_{i=1}^{m} k_i$ be the total number of coefficients in the model, and let α denote the k-dimensional vector $(\alpha_1', \ldots, \alpha_m')$ of all the coefficients. Let u be the $m \cdot T$-dimensional vector $(u_{11}, \ldots, u_{1T}, \ldots, u_{m1}, \ldots u_{mT})$. Let G' be the $k \times m \cdot T$ matrix

$$\begin{vmatrix} G_1' & 0 & \cdots & 0 \\ 0 & G_2' & & \\ \cdot & & & \\ \cdot & & & \\ \cdot & & & \\ 0 & & & G_m' \end{vmatrix}$$

Let Σ be the $m \times m$ covariance matrix of the error terms. 3SLS estimates of α are obtained by minimizing

$$u'[\hat{\Sigma}^{-1} \otimes Z(Z'Z)^{-1}Z']u = u'Du \tag{3.12}$$

with respect to α, where $\hat{\Sigma}$ is a consistent estimate of Σ and Z is a $T \times K$ matrix of FSRs. Σ is usually estimated from the 2SLS estimated residuals. An estimate of the covariance matrix of $\hat{\alpha}$ is

$$(\hat{G}'D\hat{G})^{-1}, \tag{3.13}$$

where $\hat{G}$ is G evaluated at $\hat{\alpha}$.

The 3SLS estimator that is based on minimizing (3.12) uses the same Z matrix for each equation. In small samples, this can be a disadvantage of 3SLS relative to 2SLS. It is possible to modify (3.12) to include the case of different Z_i matrices for each equation—see Fair (1984), chapter 6—although this modification requires inverting a very large matrix, which may not be feasible.

This 3SLS estimator discussed here is presented in Jorgenson and Laffont (1974) and is further discussed in Amemiya (1977). Both prove consistency and asymptotic normalality.

For FIML, let J_t denote the $n \times n$ Jacobian matrix where the i, j element is $\partial f_i(\ldots)/\partial y_{j,t}$. Under the assumption that u_t is independently and identially distributed as $N(0, \Sigma)$, it can be shown that the FIML estimates are obtained by maximizing

$$L = -(T/2)log|\Sigma| + \sum_{i=1}^{T} log|J_t| \tag{3.14}$$

with respect to α. An estimate of the covariance matrix of the FIML estimates is

$$-(\partial^2 L/\partial\alpha\partial\alpha')^{-1} \tag{3.15}$$

where the derivatives are evaluated at the optimum. There are various tricks that can be used to help maximize (3.14)—see chapter 6 in Fair (1984).

II The US Model

4 Specification and Estimation of the US Model

4.1 Overview

The US model is an example of a model in the CC tradition. There are and have been many other examples. What makes the models similar is the CC approach, not the theory used to choose the LHS and RHS variables. For example, the US model assumes disequilibrium, as discussed next, but this is not a requirement.

I have tried to write this book with as little clutter in the chapters as possible in explaining the model. The complete model is presented in table form in the appendix. There are many weeds in these tables that can be ignored unless one wants to duplicate the model. In this chapter, there is more detail than in later chapters. The core of the model is the set of estimated equations, and each estimated equation is presented in a table. These tables are presented in this chapter to be near the discussion. They are also repeated in the appendix.

The US model has 24 stochastic equations. There are about 140 identities, depending on how many variables are added for display purposes. The number of endogenous variables is equal to the number of equations, and there are about 150 exogenous variables. The sample period for which data were collected is 1952.1–2023.2, 286 quarterly observations.

In the numbering of the equations, some numbers are skipped. Like in apartment buildings there is usually no floor 13. The model has gone through many versions, and over time some equations have been dropped. It is convenient to keep the original numbering for coding and software reasons.

4.2 Disequilibrium

The theory that is behind the specification of the US model is presented in chapter 3 in Fair (1984). Households and firms make decisions by solving maximization problems, utility maximization for households and profit maximization for firms. A household's decision variables include consumption and labor supply. A firm's decision variables include its price, production, investment, employment, and wage rate. Firms are assumed to behave in a monopolistically competitive environment. Expectations are not assumed to be rational, and there is nothing in the system that insures that markets are cleared. Disequilibrium in the goods markets takes the form of unintended changes in inventories. Disequilibrium in the labor market takes the form of unemployment, where households are constrained by firms from working as much as the solutions of their unconstrained maximization problems say they want to.

4.3 Steady-State Constraints and Natural Values

Imposing steady-state restrictions on a model is not inconsistent with the CC approach. One can think of these as coefficient restrictions. Similarly, postulating natural values, like the natural value of the unemployment rate, is not inconsistent. In the spirit of the empirical nature of the CC approach, the restrictions should be tested, including restrictions imposed by the use of the natural values.

I have not imposed such restrictions in the US model. Given that the model is nonlinear and has many exogenous variables, trying to impose a steady state would be problematic if not impossible. And I am not a fan of the assumption that, say, the unemployment rate has a tendency to return to some natural value. The economy (and the model) is too complicated for this to be likely. And, as will be seen in the specification of the price equation 10, there is no need to clutter the specification with a natural unemployment rate. One can just use the unemployment rate itself and estimate a constant term. Similarly, I would argue that the concept of a natural rate of interest (sometimes called r^*) is not useful. An interest rate depends on many variables, and it is unlikely that the variables are such that there is some natural rate in the long run. A macroeconometric model can be solved each quarter for the endogenous variables, where the solution values depend on the structure of the model and the values of the predetermined variables. The solution values are whatever they are; there is no need to consider whether in some sense they are natural values or steady-state values.

So to summarize some of the philosophy behind the specification of the US model: no rational expectations, yes disequilibrium, no steady states, no natural rates.

4.4 The Pandemic

Many of the relationships among the variables were affected by the COVID-19 pandemic. This is handled by adding eight dummy variables, one for each quarter 2020.1–2021.4, to the stochastic equations. This effectively dummies out the pandemic quarters. The eight variables are *D20201*, *D20202*, *D20203*, *D20204*, *D20211*, *D20212*, *D20213*, and *D20214*, which are 1 in the respective quarter and zero otherwise.

4.5 Household Sector

The two main decision variables of a household in the theoretical model in Fair (1984) are expenditures and labor supply. The determinants of these variables include the initial value of wealth and the current and expected future values of the wage rate, the price level, the interest rate, the tax rate, the level of transfer payments, and a possible labor constraint.

In the US model, the expenditures of the household sector are disaggregated into four types: consumption of services, *CS*; consumption of nondurable goods, *CN*; consumption of durable goods, *CD*; and residential investment, *IHH*. Four labor supply variables are used: the labor force of men 25–54, *L1*, the labor force of women 25–54, *L2*; the labor force of all others 16+, *L3*, and the number of people holding more than one job, called "moonlighters," *LM*. These eight variables are determined by eight estimated equations.

Since households simultaneously determine expenditures and labor supply, if they were not constrained in how much they could work, the RHS variables in the expenditure equations would include the after-tax real wage and not the after-tax real income, which is a choice variable. If, however, the labor constraint is binding, after-tax real income, which is the constrained value of hours worked times the after-tax real wage, is a possible RHS variable. Real after-tax income in the model, *YD/PH*, where *YD* is nominal disposable income and *PH* is the price deflator for total household expenditures, is used as an explanatory variable in the expenditure equations, which implicitly assumes that the labor constraint is always binding on the household sector. The real wage is thus not an explanatory variable in the expenditure equations. Other explanatory variables, guided by the theory, include household real wealth and interest rates. Household real wealth is denoted *AA*. It is the sum of real financial wealth, *AA*1, and real housing wealth, *AA*2. More will be said about this later. When the one-quarter-lagged wealth variable is added as an explanatory variable, it is treated as endogenous in the estimation. The two-quarter-lagged wealth variable is used as an FSR.

The notation that is used in this section is presented in table 4.1. It is also repeated in table A.2 in the appendix.

Table 4.1
Variable Notation for the Household Sector

Variable	Eq.	Description	Used in Equations
AA	133	Total net wealth, h, B2012$.	1, 2, 3, 5, 6, 7, 27
*AA*1	88	Total net financial wealth, h, B2012$.	133
*AA*2	89	Total net housing wealth, h, B2012$.	133
*AG*1	exog	Percent of 16+ population 26–55 minus percent 16–25.	1, 2, 3, 4, 27
*AG*2	exog	Percent of 16+ population 56–65 minus percent 16–25.	1, 2, 3, 4, 27
*AG*3	exog	Percent of 16+ population 66+ minus percent 16–25.	1, 2, 3, 4, 27
CD	3	Consumer expenditures for durable goods, B2012$.	34, 51, 52, 58, 60, 61, 65, 96, 97, 116
CG	exog	Capital gains(+) or losses(−) on the financial assets of h, B$.	12, 66
CN	2	Consumer expenditures for nondurable goods, B2012$.	34, 51, 52, 60, 61, 65, 116
cnst2cs	exog	Time-varying constant term, 1974.1–1994.3.	1
cnst2l2	exog	Time-varying constant term, 1971.3–1989.4.	6
CS	1	Consumer expenditures for services, B2012$.	34, 51, 52, 60, 61, 65, 116
IHH	4	Residential investment, h, B2012$.	34, 59, 60, 61, 65

Table 4.1
(continued)

Variable	Eq.	Description	Used in Equations
KD	58	Stock of durable goods, B2012$.	none
KH	59	Stock of housing, h, B2012$.	89
*L*1	5	Labor force of men 25–54, millions.	86, 87
*L*2	6	Labor force of women 25–54, millions.	86, 87
*L*3	7	Labor force of all others, 16+, millions.	86, 87
LM	8	Number of "moonlighters": difference between the total number of jobs (establishment data) and the total number of people employed (household survey data), millions.	85
PF	10	Price deflator for nonfarm sales.	16, 17, 26, 27, 31, 119
PH	34	Price deflator for CS + CN + CD + IHH inclusive of indirect business taxes.	1, 2, 3, 4, 7, 88, 89
PKH	55	Market price of *KH*.	89
POP	120	Noninstitutional population 16+, millions.	1, 2, 3, 4, 5, 6, 7, 8, 26, 27, 47, 48
*POP*1	exog	Noninstitutional population of men 25–54, millions.	5, 120
*POP*2	exog	Noninstitutional population of women 25–54, millions.	6, 120
*POP*3	exog	Noninstitutional population of all others, 16+, millions.	7, 120
RSA	127	After-tax bill rate, percentage points.	1, 26
RMA	128	After-tax mortgage rate, percentage points.	2, 3, 4
T	exog	1 in 1952:1, 2 in 1952:2, etc.	3, 4, 6, 10, 14, 16
*TBL*2	exog	Time-varying time trend, 1971.3–1989.4.	6
UR	87	Civilian unemployment rate.	5, 6, 7, 8, 10, 30
WA	126	After-tax wage rate. (Includes supplements to wages and salaries except employer contributions for social insurance.)	7
YD	115	Disposable income, h, B$.	1, 2, 3, 4, 116

- B$ = Billions of dollars.
- B2012$ = Billions of 2012 dollars.

4.5.1 Equation 1. *CS*, Consumer Expenditures: Services

Equation 1 in table A1 is in real, per capita terms and is in log form. The estimates and test results are presented in the table. The equation is estimated under the assumption of first-order serial correlaion of the error term. As mentioned above, the explanatory variables include income, wealth, and an interest rate. The interest rate is the short-term after-tax interest rate, *RSA*. The interest rate is after tax since interest income is taxed. The explanatory variables also include the age variables and the eight pandemic dummy variables. The equation is estimated under the assumption of a time-varying constant, with T_1 being 1973.4 and T_2 being 1994.4. The equation includes the LDV to account for lagged adjustment and expectational effects.

As expected, the estimate of the coefficient of the LDV is large and highly significant. The income, interest rate, and wealth variables are significant, with *t*-statistics of 2.51, −4.80, and 4.78 respectively. The estimate of the serial correlation coefficient is 0.196 with a *t*-statistic of 3.03. The χ^2 test regarding the age variables shows that they are highly jointly significant. Regarding the χ^2 tests, the additional lagged values are significant at the 95 but not 99 percent confidence level. The time trend is not significant. The equation is thus fairly robust.

4.5.2 Equation 2. *CN*, Consumer Expenditures: Nondurables

Equation 2 in table A2 has the same specification as equation 1 except that it does not have a time-varying constant and uses the after-tax mortgage rate as the interest rate. The results are also similar in terms of significance. The equation is robust. The added lagged values are not significant, nor is the time trend.

Table A1: Equation 1
LHS Variable Is log(*CS*/*POP*)

Equation			χ^2 Tests			
RHS Variable	Coef.	*t*-stat.	Test	χ^2	df	*p*-value
cnst2cs	0.05774	6.08	Lags	10.53	3	0.0146
cnst	−0.11738	−3.34	*T*	0.52	1	0.4730
*AG*1	−0.07410	−2.57				
*AG*2	−0.24226	−6.66				
*AG*3	−0.04431	−0.94				
$\log(CS/POP)_{-1}$	0.82165	21.03				
$\log[YD/(POP \cdot PH)]$	0.10946	2.51				
RSA	−0.00117	−4.80				
$\log(AA/POP)_{-1}$	0.03186	4.78				
*D*20201	−0.02966	−8.00				
*D*20202	−0.15101	−20.40				
*D*20203	0.03342	3.27				
*D*20204	−0.01500	−2.30				
*D*20211	−0.03045	−2.98				
*D*20212	−0.00061	−0.09				
*D*20213	−0.00183	−0.35				
*D*20214	−0.00869	−2.06				
RHO1	0.19587	3.03				
SE	0.00359					
R^2	1.000					

χ^2 (AGE) = 64.30 (df = 3, *p*-value = 0.0000)

Lags test adds $\log(CS/POP)_{-2}$, $\log[YD/(POP \cdot PH)]_{-1}$, and RSA_{-1}.
Estimation period is 1954.1–2023.2.
$T_1 = 1973.4$; $T_2 = 1994.4$.

First-Stage Regressors

cnst2cs, *cnst*, *AG*1, *AG*2, *AG*3, $\log(CS/POP)_{-1}$, $\log(AA/POP)_{-2}$, RSA_{-1}, $cnst2cs_{-1}$, $AG1_{-1}$, $AG2_{-1}$, $AG3_{-1}$, $\log(AA/POP)_{-3}$, $\log(CS/POP)_{-2}$, $\log[(COG+COS)/POP]_{-1}$, $\log[(TRGH+TRSH)/(POP \cdot PH)]_{-1}$, $\log(EX/POP)_{-1}$, $\log POP$, $\log POP_{-1}$, *D*20201, *D*20202, *D*20203, *D*20204, *D*20211, *D*20212, *D*20213, *D*20214, $D20214_{-1}$

Table A2: Equation 2
LHS Variable Is $\log(CN/POP)$

Equation			χ^2 Tests			
RHS Variable	Coef.	*t*-stat.	Test	χ^2	df	*p*-value
cnst	−0.22546	−2.62	Lags	6.95	3	0.0736
$AG1$	0.00494	0.24	T	0.02	1	0.8963
$AG2$	−0.11311	−1.96				
$AG3$	0.00446	0.07				
$\log(CN/POP)_{-1}$	0.83507	18.98				
$\log(AA/POP)_{-1}$	0.04918	2.51				
$\log[YD/(POP \cdot PH)]$	0.04663	3.49				
RMA	−0.00109	−2.72				
$D20201$	0.00979	1.50				
$D20202$	−0.04822	−7.04				
$D20203$	0.05533	7.48				
$D20204$	−0.00487	−0.72				
$D20211$	0.02183	3.05				
$D20212$	0.02458	3.60				
$D20213$	0.00374	0.55				
$D20214$	0.00406	0.61				
RHO1	0.23187	3.53				
SE	0.00637					
R^2	0.999					

χ^2 (AGE) = 5.85 (df = 3, *p*-value = 0.1192)

Lags test adds $\log(CN/POP)_{-2}$, $\log[YD/(POP \cdot PH)]_{-1}$, and RMA_{-1}.
Estimation period is 1954.1–2023.2.

First-Stage Regressors

$cnst, AG1, AG2, AG3, \log(CN/POP)_{-1}, \log(AA/POP)_{-2}, \log[YD/(POP \cdot PH)]_{-1}, RMA_{-1}, AG1_{-1}, AG2_{-1}, AG3_{-1}, \log(AA/POP)_{-3}, \log(CN/POP)_{-2}, \log[(COG + COS)/POP]_{-1}$, $\log[(TRGH + TRSH)/(POP \cdot PH)]_{-1}$, $\log(EX/POP)_{-1}$, $D20201$, $D20202$, $D20203$, $D20204$, $D20211$, $D20212$, $D20213$, $D20214$, $D20214_{-1}$

4.5.3 Equation 3. *CD*, Consumer Expenditures: Durables

Equation 3 in table A3 has the same specification as equation 2, except that it is not estimated under the assumption of first-order serial correlation of the error term. The wealth variable is retained although it has a *t*-statistic of only 0.97. The age variables are not jointly significant. Regarding the robustness tests, the addition of the lagged values is not significant. The time trend is significant at the 95 but not 99 percent confidence level. The estimate of the serial correlation coefficient is highly significant. When the equation is estimated under the assumption of first-order serial of the error term, a number of the other coefficient estimates are not sensible. There appears to be too much collinearity, and so the serial correlation assumption was not used.

Although not shown in table A3, when the lagged per capita stock of durable goods, $\log(KD/POP)_{-1}$, is added, it is not significant, with a coefficient estimate of −0.038 and a *t*-statistic of −0.87. Thus, there is little evidence that, say, a large stock of durable goods leads to fewer purchases of durables in the future.

Table A3: Equation 3
LHS Variable Is $\log(CD/POP)$

Equation			χ^2 Tests			
RHS Variable	Coef.	*t*-stat.	Test	χ^2	df	*p*-value
cnst	−0.48389	−2.04	Lags	6.93	3	0.0742
$AG1$	−0.08633	−1.22	RHO	14.05	1	0.0002
$AG2$	−0.10283	−0.48	T	5.16	1	0.0231
$AG3$	0.20536	0.91				
$\log(CD/POP)_{-1}$	0.90717	31.24				
$\log[YD/(POP \cdot PH)]$	0.14488	2.97				
RMA	−0.00322	−2.40				
$\log(AA/POP)_{-1}$	0.03687	0.97				
$D20201$	−0.04902	−1.67				
$D20202$	−0.03289	−1.10				
$D20203$	0.14328	4.84				
$D20204$	−0.01389	−0.47				
$D20211$	0.05931	2.00				
$D20212$	0.01285	0.44				
$D20213$	−0.07190	−2.42				
$D20214$	−0.00117	−0.04				
SE	0.02864					
R^2	0.999					

χ^2 (AGE) = 1.51 (df = 3, *p*-value = 0.6791)

Lags test adds $\log(CD/POP)_{-2}$, $\log[YD/(POP \cdot PH)]_{-1}$, and RMA_{-1}.
Estimation period is 1954.1–2023.2.

First-Stage Regressors

$cnst, AG1, AG2, AG3, \log(CD/POP)_{-1}, \log(AA/POP)_{-2}, \log[YD/(POP \cdot PH)]_{-1}, RMA_{-1}, \log[(COG + COS)/POP]_{-1}, \log[(TRGH + TRSH)/(POP \cdot PH)]_{-1}, \log(EX/POP)_{-1}, T, D20201, D20202, D20203, D20204, D20211, D20212, D20213, D20214$

4.5.4 Equation 4. *IHH*, Residential Investment

Equation 4 in table A4 has the same specification as equation 3, except that the interest rate is lagged one quarter and the wealth variable is not included. The age variables are highly jointly significant. The income variable is included, although it has a *t*-statistic of only 1.62. The serial correlation of the error term is high, with a coefficient estimate of 0.91 and a *t*-statistic of 28.72. The additional lag variables are significant at the 95 but not 99 percent confidence level. The time trend is not significant.

Although not shown in the table, when the lagged per capita stock of housing, $\log(KH/POP)_{-1}$, is added to the equation, it has a coefficient estimate of -1.161 and a *t*-statistic of -1.54. Even though it is not significant, its addition has large effects on some of the other coefficient estimates that are not sensible. There appears to be too much collinarity. Equation 4 is thus somewhat fragile. The serial correlation of the error term is high, and it can be sensitive to adding other variables.

Table A4: Equation 4
LHS Variable Is log(*IHH*/*POP*)

Equation			χ^2 Tests			
RHS Variable	Coef.	*t*-stat.	Test	χ^2	df	*p*-value
cnst	−1.13917	−2.23	Lags	8.94	3	0.0301
*AG*1	0.70929	1.00	*T*	0.03	1	0.8533
*AG*2	−5.76579	−3.26				
*AG*3	2.30981	1.19				
$\log(IHH/POP)_{-1}$	0.52439	9.23				
$\log[YD/(POP \cdot PH)]$	0.23067	1.62				
RMA_{-1}	−0.03817	−6.59				
*D*20201	0.04312	1.25				
*D*20202	−0.10445	−2.11				
*D*20203	0.05815	1.09				
*D*20204	0.07003	1.29				
*D*20211	0.02872	0.49				
*D*20212	0.00189	0.04				
*D*20213	0.00012	0.00				
*D*20214	0.00783	0.23				
RHO1	0.91093	28.72				
SE	0.03510					
R^2	0.980					

χ^2 (AGE) = 5.02 (df = 3, *p*-value = 0.1702)

Lags test adds $\log(IHH/POP)_{-2}$, $\log[YD/(POP \cdot PH)]_{-1}$, and RMA_{-2}.
Estimation period is 1954.1–2023.2.

First-Stage Regressors

cnst, $\log(IHH/POP)_{-1}$, RMA_{-1}, $\log[YD/(POP \cdot PH)]_{-1}$, *AG*1, *AG*2, *AG*3, $AG1_{-1}$, $AG2_{-1}$, $AG3_{-1}$, $\log(IHH/POP)_{-2}$, RMA_{-2}, $\log[(COG+COS)/POP]_{-1}$, $\log[(TRGH+TRSH)/(POP \cdot PH)]_{-1}$, $\log(EX/POP)_{-1}$, *T*, *D*20201, *D*20202, *D*20203, *D*20204, *D*20211, *D*20212, *D*20213, *D*20214, $D20214_{-1}$

4.5.5 Equations 1–4: Nominal versus Real Interest Rates

An interest rate is significant in each of the four expenditure equations. These are nominal after-tax interest rates. Should they instead be real rates? This is easy to test. Let for period t, i_t denote the nominal interest rate, r_t the real interest rate, and $\dot{p}_t^e$ the expected future rate of inflation, where the horizon for $\dot{p}_t^e$ matches the horizon for i_t. By definition $r_t = i_t - \dot{p}_t^e$. If the real interest rate is what matters, then adding both i_t and $\dot{p}_t^e$ to the equation should result in a negative coefficient on i_t and a positive coefficient on $\dot{p}_t^e$ of roughly the same size in absolute value. The real interest rate specification can thus be tested by simply adding $\dot{p}_t^e$ to the equation with i_t included and seeing if it has a positive coefficient estimate roughly the size of the coefficient estimate of i_t in absolute value.

This test was done for each of the four equations using two measures of $\dot{p}_t^e$. One was the four-quarter change in the nonfarm price deflator, *PF*, and the other was the eight-quarter change in the deflator at annual rate. These are $100(PF_t/PF_{t-4} - 1)$ and $100(PF_t/PF_{t-8})^{.5} - 1)$. The NL2SLS estimator was used for this test. As noted in section 3.3, when the NL2SLS estimator is used, the predicted values used in the second-stage regression can be interpreted as predictions of the agents in the economy under the assumption that agents know the values of the FSRs at the time they form their expectations. Since both i_t and $\dot{p}_t^e$ are treated as endogenous in the estimation, agents can be assumed to have used the FSRs for their predictions of i_t and $\dot{p}_t^e$.

The results are presented in table 4.2. In all eight cases, the coefficient estimate of the inflation variable is negative. The estimate should be positive if the real rate matters, so there is no support for the use of real rates. The coefficient estimate of the nominal interest rate is always negative, and it is significant except for the *CD* equation with the inflation variables added and the *CN* equation with the second inflation variable added. The inflation variables are significant except for the first inflation variable in the *CS* equation and the second inflation variable in the *CN* equation. The results thus suggest that the inflation variables may have negative effects on household expenditures. This feature is not part of the specification of the four equations, and so the equations are not robust in this sense.

Why the nominal rate rather than the real rate matters is an interesting question. One possibility is that $\dot{p}_t^e$ is simply a constant, so that the nominal interest rate specification is also the real interest rate specification (with the

Table 4.2
Nominal versus Real Interest Rates

Nominal Rate			Inflation Rate			
Equation	Rate	*t*-stat	*PCPF4*	*t*-stat	*PCPF8*	*t*-stat
1 *CS*	−0.00117	(−4.80)				
	−0.00097	(−3.72)	−0.00037	(−1.93)		
	−0.00092	(−3.73)			−0.00051	(−2.56)
2 *CN*	−0.00109	(−2.72)				
	−0.00082	(−2.11)	−0.00080	(−2.51)		
	−0.00081	(−1.94)			−0.00057	(−1.52)
3 *CD*	−0.00322	(−2.40)				
	−0.00202	(−1.45)	−0.00454	(−3.57)		
	−0.00188	(−1.29)			−0.00335	(−2.38)
4 *IHH*	−0.03817	(−6.59)				
	−0.03538	(−6.15)	−0.01181	(−3.47)		
	−0.03464	(−5.99)			−0.02208	(−3.64)

$PCPF4 = 100(PF_t/PF_{t-4} - 1)$.
$PCPF8 = 100((PF_t/PF_{t-8})^{.5} - 1)$.
Base equations in tables A1–A4.
Estimation period: 1954.1–2013.2.
Estimation method: NL2SLS.

constant absorbed in the constant term of the equation). If, for example, agents think the monetary authority is targeting a fixed inflation rate, this might be a reason for $\dot{p}_t^e$ being constant. Whatever the case, the empirical results do not favor the use of $i_t - \dot{p}_t^e$ in aggregate expenditure equations when $\dot{p}_t^e$ is measured as above.

4.5.6 Equations 1–3: Financial versus Housing Wealth

The real net wealth variable in the US model is

$$AA = (AH + MH)/PH + (PKH \cdot KH)/PH = AA1 + AA2, \tag{4.1}$$

where *AH* is the nominal value of net financial assets of the household sector excluding demand deposits and currency, *MH* is the nominal value of demand deposits and currency held by the household sector, *KH* is the real stock of housing, *PKH* is the market price of *KH*, and *PH* is a price deflator relevant to household spending. $(AH + MH)/PH$, denoted $AA1$, is thus real financial wealth, and $(PKH \cdot KH)/PH$, denoted $AA2$, is real housing wealth.

The wealth variable enters equations 1–3 as $\log(AA/POP)_{-1}$, which assumes that financial and housing wealth have the same effect. This can be tested by using as the wealth variable $\log[(\lambda AA1 + (1-\lambda)AA2)/POP]_{-1}$ and estimating λ along with the other structural coefficients. If the effects are the same, then λ is 0.5. This is a nonlinear estimation problem, which NL2SLS is set up to solve.

The estimates of λ for the three equations are as follows, where *t*-statistics are in parentheses for testing the hypothesis that $\lambda = 0.5$:

Eq.	$\hat{\lambda}$
CS	0.576
	(0.82)
CN	0.459
	(−0.47)
CD	0.434
	(−0.17)

None of the three estimates of λ is significantly different from 0.5, which supports the use of the aggregate wealth variable. Both financial wealth and housing wealth appear to have the same effect.

The significance here of financial wealth in the consumption expenditure equations is contrary to results in the literature using less aggregate data. Case, Quigley, and Shiller (2012) (CQS) find stronger effects for housing wealth than for financial wealth on retail sales. In fact, for many of their estimates, financial wealth is not significant. Many assumptions have been used by CQS to create financial wealth data by state, and their negative results for financial wealth could be at least partly due to measurement error. Mian, Rao, and Sufi (2013) also do not find significant financial wealth effects on consumption, but they point out that they do not have the statistical power to estimate financial wealth effects because of lack of good data on financial assets by zip codes (p. 20). Zhou and Carroll (2012), using data by states like CQS, also find insignificant financial wealth effects but significant housing wealth effects. If constructing financial wealth by zip codes or states leads to larger measurement errors than constructing housing wealth by zip codes or states, then this could explain theinsignificance of financial wealth versus housing wealth in this literature, contrary to the results using aggregate data.

4.5.7 Equation 5. *L*1, Labor Force—Men 25–54

Equation 5 in table A5 explains the labor force participation rate of men 25–54. It is in log form and includes as explanatory variables the LDV, the wealth variable, and the unemployment rate. The unemployment rate is meant to pick up the effect of the labor constraint on labor supply—a discouraged worker effect.

The wealth variable has a negative and significant coefficient estimate, as expected. As wealth increases, labor supply falls. The unemployment rate also has a negative and significant coefficient estimate, which is reflecting the discouraged worker effect. The additional lag variables are significant at the 95 but not 99 percent confidence level. The serial correlation coefficient is not signifiant, nor is the time trend (barely).

Table A5: Equation 5
LHS Variable Is $\log(L1/POP1)$

Equation			χ^2 Tests			
RHS Variable	Coef.	*t*-stat.	Test	χ^2	df	*p*-value
cnst	0.02921	3.58	Lags	6.20	2	0.0451
$\log(L1/POP1)_{-1}$	0.90492	35.55	RHO	2.55	1	0.1101
$\log(AA/POP)_{-1}$	−0.00657	−3.58	T	3.83	1	0.0504
UR	−0.05004	−3.52				
$D20201$	0.00225	0.92				
$D20202$	−0.02223	−8.07				
$D20203$	0.01184	4.84				
$D20204$	−0.00092	−0.38				
$D20211$	0.00187	0.77				
$D20212$	0.00497	2.04				
$D20213$	0.00495	2.02				
$D20214$	−0.00005	−0.02				
SE	0.00240					
R^2	0.994					

Lags test adds $\log(L1/POP1)_{-2}$ and UR_{-1}.
Estimation period is 1954.1–2023.2.

First-Stage Regressors

$cnst$, $\log(L1/POP1)_{-1}$, $\log(AA/POP)_{-2}$, UR_{-1}, $\log[(COG+COS)/POP]_{-1}$, $\log[(TRGH+TRSH)/(POP\cdot PH)]_{-1}$, $\log(EX/POP)_{-1}$, $D20201$, $D20202$, $D20203$, $D20204$, $D20211$, $D20212$, $D20213$, $D20214$

4.5.8 Equation 6. *L2*, Labor Force—Women 25–54

Equation 6 in table A6 explains the labor force participation rate of women 25–54. It has the same specification as equation 5, except that it includes the time trend T and is estimated under the assumption of a time-varying constant term and time trend coefficient, with T_1 being 1971.4 and T_2 being

Table A6: Equation 6
LHS Variable Is $\log(L2/POP2)$

Equation			χ^2 Tests			
RHS Variable	Coef.	*t*-stat.	Test	χ^2	df	*p*-value
cnst2l2	0.09780	5.53	Lags	2.01	2	0.3666
cnst	−0.08147	−1.73	RHO	1.30	1	0.2539
TBL2	−0.00052	−6.01				
T	0.00060	7.07				
$\log(L2/POP2)_{-1}$	0.85000	32.55				
$\log(AA/POP)_{-1}$	−0.01235	−1.61				
UR	−0.14491	−4.46				
D20201	0.00013	0.03				
D20202	−0.01765	−3.19				
D20203	0.00946	1.83				
D20204	0.00167	0.33				
D20211	0.00445	0.87				
D20212	0.00441	0.86				
D20213	0.00410	0.80				
D20214	0.00496	0.98				
SE	0.00491					
R^2	1.000					

Lags test adds $\log(L2/POP2)_{-2}$ and UR_{-1}
Estimation period is 1954.1–2023.2.
$T_1 = 1971.4$; $T_2 = 1989.4$.

First-Stage Regressors

cnst2l2, *cnst*, *TBL2*, *T*, $\log(L2/POP2)_{-1})$, $\log(AA/POP)_{-2}$, UR_{-1}, $\log[(COG+COS)/POP]_{-1}$, $\log[(TRGH+TRSH)/(POP \cdot PH)]_{-1}$, $\log(EX/POP)_{-1}$, *D20201*, *D20202*, *D20203*, *D20204*, *D20211*, *D20212*, *D20213*, *D20214*

1989.4. There is an economically unexplained trend in *L2*, especially in the 1970s, due to social movements, which is the reason *T* and *TB* are added. The results show a significant discouraged worker effect, but the *t*-statistic on the wealth variable is only −1.61. The equation is robust to the Lags and RHO tests.

4.5.9 Equation 7. *L3*, Labor Force—All Others 16+

Equation 7 in table A7 explains the labor force participation rate of all others 16+. It has the same specification as equation 5, except that the real wage is added. The discouraged worker effect is significant. The wealth variable has

Table A7: Equation 7

LHS Variable Is log(*L3*/*POP3*)

Equation			χ^2 Tests			
RHS Variable	Coef.	*t*-stat.	Test	χ^2	df	*p*-value
cnst	0.03767	2.02	Lags	3.13	3	0.3713
$\log(L3/POP3)_{-1}$	0.97257	70.63	RHO	4.15	1	0.0415
$\log(WA/PH)$	0.01612	2.18	*T*	2.06	1	0.1514
$\log(AA/POP)_{-1}$	−0.01207	−2.30	log *PH*	2.20	1	0.1382
UR	−0.12130	−3.95				
D20201	−0.00770	−1.48				
D20202	−0.04469	−8.10				
D20203	0.02638	5.04				
D20204	0.00738	1.42				
D20211	−0.01011	−1.93				
D20212	0.00661	1.26				
D20213	0.00287	0.55				
D20214	0.00576	1.10				
SE	0.00512					
R^2	0.989					

Lags test adds $\log(L3/POP3)_{-2}$, $\log(WA/PH)_{-1}$, and UR_{-1}.
Estimation period is 1954.1–2023.2.

First-Stage Regressors

cnst, $\log(L3/POP3)_{-1})$, $\log(AA/POP)_{-2}$, $\log(WA/PH)_{-1}$, UR_{-1}, $\log[(COG+COS)/POP]_{-1}$, $\log[(TRGH+TRSH)/(POP \cdot PH)]_{-1}$, $\log(EX/POP)_{-1}$, D20201, D20202, D20203, D20204, D20211, D20212, D20213, D20214

a *t*-statistic of −2.30. The real wage variable has a positive coefficient with a *t*-statistic of 2.18. This means a positive substitution effect.

The equation is robust to the Lags and T tests. The *p*-value for the RHO test is 0.0415, and so serial correlation is significant at the 95 but not 99 percent confidence level. The last χ^2 test adds $\log PH$ to the equation. This is a test of the use of the real wage in the equation. If $\log PH$ is significant, this is a rejection of the hypothesis that the coefficient of $\log WA$ is equal to the negative of the coefficient of $\log PH$, which is implied by the use of the real wage. The test shows that $\log PH$ is not significant.

4.5.10 Equation 8. *LM*, Number of Moonlighters

Equation 8 in table A8 determines the number of moonlighters. It is in log form and includes the LDV variable and the unemployment rate as

Table A8: Equation 8

LHS Variable Is $\log(LM/POP)$

Equation			χ^2 Tests			
RHS Variable	Coef.	*t*-stat.	Test	χ^2	df	*p*-value
cnst	−0.30620	−4.34	Lags	1.07	2	0.5865
$\log(LM/POP)_{-1}$	0.89168	39.92	RHO	0.00	1	0.9901
UR	−1.47326	−4.42	*T*	1.17	1	0.2802
*D*20201	−0.16958	−2.51				
*D*20202	0.39594	5.67				
*D*20203	−0.12685	−1.88				
*D*20204	−0.33893	−5.07				
*D*20211	0.09747	1.44				
*D*20212	0.07786	1.16				
*D*20213	0.02061	0.31				
*D*20214	−0.09655	−1.43				
SE	0.06672					
R^2	0.922					

Lags test adds $\log(LM/POP)_{-2}$ and UR_{-1}.
Estimation period is 1954.1–2023.2.

First-Stage Regressors

cnst, $\log(LM/POP)_{-1}$, UR_{-1}, $\log[(COG+COS)/POP]_{-1}$, $\log[(TRGH+TRSH)/(POP\cdot PH)]_{-1}$, $\log(EX/POP)_{-1}$, *D*20201, *D*20202, *D*20203, *D*20204, *D*20211, *D*20212, *D*20213, *D*20214

explanatory variables. The unemployment rate has a negative and significant coefficient estimate, which means there is a discouraged worker effect regarding moonlighters, as would be expected. The equation is robust to all three tests.

4.6 Firm Sector

In the maximization problem of a firm in the theoretical model in chapter 3 in Fair (1984) there are five main decision variables: the firm's price, production, investment, demand for employment, and wage rate. These five decision variables are determined jointly in that they are the result of solving one maximization problem. The variables that affect this solution include (1) the initial stocks of excess capital, excess labor, and inventories; (2) the current and expected future values of the interest rate; (3) the current and expected future demand schedules for the firm's output; (4) the current and expected future supply schedules of labor facing the firm; and (5) the firm's expectations of other firms' future price and wage decisions.

In the US model, seven variables are chosen to represent the five decisions: (1) the price level for the firm sector, *PF*; (2) production, *Y*; (3) nonresidential fixed investment, *IKF*; (4) the number of jobs in the firm sector, *JF*; (5) the average number of hours paid per job, *HF*; (6) the average number of overtime hours paid per job, *HO*; and (7) the wage rate of the firm sector, *WF*. Each of these variables is determined by a stochastic equation, and these are the main stochastic equations of the firm sector.

Moving from the theoretical model of firm behavior to the econometric specifications is not straightforward, and a number of approximations have been made. One of the key approximations is to assume that the five decisions of a firm are made sequentially rather than jointly. The sequence is from the price decision, to the production decision, to the investment and employment decisions, and to the wage rate decision. In this way of looking at the problem, the firm first chooses its optimal price path. This path implies a certain expected sales path, from which the optimal production path is chosen. Given the optimal production path, the optimal paths of investment and employment are chosen.

Finally, given the optimal employment path, the optimal wage path is chosen.

The notation that is used in this section is presented in table 4.3. It is also repeated in table A.2 in the appendix.

Table 4.3
Variable Notation for the Firm Sector

Variable	Eq.	Description	Used in Equations
cnst2kk	exog	Time-varying constant term, 1981.3–1986.2.	12
D2G	exog	Profit tax rate, g.	12, 17, 49, 121
D2S	exog	Profit tax rate, s.	12, 17, 50, 121
D5G	exog	Employer social security tax rate, g.	10, 54
D593	exog	1 in 1959:3; 0 otherwise.	11, 13
D594	exog	1 in 1959:4; 0 otherwise.	11
D601	exog	1 in 1960:1; 0 otherwise.	11
DF	18	Net dividends paid, f, B$.	64, 69, 115
HF	14	Average number of hours paid per job, f, hours per quarter.	62, 100, 118
HFF	100	Deviation of *HFF* from *HFS*.	15
HFS	exog	Potential value of *HF*.	13, 14, 100
HO	15	Average number of overtime hours paid per job, f, hours per quarter.	43, 53, 54, 62, 67, 68, 115, 121, 126
JF	13	Number of jobs, f, millions.	14, 43, 53, 54, 64, 68, 69, 85, 115, 118, 121
JHMIN	94	Number of worker hours required to produce Y, millions.	13, 14
KK	12	Stock of capital, f, B2012$.	92
KKMIN	93	Amount of capital required to produce Y, B2012$.	12
LAM	exog	Amount of output capable of being produced per worker hour.	10, 16, 94
MF	17	Demand deposits and currency, f, B$.	70, 71, 81
PF	10	Price deflator for nonfarm sales.	16, 17, 26, 27, 31, 119
PIEF	67	Before-tax profits, f, B$.	18, 49, 50, 121, 132

Table 4.3
(continued)

Variable	Eq.	Description	Used in Equations
PIM	exog	Price deflator for IM.	10, 27, 33, 61, 74
PX	31	Price deflator for total sales.	12, 32, 33, 61, 72, 82, 119
RS	30	Three-month Treasury bill rate, percentage points.	17, 23, 24, 29, 127
T	exog	1 in 1952:1, 2 in 1952:2, etc.	3, 4, 6, 10, 14, 16
UR	87	Civilian unemployment rate.	5, 6, 7, 8, 10, 30
V	63	Stock of inventories, f, B2012$.	11, 82, 117
WF	16	Average hourly earnings excluding overtime of workers in f. (Includes supplements to wages and salaries except employer contributions for social insurance.)	10, 11, 28, 43, 44, 45, 46, 53, 54, 64, 68, 69, 121, 126
X	60	Total sales, B2012$.	11, 17, 26, 31, 33, 63
Y	11	Total production, B2012$.	10, 12, 13, 14, 27, 63, 83, 93, 94, 118
YS	exog	Potential output, B2012$.	12

- B$ = Billions of dollars.
- B2012$ = Billions of 2012 dollars.

4.6.1 Equation 10. *PF*, Private Nonfarm Price Deflator

Equation 10 in table A10 determines the price deflator of the firm sector, *PF*, the private nonfarm price deflator. A widely cited price deflator in the media is the price deflator for personal consumption expenditures (PCE). This is the price deflator targeted by the Federal Reserve (Fed). If, however, one is interested in explaining the pricing behavior of agents in the US economy, PCE is not appropriate because it includes import prices (as well as excluding export prices). The same is true of the consumer price index. Import prices reflect decisions of foreign agents and the behavior of exchange rates, which are not decision variables of domestic agents. The price deflator of the firm sector used here reflects private, domestic decisions. Its use is consistent with the theoretical model outlined above.

Equation 10 is in log form. The price level is a function of the lagged price level, the wage rate inclusive of the employer social security tax rate, the price of imports, the time trend, and the reciprocal of the unemployment

Table A10: Equation 10
LHS Variable Is $\log PF$

Equation			χ^2 Tests			
RHS Variable	Coef.	*t*-stat.	Test	χ^2	df	*p*-value
$\log PF_{-1}$	0.85948	60.77	Lags	16.37	3	0.0010
$\log[WF(1+D5G)/LAM]$	0.07627	4.88	*UR*	1.21	1	0.2716
cnst	−0.01418	−1.08	*GAP*	3.58	1	0.0584
T	0.00021	7.37	$1/(GAP+.07)$	1.57	1	0.2098
$\log PIM$	0.04918	16.46				
$1/UR$	0.00059	6.96				
D20201	−0.00649	−1.71				
D20202	−0.01230	−2.81				
D20203	0.00317	0.75				
D20204	0.00068	0.16				
D20211	0.00418	1.02				
D20212	0.00187	0.46				
D20213	0.00760	1.88				
D20214	0.00453	1.18				
RHO1	0.25956	4.25				
SE	0.00372					
R^2	1.000					

Lags test adds $\log PF_{-2}$, $\log PIM_{-1}$, and $1/UR_{-1}$.
Estimation period is 1954.1–2023.2.

First-Stage Regressors
$\log PF_{-1}$, $\log[[WF(1+D5G)/LAM]_{-1}$, *cnst*, *T*, $\log PIM_{-1}$, $1/UR_{-1}$, UR_{-1}, $\log[(COG+COS)/POP]_{-1}$, $\log[(TRGH+TRSH)/(POP\cdot PH)]_{-1}$, $\log(EX/POP)_{-1}$, $\log PF_{-2}$, *D20201*, *D20202*, *D20203*, *D20204*, *D20211*, *D20212*, *D20213*, *D20214*

rate. The unemployment rate is taken as a measure of demand pressure. The lagged price level is meant to pick up expectational effects, and the wage rate and import price variables are meant to pick up cost effects. (More will be said about expectations in the next subsection.) The log of the wage rate variable has subtracted from it $\log LAM$, where *LAM* is a measure of potential labor productivity. The construction of *LAM* is explained in chapter 5; it is computed from a peak-to-peak interpolation of measured productivity.

An important feature of the price equation is that the price *level* is explained by the equation, not the price *change*. This treatment is contrary to the standard Phillips-curve treatment, where the price (or wage) *change* is explained by the equation. It is also contrary to the standard NAIRU specification, where the change in the change in the price level (i.e., the change in the inflation rate) is explained. In the theoretical model, the natural decision variables of a firm are the levels of prices and wages. For example, the market share equations in the theoretical model have a firm's market share as a function of the ratio of the firm's price to the average price of other firms. These are price levels, and the objective of the firm is to choose the price level path (along with the paths of the other decision variables) that maximizes the multiperiod objective function. A firm decides what its price *level* should be relative to the price *levels* of other firms. This thus argues for a specification in levels, which is used here.

The time trend, T, is meant to pick up any trend effects on the price level not captured by the other variables. Adding the time trend to an equation like 10 is similar to adding the constant term to an equation specified in terms of changes rather than levels. The time trend will also pick up any trend mistakes made in constructing LAM. If, for example, $LAM_t = LAM_t^a + \alpha_1 t$, where LAM_t^a is the correct variable to subtract from the wage rate variable to adjust for potential productivity, then the time trend will absorb this error.

The variables in equation 10 are all highly significant. Regarding the cost variables, the wage variable has a t-statistic of 4.88 and the price of imports has a t-statistic of 16.46. On the demand side, the reciprocal of the unemployment rate has a t-statistic of 6.96. The equation is estimated under the assumption of first-order serial correlation of the error term. The serial correlation coefficient estimate is 0.26 with a t-statistic of 4.25.

The price of imports is a key explanatory variable in the equation. It is plotted relative to *PF* in figure 7.5. There was a huge increase in *PIM* relative to *PF* in the 1970s. A common view in the literature is that price equations (in particular Phillips curves) "broke down" in the 1970s when there was stagflation. In fact, the high inflation in the 1970s is well explained by cost shocks, particularly oil price shocks, which are picked up here by the price of imports. Note also from figure 7.5 that the relative price of imports fell in the 1980s, which is a factor leading to the falling inflation in the 1980s aside from aggregate demand effects. Volcker was help by favorable cost shocks during this period.

Regarding the χ^2 tests, the first test shows that the added lagged variables are highly significant. The lagged values are highly correlated with the included explanatory variables, and the resulting equation with the lagged values included does not have sensible estimates. The second test adds the level of *UR*, so that both *UR* and $1/UR$ are explanatory variables. *UR* is not significant and does not added explanatory power beyond $1/UR$. Adding the *GAP* variable in the third test also does not add explanatory power, with a p-value of 0.0584. Although not shown, $1/UR$ is still significant when *GAP* is added. For the fourth test, the reciprocal of *GAP* is added (after adjusting for the mean of *GAP*), and it is also not significant. $1/UR$ is also still significant for this test.

Regarding robustness, an interesting question in the current literature is whether the Phillips curve has become flatter. For equation 10, the question is whether the coefficient of $1/UR$ has become smaller over time. The coefficient estimate is in fact relatively stable, as can be seen as follows. When the equation is estimated only through 1975.4 (the sample period beginning in 1954.1), 88 observations, the coefficient estimate is 0.00080, which compares to 0.00059 in table A10. When the end point is extended one quarter at a time, the largest estimate is in fact 0.00080 in 1975.4. The the smallest estimate is 0.00055 in 2008.2. All the coefficient estimates are significant. This is a fairly small range for this kind of work.

What does not work, however, is to do a rolling regression of, say, 20 years (80 quarters). Here, the variation in the coefficient estimates is large. The problem with this procedure in my view is that the sample size is too small. As one rolls out of the mid 1980s, the inflation experience in the late 1960s, 1970s, and mid 1980s is lost, and one enters a much smoother period regarding inflation. Many of the 80-quarter estimation periods are not typical of the historical experience of inflation. It should not be surprising that price equations estimated for this period are considerably different from ones estimated earlier or for a longer period. Not using information through the 1980s is problematic.

The discussion next shows that equation 10 dominates traditional Phillips curves.

4.6.2 Equation 10: Expectations, Dynamics, and the NAIRU Model

The lagged price level in equation 10 is meant to pick up expectational effects, consistent with the assumption in the US model that expectations are not rational and depend on lagged values. A key question about price or inflation expectations is whether the Fed can influence them. The inflation expectations that matter for price equations are the expectations of firms, since firms are the agents setting prices.

My reading of the literature on firms' inflation expectations is that they are largely determined by firms' perceptions of current and past inflation. An early paper supporting the view that expectations of future inflation depend mostly on past inflation is Fuhrer (1997). Fast forward to the present, Coibion et al. (2020) have an informative review of the recent literature on how inflation expectations are formed. The evidence shows that household and firm expectations tend to differ considerably from market expectations and those of professional forecasters. The evidence also shows that the strongest predictor of households' and firms' inflation forecasts are what households and firms believe inflation has been in the recent past. There is also little evidence that firms know much about monetary policy targets. Further evidence from a survey of firms that began in 2018 is presented in Candia, Coibion, and Goroodnichenko (2021). This survey finds no evidence that firms' expectations of future inflation are anchored. The findings suggest that there is systematic inattention to monetary policy: "...we find that most CEOs are unaware of the Federal Reserve's inflation target. The fraction of CEOs that correctly identifies 2 percent as the inflation target is less than 20 percent. Nearly two thirds of CEOs are unwilling to even guess what the target is. Of those who dare, less than 50 percent think it is between 1.5 and 2.5 percent" (Candia et al., 2021, p. 4).

Another recent survey, of firms in France, described in Savignac et al. (2021), shows that firms' inflation expectations depend in large part on their perceptions of past inflation. The results also suggest that firms are not that knowledgeable about macroeconomics in that they perceive little link between price and wage inflation.

D'Acunto, Malmendier, and Weber (2022) review the literature on households' inflation expectations. The story is the same for households as it is for firms. Households' inflation expectations appear to be primarily determined by observations of current and past inflation, particularily of grocery store prices and gasoline prices. There is no evidence that monetary authorities' announcements play any role in determining these expectations.

This literature thus supports the use of lagged prices or lagged inflation as proxies for firms' expectations of future inflation. Conditional on this assumption, the following results show that the data do not support the dynamics of the expectations augmented Phillips curve. It will be seen that the data support the specification of price equations in level form rather than in first difference or second difference form.

The expectations augmented Phillips curve is

$$\pi_t = \pi^e_{t+1} + \beta(u_t - u^*) + \gamma s_t + \epsilon_t, \quad \beta < 0, \quad \gamma > 0, \tag{4.2}$$

where π_t is the rate of inflation, π^e_{t+1} is the expected rate of inflation for period $t+1$, u_t is the unemployment rate, s_t is a cost shock variable, ϵ_t is an error term, and u^* is the NAIRU.[1]

A key question, of course, is how π^e_{t+1} is determined. If it is assumed that agents look only at past inflation in forming their expectations of future inflation, a common specification is

$$\pi^e_{t+1} = \sum_{i=1}^{n} \delta_i \pi_{t-i}, \quad \sum_{i=1}^{n} \delta_i = 1. \tag{4.3}$$

Combining (4.2) and (4.3) yields:

$$\pi_t = \sum_{i=1}^{n} \delta_i \pi_{t-i} + \beta(u_t - u^*) + \gamma s_t + \epsilon_t, \quad \sum_{i=1}^{n} \delta_i = 1. \tag{4.4}$$

Equation (4.4) says that current inflation depends on past inflation, the unemployment rate, and a supply shock, where the coefficients on the past inflation rates sum to 1.

One restriction in equation (4.4) is that the δ_i coefficients sum to one. A second restriction is that each price level is subtracted from the previous price level before entering the equation. These two restrictions are straightforward to test. The test is simply to add p_{t-1} and p_{t-2} to equation (4.4) and see if they are significant, where p_t be the log of the price level for period t. Using this notation, equation (4.4) can be written in terms of p rather than π. If, for example, $n=1$, equation (4.4) becomes

$$p_t = 2p_{t-1} - p_{t-2} + \beta(u_t - u^*) + \gamma s_t + \epsilon_t. \tag{4.5}$$

In other words, equation (4.4) can be written in terms of the current and past two price levels,[2] with restrictions on the coefficients of the past two price levels. Similarly, if, say, $n=4$, equation (4.4) can be written in terms of the current and past five price levels, with two restrictions on the coefficients of the five past price levels. (Denoting the coefficients on the past five price levels as a_1 through a_5, the two restrictions are $a_4 = 5 - 4a_1 - 3a_2 - 2a_3$ and $a_5 = -4 + 3a_1 + 2a_2 + a_3$.)

An equivalent test to adding p_{t-1} and p_{t-2} is to add π_{t-1} (i.e., $p_{t-1} - p_{t-2}$) and p_{t-1}. Adding π_{t-1} breaks the restriction that the δ_i coefficients sum to one, and adding both π_{t-1} and p_{t-1} breaks the summation restriction and the restriction that each price level is subtracted from the previous price level before entering the equation. This latter restriction can be thought of as a first-derivative restriction, and the summation restriction can be thought of as a second-derivative restriction.

I have performed this test using a modified version of equation 10. I have dropped the wage variable and taken the demand variable to be *UR* rather than 1/*UR*. The estimation period is 1954.1–2023.1. I have used the OLS technique since this is what is done in the literature. For the estimation, n was taken to be 4, $p_t = \log PF_t$. $\pi_t = p_t - p_{t-1}$, and $u_t = UR_t$. s_t is postulated to be $\log PIM_t - \tau_0 - \tau_1 t$, the deviation of $\log PIM$ from a trend line. Given these variables and the restriction on the δ_i coefficients, the equation estimated is

$$\Delta\pi_t = \lambda_0 + \lambda_1 t + \sum_{i=2}^{4} \delta_i(\pi_{t-i} - \pi_{t-1}) + \beta UR_t + \gamma \log PIM_t + \epsilon_t, \tag{4.6}$$

where $\lambda_0 = -\beta u^* - \gamma\tau_0$ and $\lambda_1 = \gamma\tau_1$. u^* is not identified in equation (4.6), but for purposes of the tests this does not matter. If, however, one wanted to compute the NAIRU (i.e., u^*), one would need a separate estimate of τ_0 in order to estimate u^*.[3]

The results of estimating equation (4.6) are presented in column (1) in table 4.4. In column (2), π_{t-1} is added, and in column (3), both π_{t-1} and p_{t-1} are added. Comparing columns (1) and (2), table 4.4 shows that when π_{t-1} is added, it is significant with a t-statistic of −3.76. When both π_{t-1} and p_{t-1} are added in column (3), both are significant with t-statistics of −8.76 and −8.28, respectively. The χ^2 value for the hypothesis that the coefficients of both variables are zero is 82.01.[4]

The results thus strongly reject equation (4.6) and equation (4.6) with π_{t-1} added. Only the lagged inflation variables are significant, and there are very large changes in the coefficient estimates when π_{t-1} and

Table 4.4: Equation Estimates
Dependent Variable Is $\Delta\pi_t$

Variable	(1) Equation (4.6) Estimate	t-stat.	(2) Equation (4.6) π_{t-1} added Estimate	t-stat.	(3) Equation (4.6) π_{t-1} added and p_{t-1} added Estimate	t-stat.
cnst	0.0016	0.57	0.0072	2.20	−0.0344	−5.92
t	0.0000003	0.03	−0.0000180	−1.68	0.0001829	7.01
UR_t	−0.0303	−1.48	−0.0357	−1.76	−0.1278	−6.04
$\log PIM_t$	−0.0002	−0.17	0.0018	1.43	0.0344	8.41
$\pi_{t-2} - \pi_{t-1}$	0.272	4.16	0.233	3.56	0.084	1.37
$\pi_{t-3} - \pi_{t-1}$	0.208	3.17	0.167	2.96	0.076	1.29
$\pi_{t-4} - \pi_{t-1}$	0.124	1.99	0.075	1.19	0.030	0.54
π_{t-1}			−0.175	−3.26	−0.668	−8.76
p_{t-1}					−0.053	−8.28
SE	0.00439		0.00431		0.00383	
χ^2					82.01	

- $p_t = \log PF_t$, $\pi_t = \log(PF_t/PF_{t-1})$, UR_t = unemployment rate, $\log PIM$ = log of the price of imports.
- Estimation method: OLS.
- Estimation period: 1954.1–2019.4.
- Five percent χ^2 critical value = 5.99; one percent χ^2 critical value = 9.21.

p_{t-1} are added. In particular, the coefficient estimates of the unemployment rate are much smaller in absolute value without the two variables added.

The three equations in table 4.4 have quite different dynamics, and it is useful to examine the differences. The question considered is the following: If the unemployment rate were permanently lowered by one percentage point, what would the price level and inflation consequences be? To answer this question, the following experiment was performed for each equation. A dynamic simulation was run beginning in 2023.3 using the actual values of all the variables from 2023.2 back. The values of *UR*, *PIM*, and *t* from 2023.3 forward were taken to be the actual values for 2023.2. Call this simulation the "base" simulation. A second dynamic simulation was then run where the only change was that the unemployment rate was decreased permanently by one percentage point from 2023.3 on. The difference between

Table 4.5
Effects of a One Percentage Point Fall in *UR*

	Equation (4.6)		Equation (4.6) π_{t-1} added		Equation (4.6) π_{t-1} and p_{t-1} added	
Quar.	$p^{new} - p^{base}$	$\pi^{new} - \pi^{base}$	$p^{new} - p^{base}$	$\pi^{new} - \pi^{base}$	$p^{new} - p^{base}$	$\pi^{new} - \pi^{base}$
1	0.0004	0.12	0.0004	0.14	0.0016	0.51
2	0.0009	0.17	0.0010	0.19	0.0033	0.56
3	0.0016	0.22	0.0018	0.24	0.0051	0.58
4	0.0025	0.28	0.0027	0.30	0.0069	0.59
5	0.0036	0.34	0.0038	0.35	0.0088	0.58
6	0.0049	0.40	0.0051	0.39	0.0105	0.55
7	0.0065	0.46	0.0065	0.43	0.0122	0.52
8	0.0083	0.52	0.0080	0.46	0.0138	0.49
12	0.0179	0.75	0.0153	0.58	0.0189	0.35
40	0.2951	2.40	0.0982	0.80	0.0298	0.03
80	4.1287	4.76	0.2816	0.82	0.0311	0.00
120	63.0140	7.11	0.5529	0.82	0.0311	0.00

• P = price level (PF), $\pi = \log PF - \log PF_{-1}$.

the predicted value of π from this simulation and that from the base simulation for a given quarter is the estimated effect of the change in *UR* on π. Similarly for p.[5]

The results for the three equations are presented in table 4.5. It should be stressed that these experiments are not meant to be realistic. For example, there is no Fed reaction to the rise in inflation. The experiments are simply meant to help illustrate how the equations differ in a particular dimension.

Consider the very long-run properties in table 4.5 first. For equation (4.6), the new price level grows without bounds relative to the base price level and the new inflation rate grows without bounds relative to the base inflation rate. For equation (4.6) with π_{t-1} added, the new price level grows without bounds relative to the base, but the inflation rate does not. It is 0.82 percentage points higher in the long run. For equation (4.6) with both π_{t-1} and p_{t-1} added, the new price level is higher by 3.11 percent in the limit and the new inflation rate is back to the base.

The long-run properties are thus vastly different, as is, of course, obvious from the specifications. What is interesting, however, is that the effects on inflation are close after, say, eight quarters. The inflation differences, new minus base, are 0.52, 0.46, and 0.49, respectively. It is hard to distinguish among the equations based only on their short-run properties.

Finally, note that equation (4.6) in table 4.4 with both π_{t-1} and p_{t-1} added is not exactly equation 10. It is missing the wage variable, has three lagged explanatory inflation variables, uses *UR* instead of $1/UR$, is not estimated under the assumption of first-order serial correlation of the error term, and is estimated by OLS. However, adding π_{t-1} and p_{t-1} to equation (4.6) puts the equation in log level terms, as is equation 10. The two equations thus have similar dynamic properties.

4.6.3 Equation 11. *Y*, Production

The specification of the production equation is where the assumption that a firm's decisions are made sequentially begins to be used. The equation is based on the assumption that the firm sector first sets it price, then knows what its sales for the current period will be, and from this latter information decides on what its production for the current period will be.

In the theoretical model production is smoothed relative to sales. The reason for this is various costs of adjustment, which include costs of changing employment, costs of changing the capital stock, and costs of having the stock of inventories deviate from some proportion of sales. If a firm were only interested in minimizing inventory costs, it would produce according to the following equation (assuming that sales for the current period are known):

$$Y = X + \beta X - V_{-1}, \tag{4.7}$$

where Y is the level of production, X is the level of sales, V_{-1} is the stock of inventories at the end of the previous period, and β is the inventory-sales ratio that minimizes inventory costs. The construction of V is explained in chapter 5. Since by definition $V - V_{-1} = Y - X$, producing according to equation (4.7) would ensure that $V = \beta X$. Because of the other adjustment costs, it is generally not optimal for a firm to produce according to equation (4.7). In the theoretical model, there was no need to postulate explicitly how a firm's production plan deviated from equation (4.7) because its optimal production plan just results, along with the other optimal paths, from the direct solution of its maximization problem. For the empirical work, however, it is necessary to make further assumptions.

The estimated production equation is based on the following three assumptions:

$$\log V^* = \beta \log X, \tag{4.8}$$

$$\log Y^* = \log X + \alpha(\log V^* - \log V_{-1}), \tag{4.9}$$

$$\log Y - \log Y_{-1} = \lambda(\log Y^* - \log Y_{-1}) + \epsilon, \tag{4.10}$$

where * denotes a desired value. (In the following discussion, all variables are assumed to be in logs.) Equation (4.8) states that the desired stock of inventories is proportional to current sales. Equation (4.9) states that the desired level of production is equal to sales plus some fraction of the difference between the desired stock of inventories and the stock on hand at the end of the previous period. Equation (4.10) states that actual production partially adjusts to desired production each period.

Combining equations (4.8)–(4.10) yields:

$$\log Y = (1 - \lambda) \log Y_{-1} + \lambda(1 + \alpha\beta) \log X - \lambda\alpha \log V_{-1} + \epsilon. \tag{4.11}$$

Equation 11 in table A11 is the estimated version of equation (4.11). The equation is estimated under the assumption of a third-order autoregressive process of the error term, and three dummy variables are added to account for the effects of a steel strike in the last half of 1959.

The estimate of $1 - \lambda$ is .318, and so the implied value of λ is .682, which means that actual production adjusts 68.2 percent of the way to desired production in the current quarter. The estimate of $\lambda\alpha$ is .220, and so the implied value of α is .323. This means that (in logs) desired production is equal to sales plus 32.3 percent of the desired change in inventories. The estimate of $\lambda(1 + \alpha\beta)$ is .855, and so the implied value of β is .785.

The χ^2 tests show that equation 11 is robust in that the lagged values are not significant and the time trend is not significant.

The estimates of equation 11 are consistent with the view that firms smooth production relative to sales. The view that production is smoothed relative to sales was challenged by Blinder (1981) and others. This work was in turn challenged in Fair (1989) as being based on faulty data. The results in Fair (1989), which use data in physical units, suggest that production is smoothed relative to sales. The results using the physical units data thus provide some support for the current aggregate estimates.

Table A11: Equation 11
LHS Variable Is log Y

Equation			χ^2 Tests			
RHS Variable	Coef.	*t*-stat.	Test	χ^2	df	*p*-value
cnst	0.29989	4.55	Lags	3.67	2	0.1595
$\log Y_{-1}$	0.31759	6.58	T	1.69	1	0.1939
$\log X$	0.85539	15.60				
$\log V_{-1}$	−0.21962	−8.55				
*D*593	−0.00966	−2.61				
*D*594	−0.00375	−1.03				
*D*601	0.00953	2.58				
*D*20201	−0.00640	−1.59				
*D*20202	−0.02745	−4.70				
*D*20203	0.02451	4.21				
*D*20204	0.00222	0.49				
*D*20211	−0.00298	−0.63				
*D*20212	−0.00993	−2.12				
*D*20213	−0.01258	−2.97				
*D*20214	−0.00012	−0.03				
RHO1	0.40195	5.27				
RHO2	0.37467	5.85				
RHO3	0.16696	2.44				
SE	0.00406					
R^2	1.000					

Lags test adds $\log Y_{-2}$ and $\log X_{-1}$.
Estimation period is 1954.1–2023.2.

First-Stage Regressors

cnst, $\log Y_{-1}$, $\log V_{-1}$, *D*593, *D*594, *D*601, $\log Y_{-2}$, $\log Y_{-3}$, $\log Y_{-4}$, $\log V_{-2}$, $\log V_{-3}$, $\log V_{-4}$, $D601_{-1}$, $D601_{-2}$, $D601_{-3}$, $\log[(COG+COS)/POP]_{-1}$, $\log[(TRGH+TRSH)/(POP \cdot PH)]_{-1}$, $\log(EX/POP)_{-1}$, *D*20201, *D*20202, *D*20203, *D*20204, *D*20211, *D*20212, *D*20213, *D*20214, $D20214_{-1}$, $D20214_{-2}$, $D20214_{-3}$

4.6.4 Equation 12. *KK*, Stock of Capital

Equation 12 explains the stock of capital of the firm sector, *KK*. Given *KK*, nonresidential fixed investment of the firm sector, *IKF*, is determined by identity 92:

$$IKF = KK - (1 - DELK)KK_{-1}, \tag{4.12}$$

where *DELK* is the depreciation rate. The construction of *KK* and *DELK* is explained in chapter 5. Equation 12 will sometimes be referred to as an "investment" equation, since *IKF* is determined once *KK* is.

Equation 12 is based on the assumption that the production decision has already been made. In the theoretical model, because of costs of changing the capital stock, it may sometimes be optimal for a firm to hold excess capital. If there were no such costs, investment each period would merely be the amount needed to have enough capital to produce the output of the period. In the theoretical model, there was no need to postulate explicitly how investment deviates from this amount, but for the empirical work, this must be done.

The estimated equation for *KK* is based on the following two equations:

$$\begin{aligned} \log(KK^*/KK_{-1}) = {} & \alpha_0 \log(KK_{-1}/KKMIN_{-1}) + \alpha_1 \Delta \log Y \\ & + \alpha_2 \Delta \log Y_{-1} + \alpha_3 \Delta \log Y_{-2} + \alpha_4 \Delta \log Y_{-3} \\ & + \alpha_5 \Delta \log Y_{-4} + \alpha_6 r, \end{aligned} \tag{4.12}$$

$$\begin{aligned} \log(KK/KK_{-1}) - \log(KK_{-1}/KK_{-2}) = {} & \lambda[\log(KK^*/KK_{-1}) - \\ & - \log(KK_{-1}/KK_{-2})] + \epsilon, \end{aligned} \tag{4.13}$$

where r is some measure of the cost of capital, α_0 and α_6 are negative, and the other coefficients are positive. The construction of *KKMIN* is explained in chapter 5. It is, under the assumption of a putty-clay technology, an estimate of the minimum amount of capital required to produce the current level of output, Y. $KK_{-1}/KKMIN_{-1}$ is thus the ratio of the actual capital stock on hand at the end of the previous period to the minimum required to produce the output of that period. $\log(KK_{-1}/KKMIN_{-1})$ will be referred to as the amount of "excess capital" on hand.

KK^* in equation (4.12) is the value of the capital stock that the firm would desire to have on hand in the current period if there were no costs of changing the capital stock. The desired change, $\log(KK^*/KK_{-1})$, depends on (1) the amount of excess capital on hand, (2) five change-in-output terms, and (3) the cost of capital. The lagged output changes are meant to be proxies for expected future output changes. Other things equal, the firm desires to increase the capital stock if the output changes are positive. Equation (4.13) is a partial adjustment equation of the actual capital stock to the desired stock. It states that the actual percentage change in the capital stock is a fraction of the desired percentage change.

Ignoring the cost of capital term in equation (4.12), the equation says that the desired capital stock approaches *KKMIN* in the long run if output is not changing. How can the cost of capital term be justified? In the theoretical model, the cost of capital affects the capital stock by affecting the kinds of machines that are purchased. If the cost of capital falls, machines with lower labor requirements are purchased, other things being equal. For the empirical work, data are not available by types of machines, and approximations have to be made. A key approximation, discussed in chapter 5, is that the postulation of a putty-clay technology in the construction of *KKMIN*. If there is in fact some substitution of capital for labor in the short run, the cost of capital is likely to affect the firm's desired capital stock, and this is the reason for including a cost of capital term in equation (4.12).

Combining equations (4.12) and (4.13) yields:

$$\begin{aligned}\Delta \log KK = {} & \lambda\alpha_0 \log(KK_{-1}/KKMIN_{-1}) + (1-\lambda)\Delta \log KK_{-1} \\ & + \lambda\alpha_1 \Delta \log Y + \lambda\alpha_2 \Delta \log Y_{-1} + \lambda\alpha_3 \Delta \log Y_{-2} \\ & + \lambda\alpha_4 \Delta \log Y_{-3} + \lambda\alpha_5 \Delta \log Y_{-4} + \lambda\alpha_6 r + \epsilon.\end{aligned} \tag{4.14}$$

Equation 12 in table A12 is the estimated version of equation (4.14). The equation is estimated under the assumption of first-order serial correlaion of the error term. The equation is also estimated under the assumption of a time-varying constant, with T_1 being 1978.4 and T_2 being 1987.4.

The estimate of $1-\lambda$ is 0.873, and so the implied value of λ is 0.127. The estimate of $\lambda\alpha_0$ is $-.0084$, and so the implied value of α_0 is $-.066$. This is the estimate of the size of the effect of excess capital on the desired stock of capital. The cost of capital variable in the equation that is used is a function of stock price changes. It is the ratio of capital gains or losses on the financial assets of the household sector (mostly from corporate stocks) over three quarters to nominal potential output. This ratio is a measure of how well or poorly the stock market is doing. If the stock market is doing well, for example, the ratio is high, which should in general lower the cost of capital to firms. This variable is significant with a t-statistic of 4.08. Various interest rates were tried as another cost of capital variable, but none were

Table A12: Equation 12
LHS Variable Is $\Delta \log KK$

Equation			χ^2 Tests			
RHS Variable	Coef.	t-stat.	Test	χ^2	df	p-value
cnst2kk	−0.00043	−3.82	Lags	5.15	3	0.1614
cnst	0.00094	3.60	T	3.41	1	0.0648
$\log(KK/KKMIN)_{-1}$	−0.00836	−3.43				
$\Delta \log KK_{-1}$	0.87323	42.07				
$\Delta \log Y$	0.01366	1.53				
$\Delta \log Y_{-1}$	0.00867	2.20				
$\Delta \log Y_{-2}$	0.00332	0.82				
$\Delta \log Y_{-3}$	0.00406	1.12				
$\Delta \log Y_{-4}$	0.00686	1.94				
a	0.00074	4.08				
D20201	−0.00092	−1.94				
D20202	−0.00117	−1.23				
D20203	0.00137	1.50				
D20204	0.00013	0.20				
D20211	−0.00051	−0.84				
D20212	−0.00021	−0.35				
D20213	−0.00159	−2.97				
D20214	−0.00122	−2.67				
RHO1	0.15657	2.27				
SE	0.00043					
R^2	0.977					

[a] Variable is $(CG_{-2}+CG_{-3}+CG_{-4})/(PX_{-2}YS_{-2}+PX_{-3}YS_{-3}+PX_{-4}YS_{-4})$
Lags test adds $\log(KK/KKMIN)_{-2}$, $\Delta \log Y_{-5}$, and [a] lagged once.
Estimation period is 1954.1–2023.2.
T_1 = 1978.4; T_2 = 1987.4.

First-Stage Regressors

cnst2kk, *cnst*, $\log KK_{-1}$, $\log KK_{-2}$, $\log Y_{-1}$, $\log Y_{-2}$, $\log Y_{-3}$, $\log Y_{-4}$, $\log Y_{-5}$, $\log(KK/KKMIN)_{-1}$, $\Delta \log Y_{-5}$, [a] lagged twice, $\log[(COG+COS)/POP]_{-1}$, $\log[(TRGH+TRSH)/(POP\cdot PH)]_{-1}$, $\log(EX/POP)_{-1}$, $\log(KK/KKMIN)_{-2}$, $\Delta \log KK_{-2}$, *D20201*, *D20202*, *D20203*, *D20204*, *D20211*, *D20212*, *D20213*, *D20214*, $D20214_{-1}$

significant. This is a common result. It is hard to find significant interest rate effects on nonresidential fixed investment.

Equation 12 is robust. The lagged variables are not significant, nor is the time trend.

4.6.5 Equation 13. *JF*, Number of Jobs

The employment equation 13 and the hours equation 14 are similar in spirit to the capital stock equation 12. They are also based on the assumption that the production decision is made first. Because of adjustment costs, it is sometimes optimal in the theoretical model for firms to hold excess labor. Were it not for the costs of changing employment, the optimal level of employment would merely be the amount needed to produce the output of the period. In the theoretical model, there was no need to postulate explicitly how employment deviates from this amount, but this must be done for the empirical work.

The estimated employment equation is based on the following two equations:

$$\log(JF^*/JF_{-1}) = \alpha_0 \log[JF_{-1}/(JHMIN_{-1}/HFS_{-1})] + \alpha_1 \Delta \log Y, \tag{4.15}$$

$$\log(JF/JF_{-1}) - \log(JF_{-1}/JF_{-2}) = \lambda[\log(JF^*/JF_{-1}) - \log(JF_{-1}/JF_{-2})] + \epsilon, \tag{4.16}$$

where α_0 is negative and the other coefficients are positive. The construction of *JHMIN* and *HFS* is explained in chapter 5. *JHMIN* is, under the assumption of a putty-clay technology, an estimate of the minimum number of worker hours required to produce the current level of output, Y. *HFS* is an estimate of the desired number of hours worked per worker. $JF_{-1}/(JHMIN_{-1}/HFS_{-1})$ is the ratio of the actual number of workers on hand at the end of the previous period to the minimum number required to produce the output of that period if the average number of hours worked were HFS_{-1}. $\log[JF_{-1}/JHMIN_{-1}/HFS_{-1})]$ will be referred to as the amount of "excess labor" on hand.

JF^* in equation (4.15) is the number of workers that the firm would desire to have on hand in the current period if there were no costs of changing employment. The desired change, $\log(JF^*/JF_{-1})$, depends on the amount of excess labor on hand and the change in output. This equation says that the desired number of workers approaches *JHMIN*/*HFS* in the long run if output is not changing. Equation (4.16) is a partial adjustment equation of the actual number of workers to the desired number.

Combining equations (4.15) and (4.16) yields:

$$\Delta \log JF = \lambda\alpha_0 \log[JF_{-1}/(JHMIN_{-1}/HFS_{-1})] + (1-\lambda)\Delta \log JF_{-1} + \lambda\alpha_1 \Delta \log Y + \epsilon. \quad (4.17)$$

Equation 13 in table A13 is the estimated version of equation (4.17). It has a dummy variable, *D*593, added to pick up the effects of a steel strike. The estimate of $1-\lambda$ is 0.590, and so the implied value of λ is 0.410. The estimate of $\lambda\alpha_0$ is −0.053, and so the implied value of α_0 is −0.129. This is the

Table A13: Equation 13
LHS Variable Is $\Delta \log JF$

Equation			χ^2 Tests			
RHS Variable	Coef.	*t*-stat.	Test	χ^2	df	*p*-value
cnst	0.00082	1.17	Lags	14.87	3	0.0019
$\log JF/(JHMIN/HFS)_{-1}$	−0.05320	−4.50	RHO	2.63	1	0.1045
$\Delta \log JF_{-1}$	0.58951	13.72	*T*	1.81	1	0.1785
$\Delta \log Y$	0.28270	3.57				
*D*593	−0.01810	−5.30				
*D*20201	−0.00564	−1.55				
*D*20202	−0.09792	−12.32				
*D*20203	0.11085	10.20				
*D*20204	−0.02327	−5.87				
*D*20211	−0.00824	−2.48				
*D*20212	0.00014	0.04				
*D*20213	0.00467	1.39				
*D*20214	−0.00254	−0.77				
SE	0.00322					
R^2	0.911					

Lags test adds $\log JF/(JHMIN/HFS)_{-2}$, $\Delta \log JF_{-2}$, and $\Delta \log Y_{-1}$.
Estimation period is 1954.1–2023.2.

First-Stage Regressors

cnst, $\log[JF/(JHMIN/HFS)]_{-1}$, $\Delta \log JF_{-1}$, $\Delta \log Y_{-1}$, *D*593, $\log[(COG + COS)/POP]_{-1}$, $\log[(TRGH + TRSH)/(POP \cdot PH)]_{-1}$, $\log(EX/POP)_{-1}$, *D*20201, *D*20202, *D*20203, *D*20204, *D*20211, *D*20212, *D*20213, *D*20214

estimate of the size of the effect of excess labor on the desired number of workers.

Regarding the χ^2 tests, the serial correlation coefficieint is not significant, nor is the time trend. The lagged values are, however, significant, with a p-value of 0.0019.

The ideas behind the employment demand equation 13 and the hours demand equation 14 discussed next go back to my PhD dissertation, Fair (1969). See also Fair (1985), which shows that the aggregate equations are consistent with the survey results of Fay and Medoff (1985). These two equations have held up remarkably well over the years.

The fact that firms are not always on their production function regarding labor, holding excess labor at times, means that labor productivity defined as actual output divided by actual jobs is procyclical. As output expands, some of the increase in labor requirements is met by drawing down excess labor, so measured productivity increases. When output falls, excess labor is built up, and so measured productivity decreases. Productivity changes are not exogenous shocks, but endogenous responses by firms to output changes.

4.6.6 Equation 14. *HF*, Average Number of Hours Paid per Job

The estimated hours equation is

$$\begin{aligned}\Delta \log HF &= \lambda \log(HF_{-1}/HFS_{-1}) \\ &+ \alpha_0 \log[JF_{-1}/(JHMIN-1/HFS_{-1})] + \alpha_1 \Delta \log Y + \epsilon.\end{aligned} \tag{4.18}$$

The first term on the RHS of equation (4.18) is the (logarithmic) difference between the actual number of hours paid for in the previous period and the desired number. The reason for the inclusion of this term in the hours equation but not in the employment equation is that, unlike *JF*, *HF* fluctuates around a slowly trending level of hours. This restriction is captured by the first term in (4.18). It could be that the term does not exactly capture the slowly trending effect, and the time trend has been added to the estimated equation to pick up any missing trend effects. The other two terms are the amount of excess labor on hand and the current change in output. Both of these terms affect the employment decision, and they should also affect the hours decision since the two are closely related.

Equation 14 in table A14 is the estimated version of equation (4.18). The estimate of λ is −0.130. The estimate of α_0 is −0.014. This estimate is small and not significant, which means that most of the effect of excess labor on employment decisions is estimated to be through jobs rather than hours per job. The equation is robust in that neither the added lags nor the estimate of the serial correlation coefficient is significant.

Table A14: Equation 14
LHS Variable Is $\Delta \log HF$

Equation			χ^2 Tests			
RHS Variable	Coef.	*t*-stat.	Test	χ^2	df	*p*-value
cnst	−0.00438	−4.92	Lags	6.61	3	0.0854
$\log(HF/HFS)_{-1}$	−0.12962	−4.66	RHO	1.84	1	0.1745
$\log JF/(JHMIN/HFS)_{-1}$	−0.01405	−1.41				
$\Delta \log Y$	0.26874	4.16				
T	0.00001	4.13				
D20201	−0.00157	−0.52				
D20202	0.01109	1.68				
D20203	−0.00852	−1.51				
D20204	0.00313	1.11				
D20211	−0.00294	−1.01				
D20212	−0.00275	−0.95				
D20213	−0.00239	−0.85				
D20214	−0.00342	−1.19				
SE	0.00273					
R^2	0.398					

Lags test adds $\log(HF/HFS)_{-2}$, $\log JF/(JHMIN/HFS)_{-2}$, and $\Delta \log Y_{-1}$.
Estimation period is 1954.1–2023.2.

First-Stage Regressors

cnst, $\log(HF/HFS)_{-1}$, $\log[JF/(JHMIN/HFS)]_{-1}$, $\Delta \log Y_{-1}$, T, $\log[(COG+COS)/POP]_{-1}$, $\log[(TRGH+TRSH)/(POP \cdot PH)]_{-1}$, $\log(EX/POP)_{-1}$, *D20201*, *D20202*, *D20203*, *D20204*, *D20211*, *D20212*, *D20213*, *D20214*

4.6.7 Equation 15. *HO*, Average Number of Overtime Hours Paid per Job

Equation 15 explains overtime hours, *HO*. Let $HFF = HF - HFS$, which is the deviation of actual hours per worker from desired hours. One would expect *HO* to be close to zero for low values of *HFF* (i.e., when actual hours are much below desired hours), and to increase roughly one for one for high values of *HFF*. An approximation to this relationship is

$$HO = e^{\alpha_1 + \alpha_2 HFF + \epsilon}, \tag{4.19}$$

which in log form is

$$\log HO = \alpha_1 + \alpha_2 HFF + \epsilon. \tag{4.20}$$

Equation 15 in table A15 is the estimated version of equation (4.20). Both *HFF* and HFF_{-1} are included in the equation, which appears to capture the dynamics better. The equation is estimated under the assumption of

Table A15: Equation 15

LHS Variable Is $\log HO$

Equation			χ^2 Tests			
RHS Variable	Coef.	*t*-stat.	Test	χ^2	df	*p*-value
cnst	3.93658	46.84	Lags	0.07	1	0.7954
HFF	0.01655	8.39	*T*	3.70	1	0.0545
HFF_{-1}	0.00827	4.19				
D20201	0.01431	0.34				
D20202	−0.12866	−2.20				
D20203	0.01712	0.26				
D20204	−0.01540	−0.23				
D20211	−0.03512	−0.53				
D20212	−0.04670	−0.73				
D20213	−0.06485	−1.16				
D20214	−0.05851	−1.38				
RHO1	0.96722	62.71				
SE	0.04425					
R^2	0.961					

Lags test adds HFF_{-2}.
Estimation period is 1956.1–2023.2.
OLS estimation.

first-order serial correlation of error term. The estimate of the serial correlation coefficient is large at 0.967. Regarding the χ^2 tests, the added lagged value is not significant, nor is the time trend.

4.6.8 Equation 16. *WF*, Average Hourly Earnings Excluding Overtime

Equation 16 is the wage rate equation. It is in log form. In the final specification, the wage rate was simply taken to be a function of the constant term, the current value of the price level, the lagged value of the price level, and the lagged value of the wage rate. The potential productivity variable, *LAM*, is subtracted from the wage rate in equation 16. The price equation, equation 10, is identified because the wage rate equation includes the lagged wage rate, which the price equation does not. The wage rate equation is identified because the price equation includes the price of imports and the reciprocal of the unemployment rate, which the wage rate equation does not.

A constraint was imposed on the coefficients in the wage equation to ensure that the determination of the real wage implied by equations 10 and 16 is sensible. Let $p = \log PF$ and $w = \log WF$. The relevant parts of the price and wage equations regarding the constraints are

$$p = \beta_1 p_{-1} + \beta_2 w + \ldots, \tag{4.21}$$

$$w = \gamma_1 w_{-1} + \gamma_2 p + \gamma_3 p_{-1} + \ldots. \tag{4.22}$$

The implied real wage equation from these two equations should not have $w - p$ as a function of either w or p separately, since one does not expect the real wage to grow simply because the levels of w and p are growing. The desired form of the real wage equation is thus

$$w - p = \delta_1 (w_{-1} - p_{-1}) + \ldots, \tag{4.23}$$

which says that the real wage is a function of its own lagged value plus other terms. The real wage is *not* a function of the level of w or p separately. The constraint on the coefficients in equations (4.21) and (4.22) that imposes this restriction is

$$\gamma_3 = [\beta_1/(1 - \beta_2)](1 - \gamma_2) - \gamma_1. \tag{4.24}$$

This constraint is imposed in the estimation by first estimating the price equation to get estimates of β_1 and β_2 and then using these estimates to impose the constraint on γ_3 in the wage equation.

The coefficient estimates of the lagged wage and the price level are highly significant in equation 16 in table A16. The implied coefficient on the lagged price level is −0.862. The first χ^2 test tests the hypothesis that the real wage restriction discussed above is true. The hypothesis is rejected at the 95 but not 99 percent confidence level. The added lagged value is not significant, although the time trend is. The estimate of the serial correlation coefficient is not significant.

Table A16: Equation 16
LHS Variable Is $\log(WF/LAM)$

Equation			χ^2 Tests			
RHS Variable	Coef.	*t*-stat.	Test	χ^2	df	*p*-value
$\log(WF/LAM)_{-1}$	0.93573	54.28	[b]RealWage Res	5.50	1	0.0190
$\log PF$	0.92099	36.68	Lags	0.02	1	0.8784
cnst	−0.04083	−3.77	T	7.41	1	0.0065
$D20201$	0.02788	3.53	RHO	0.03	1	0.8662
$D20202$	0.08456	10.71	$1/UR$	6.29	1	0.0122
$D20203$	−0.01615	−1.96	$1/(GAP+.07)$	2.64	1	0.1041
$D20204$	0.00337	0.41				
$D20211$	−0.01587	−1.95				
$D20212$	0.01336	1.66				
$D20213$	−0.00228	−0.28				
$D20214$	−0.00073	−0.09				
[a]$\log PF_{-1}$	−0.86221					
SE	0.00785					
R^2	0.947					

[a]Coefficient constrained. See the discussion in the text.
[b]Equation estimated with no restrictions on the coefficients.
Lags test adds $\log(WF/LAM)_{-2}$.
Estimation period is 1954.1–2023.2.

First-Stage Regressors

cnst, T, $\log WF_{-1} - \log LAM_{-1} - \log PF_{-1}$, $\log PF_{-1}$, $\log PF_{-2}$, $\log PIM_{-1}$, $\log[(COG+COS)/POP]_{-1}$, $\log[(TRGH+TRSH)/(POP \cdot PH)]_{-1}$, $\log(EX/POP)_{-1}$, $1/UR_{-1}$, UR_{-1}, $D20201$, $D20202$, $D20203$, $D20204$, $D20211$, $D20212$, $D20213$, $D20214$

An interesting question is whether a demand pressure variable should be added to the wage equation. The fifth χ^2 test shows that the reciprocal of the unemployment is significant, with a p-value of 0.0190. In the next test, the reciprocal of the gap variable is not significant. I have chosen not to add $1/UR$ to the equation. Having $1/UR$ in both equations 10 and 16 can be problematic in the price level affecting the wage rate and vice versa. But this is an area for further research.

4.6.9 Equation 17. *MF*, Demand Deposits and Currency, Firm Sector

Equation 17 is the demand for money equation of the firm sector. In earlier versions of the US model, a demand for money equation of the household sector was also estimated (old equation 9). The data became unreliable, and this equation is no longer in the model. The model now contains two demand for money equations: equation 17 and a demand for currency equation, which is equation 26 below. These two equations are not in fact important in the model because of the use of the interest rate rule (equation 30 below). They are included more for historical reasons than anything else. When the interest rate rule is used, the short-term interest rate is determined by the rule and the overall money supply is whatever is needed to have the demand for money equations be met.

Before presenting these two equations, it is necessary to discuss how the dynamics are handled. The key question about the dynamics is whether the adjustment of actual to desired values is in nominal or real terms. Let M_t^*/P_t denote the desired level of real money balances, let y_t denote a measure of real transactions, and let r_t denote a short-term interest rate. Assume that the equation determining desired money balances is in log form and write

$$\log(M_t^*/P_t) = \alpha + \beta \log y_t + \gamma r_t. \tag{4.25}$$

Note that the log form has not been used for the interest rate. Interest rates can at times be quite low, and it may not be sensible to take the log of the interest rate. If, for example, the interest rate rises from .02 to .03, the log of the rate rises from −3.91 to −3.51, a change of .40. If, on the other hand, the interest rate rises from .10 to .11, the log of the rate rises from −2.30 to −2.21, a change of only .09. One does not necessarily expect a one percentage point rise in the interest rate to have four times the effect on the log of desired money holdings when the change is from a base of .02 rather than .10.

If the adjustment of actual to desired money holdings is in real terms, the adjustment equation is

$$\log(M_t/P_t) - \log(M_{t-1}/P_{t-1}) = \lambda[\log(M_t^*/P_t) - \log(M_{t-1}/P_{t-1})] + \epsilon. \quad (4.26)$$

If the adjustment is in nominal terms, the adjustment equation is

$$\log M_t - \log M_{t-1} = \lambda(\log M_t^* - \log M_{t-1}) + \mu. \quad (4.27)$$

Combining (4.25) and (4.26) yields :

$$\log(M_t/P_t) = \lambda\alpha + \lambda\beta \log y_t + \lambda\gamma r_t + (1-\lambda)\log(M_{t-1}/P_{t-1}) + \epsilon. \quad (4.28)$$

Combining (4.25) and (4.27) yields:

$$\log(M_t/P_t) = \lambda\alpha + \lambda\beta \log y_t + \lambda\gamma r_t + (1-\lambda)\log(M_{t-1}/P_t) + \mu. \quad (4.29)$$

Equations (4.28) and (4.29) differ in the lagged money term. In (4.28), which is the real adjustment specification, M_{t-1} is divided by P_{t-1}, whereas in (4.29), which is the nominal adjustment specification, M_{t-1} is divided by P_t.

A test of the two hypotheses is simply to put both lagged money variables in the equation and see which one dominates. If the real adjustment specification is correct, $\log(M_{t-1}/P_{t-1})$ should be significant and $\log(M_{t-1}/P_t)$ should not, and vice versa if the nominal adjustment specification is correct. This test may, of course, be inconclusive in that both terms may be significant or insignificant. It turns out that the real adjustment specification dominates.

Equation 17 in table A17 is the estimated version of equation (4.28) for the firm sector. The transactions variable is the level of nonfarm firm sales, $X - FA$, and the interest rate variable is the after-tax three-month Treasury bill rate. The tax rates used in this equation are the corporate tax rates, *D2G* and *D2S*.

All the variables are significant in the equation. The first test result shows that the lagged dependent variable that pertains to the nominal adjustment specification, $\log(MF_{-1}/PF)$, is not significant. The lagged values are not significant, nor is the estimate of the serial correlation coefficient. The time trend is significant.

Table A17: Equation 17
LHS Variable Is $\log(MF/PF)$

Equation			χ^2 Tests			
RHS Variable	Coef.	*t*-stat.	Test	χ^2	df	*p*-value
cnst	0.04187	0.87	$\log(MF_{-1}/PF)$	1.22	1	0.2690
$\log(MF/PF)_{-1}$	0.97796	92.20	Lags	6.67	3	0.0830
$\log(X-FA)$	0.01519	2.39	RHO	1.29	1	0.2560
$RS(1-D2G-D2S)$	−0.00502	−3.18	T	8.13	1	0.0044
D20201	0.19143	4.21				
D20202	0.16598	3.62				
D20203	−0.05346	−1.16				
D20204	−0.04510	−0.98				
D20211	0.01761	0.38				
D20212	0.00083	0.02				
D20213	0.03357	0.73				
D20214	0.03288	0.71				
SE	0.04465					
R^2	0.992					

Lags test adds $\log(MF/PF)_{-2}$, $\log(X-FA)_{-1}$, and $RS(1-D2G-D2S)_{-1}$.
Estimation period is 1954.1–2023.2.

First-Stage Regressors

cnst, $\log(MF/PF)_{-1}$, $\log(X-FA)_{-1}$, $RS(1-D2G-D2S)_{-1}$, $\log[(COG+COS)/POP]_{-1}$, $\log[(TRGH+TRSH)/(POP\cdot PH)]_{-1}$, $\log(EX/POP)_{-1}$, $\log(MF_{-2}/PF_{-1})$, *D20201*, *D20202*, *D20203*, *D20204*, *D20211*, *D20212*, *D20213*, *D20214*

4.6.10 Equation 18. *DF*, Dividends Paid

Let Π denote after-tax profits. If in the long run firms desire to pay out all of their after-tax profits in dividends, one can write $DF^* = \Pi$, where DF^* is the long-run desired value of dividends for profit level Π. If it is assumed that actual dividends are partially adjusted to desired dividends each period as

$$DF/DF_{-1} = (DF^*/DF_{-1})^{\lambda} e^{\epsilon}, \tag{4.30}$$

then the equation to be estimated is

$$\Delta \log DF = \lambda \log(\Pi/DF_{-1}) + \epsilon. \tag{4.31}$$

Equation 18 in table A18 is the estimated version of equation (4.31). The level of after-tax profits in the notation of the model is *PIEF* – *TFG* – *TFS* – *TFR*. The estimate of λ is .023, with a *t*-statistic of 3.74. This estimate implies a slow adjustment of actual to desired dividends, which is not surprising. The equation does well in the tests. For the first test, the hypothesis that the restriction discussed above is valid is not rejected. (This restriction is tested by simply adding $\log DF_{-1}$ to the equation.) The added lagged value is not significant, nor is the estimate of the serial correlation coefficient and the time trend. The last test shows that the constant term is not significant. The above specification does not call for the constant term, and this is supported by the data.

Table A18: Equation 18
LHS Variable Is $\Delta \log DF$

Equation			χ^2 Tests			
RHS Variable	Coef.	*t*-stat.	Test	χ^2	df	*p*-value
a	0.02342	3.74	[b]Restriction	0.11	1	0.7427
D20201	0.12679	1.56	Lags	0.78	1	0.3762
D20202	−0.11292	−1.39	RHO	0.85	1	0.3565
D20203	0.12617	1.55	*T*	0.00	1	0.9981
D20204	−0.03468	−0.43	cnst	0.14	1	0.7096
D20211	0.06341	0.78				
D20212	0.07981	0.98				
D20213	−0.08404	−1.03				
D20214	0.10650	1.31				
SE	0.08114					
R^2	0.062					

[a]Variable is $\log[(PIEF - TFG - TFS - TFR)/DF_{-1}]$
[b]$\log DF_{-1}$ added.
Lags test adds [a] lagged once.
Estimation period is 1954.1–2023.2.

First-Stage Regressors

cnst, $\log[(PIEF-TFG-TFS)/DF_{-1}]_{-1}$, $\log[(COG+COS)/POP]_{-1}$, $\log[(TRGH+TRSH)/(POP \cdot PH)]_{-1}$, $\log(EX/POP)_{-1}$ *D20201*, *D20202*, *D20203*, *D20204*, *D20211*, *D20212*, *D20213*, *D20214*

4.7 Financial Sector

The stochastic equations for the financial sector consist of two-term structure equations and a demand for currency equation. The notation that is used for the financial sector and also for the import equation and government sectors below is presented in table 4.6. It is also repeated in table A.2 in the appendix.

Table 4.6
Variable Notation for Financial and Government Sectors and Import Equation

Variable	Eq.	Description	Used in Equations
AA	133	Total net wealth, h, B2012$.	1, 2, 3, 5, 6, 7, 27
*AG*1	exog	Percent of 16+ population 26–55 minus percent 16–25.	1, 2, 3, 4, 27
*AG*2	exog	Percent of 16+ population 56–65 minus percent 16–25.	1, 2, 3, 4, 27
*AG*3	exog	Percent of 16+ population 66+ minus percent 16–25.	1, 2, 3, 4, 27
*D*691	exog	1 in 1969:1; 0 otherwise.	27
*D*692	exog	1 in 1969:2; 0 otherwise.	27
*D*714	exog	1 in 1971:4; 0 otherwise.	27
*D*721	exog	1 in 1972:1; 0 otherwise.	27
*D*794823	exog	1 in 1979:4-1982:3; 0 otherwise.	30
*D*20083	exog	1 in 1952.1-2008.3; 0 otherwise.	30
DF	18	Net dividends paid, f, B$.	64, 69, 115
IM	27	Imports, B2012$.	33, 60, 61, 74
INTG	29	Net interest payments, g, B$.	56, 64, 76, 106, 115
*PCM*1	124	Percentage change in M1, annual rate, percentage points.	30
PF	10	Price deflator for nonfarm sales.	16, 17, 26, 27, 31, 119
PIEF	67	Before-tax profits, f, B$.	18, 49, 50, 121, 132
PIM	exog	Price deflator for IM.	10, 27, 33, 61, 74
POP	120	Noninstitutional population 16+, millions.	1, 2, 3, 4, 5, 6, 7, 8, 26, 27, 47, 48
RB	23	Bond rate, percentage points.	29
RM	24	Mortgage rate, percentage points.	128
RMA	128	After-tax mortgage rate, percentage points.	2, 3, 4

Table 4.6
(continued)

Variable	Eq.	Description	Used in Equations
RS	30	Three-month Treasury bill rate, percentage points.	17, 23, 24, 29, 127
RSA	127	After-tax bill rate, percentage points.	1, 26
U	86	Number of people unemployed, millions.	28, 87
UB	28	Unemployment insurance benefits, B$.	65, 78, 111, 115
UR	87	Civilian unemployment rate.	5, 6, 7, 8, 10, 30
WF	16	Average hourly earnings excluding overtime of workers in f. (Includes supplements to wages and salaries except employer contributions for social insurance.)	10, 11, 28, 43, 44, 45, 46, 53, 54, 64, 68, 69, 121, 126
X	60	Total sales, B2012$.	11, 17, 26, 31, 33, 63
Y	11	Total production, B2012$.	10, 12, 13, 14, 27, 63, 83, 93, 94, 118

- B$ = Billions of dollars.
- B2012$ = Billions of 2012 dollars.

4.7.1 Equation 23. *RB*, Bond Rate; Equation 24. *RM*, Mortgage Rate

The expectations theory of the term structure of interest rates states that long-term rates are a function of current and expected future short-term rates. The two long-term interest rates in the model are the bond rate, *RB*, and the mortgage rate, *RM*. These rates are assumed to be determined according to the expectations theory, where the current and past values of the short-term interest rate (the three-month Treasury bill rate, *RS*) are used as proxies for expected future values. Equations 23 and 24 are the two estimated equations. The lagged dependent variable is used in each of these equations, which implies a fairly complicated lag structure relating each long-term rate to the past values of the short-term rate. In addition, a constraint has been imposed on the coefficient estimates. The sum of the coefficients of the current and lagged values of the short-term rate has been constrained to be equal to one minus the coefficient of the lagged long-term rate. This means that, for example, a sustained one percentage point increase in the short-term rate eventually results in a one percentage point increase in the long-term rate. (This restriction is imposed by subtracting RS_{-2} from each of the other interest rates in the equations.) Equation 23 (but not 24) is estimated under the assumption of first-order serial correlation of the error term.

The results for the two equations are in tables A23 and A24. They are quite good. The short-term interest rates are significant in the two

Table A23: Equation 23

LHS Variable Is $RB - RS_{-2}$

Equation			χ^2 Tests			
RHS Variable	Coef.	*t*-stat.	Test	χ^2	df	*p*-value
cnst	0.19660	4.54	[a]Restriction	0.06	1	0.8099
$RB_{-1} - RS_{-2}$	0.91834	57.85	Lags	0.42	2	0.8105
$RS - RS_{-2}$	0.32027	4.93	T	2.50	1	0.1138
$RS_{-1} - RS_{-2}$	−0.26142	−3.51	[b]	0.75	1	0.3854
D20201	−0.03960	−0.14	[c]	0.50	1	0.4787
D20202	−0.20465	−0.70				
D20203	−0.24300	−0.85				
D20204	0.05216	0.18				
D20211	0.42309	1.49				
D20212	0.17777	0.62				
D20213	−0.32446	−1.14				
D20214	0.00161	0.01				
RHO1	0.20616	3.26				
SE	0.27749					
R^2	0.962					

[a] RS_{-2} added.
[b] $100 \cdot (PD/PD(-4) - 1)$
[c] $100 \cdot [(PD/PD(-8))^{.5} - 1]$
Lags test adds RS_{-3} and RB_{-2}.
Estimation period is 1954.1–2023.2.

First-Stage Regressors

$cnst$, RB_{-1}, RB_{-2}, RS_{-1}, RS_{-2}, RS_{-3}, $100[(PD/PD_{-1})^4 - 1]_{-1}$, UR_{-1}, $\log(PIM/PF)_{-1}$, $\log[(COG + COS)/POP]_{-1}$, $\log[(TRGH + TRSH)/(POP \cdot PH)]_{-1}$, $\log(EX/POP)_{-1}$, T, $D20201$, $D20202$, $D20203$, $D20204$, $D20211$, $D20212$, $D20213$, $D20214$, $D20214_{-1}$

Table A24: Equation 24
LHS Variable Is $RM - RS_{-2}$

Equation			χ^2 Tests			
RHS Variable	Coef.	t-stat.	Test	χ^2	df	p-value
cnst	0.38677	5.54	[a]Restriction	0.12	1	0.7254
$RM_{-1} - RS_{-2}$	0.87750	41.75	Lags	0.60	2	0.7397
$RS - RS_{-2}$	0.37969	3.92	RHO	2.04	1	0.1532
$RS_{-1} - RS_{-2}$	−0.19275	−1.54	T	1.66	1	0.1975
D20201	−0.11308	−0.31	[b]	1.34	1	0.2470
D20202	0.02473	0.07	[c]	1.09	1	0.2957
D20203	−0.21791	−0.59				
D20204	−0.21976	−0.60				
D20211	0.07430	0.20				
D20212	0.09447	0.26				
D20213	−0.15864	−0.44				
D20214	0.16526	0.45				
SE	0.36338					
R^2	0.899					

[a]RS_{-2} added.
[b]$100 \cdot (PD/PD(-4) - 1)$
[c]$100 \cdot [(PD/PD(-8))^{.5} - 1]$
Lags test adds RS_{-3} and RM_{-2}.
Estimation period is 1954.1–2023.2.

First-Stage Regressors

$cnst, RM_{-1}, RS_{-1}, 100[(PD/PD_{-1})^4 - 1]_{-1}, UR_{-1}, \log(PIM/PF)_{-1}, \log[(COG + COS)/POP]_{-1}, \log[(TRGH + TRSH)/(POP \cdot PH)]_{-1}, \log(EX/POP)_{-1}, T, D20201,$ $D20202, D20203, D20204, D20211, D20212, D20213, D20214$

equations except for RS_{-1} in equation 24. The first χ^2 test for each equation shows that the coefficient restriction is not rejected for either equation. The added lagged value is not significant in either equation, nor is the time trend and the serial correlation coefficient in equation 24. Two inflation expectations variables, $\dot{p}^e_{4t}$ and $\dot{p}^e_{8t}$, were added to the equations to see if inflation expectations might matter. Neither was significnt in either equation.

4.7.2 Equation 26. *CUR*, Currency Held Outside Banks

Equation 26 in table A26 is the demand for currency equation. It is in per capita terms and is in log form. The transactions variable that is used is the level of nonfarm firm sales. The interest rate variable used is *RSA*. The lagged dependent variable reflects the real adjustment specification—see the discussion above on equation 17.

Table A26: Equation 26

LHS Variable Is $\log[CUR/(POP \cdot PF)]$

Equation			χ^2 Tests			
RHS Variable	Coef.	*t*-stat.	Test	χ^2	df	*p*-value
cnst	−0.05391	−7.10	$\log(CUR_{-1}/$ $(POP_{-1}PF)$	2.07	1	0.1501
$\log[CUR/(POP \cdot PF)]_{-1}$	0.96732	187.17				
$\log[(X - FA)/POP]$	0.04278	7.66	Lags	10.00	3	0.0186
RSA	−0.00244	−5.90	RHO	0.62	1	0.4317
D20201	0.02583	2.48	*T*	10.20	1	0.0014
D20202	0.06335	6.07				
D20203	0.02217	2.12				
D20204	0.00945	0.90				
D20211	0.01345	1.29				
D20212	0.00673	0.65				
D20213	−0.01336	−1.28				
D20214	−0.00804	−0.77				
SE	0.01026					
R^2	1.000					

Lags test adds $\log[CUR/(POP \cdot PF)]_{-2}$, $\log[(X - FA)/POP]_{-1}$, and RSA_{-1}.
Estimation period is 1954.1–2023.2.

First-Stage Regressors

cnst, $\log[CUR/(POP \cdot PF)]_{-1}$, $\log[(X - FA)/POP]_{-1}$, RSA_{-1}, $\log[CUR_{-2}/(POP_{-2} \cdot PF_{-1})]$, $\log[(COG + COS)/POP]_{-1}$, $\log[(TRGH + TRSH)/(POP \cdot PH)]_{-1}$, $\log(EX/POP)_{-1}$, *D20201*, *D20202*, *D20203*, *D20204*, *D20211*, *D20212*, *D20213*, *D20214*

The coefficient estimates are all highly significant. The first χ^2 test shows that the addition reflecting the nominal adjustment specification is not significant. The additions of the lagged values and the time trend are significant, but not the estimate of the serial correlation coefficient. There is thus some lack of robustness.

4.8 Imports

4.8.1 Equation 27. *IM*, Imports

The import equation 27 in table A27 is in real, per capita, and log terms. The explanatory variables include income; wealth; the age variables, the price deflator for domestically produced goods, *PF*; relative to the import price deflator, *PIM*; the time trend; and four dummy variables to account for two dock strikes. The wealth and age variables are the same as in the three consumption equations, 1, 2, and 3. Many imports are purchased by the household sector, and so one would expect the same variables that affect consumption also affect imports. The income variable is total income (output), Y, rather than disposable income, YD/PH, since some imports are purchased by other sectors. The time trend has been added to pick up the fact that imports have been rising relative to total output over time for reasons not related to the economic variables in the equation.

The age variables in table A27 are jointly significant, and the other variables are significant except for the wealth variable, which has a t-statistic of only 0.20. The tests show that the equation is fragile in that the added lagged values are significant, as is the estimate of the serial correlation coefficient. Although not shown in the table, when the serial correlation coefficient is estimated, some of the other coefficient estimates are not sensible—there appears to be too much collinearity—and so this specification was not used. The import equation is one of the more problematic equations in the model. It is sensitive to alternative specifications.

The last test adds $\log PF$ to the equation, which is a test of the restriction that the coefficient of $\log PF$ is equal to the negative of the coefficient of $\log PIM$. The $\log PF$ variable is not significant, and so the restriction is not rejected.

Table A27: Equation 27
LHS Variable Is $\log(IM/POP)$

Equation			χ^2 Tests			
RHS Variable	Coef.	t-stat.	Test	χ^2	df	p-value
cnst	−1.28726	−4.57	Lags	24.69	3	0.0000
$AG1$	0.51852	4.06	RHO	39.22	1	0.0000
$AG2$	0.26326	1.02	$\log PF$	3.46	1	0.0629
$AG3$	−1.12203	−3.79				
$\log(IM/POP)_{-1}$	0.77187	21.42				
$\log(Y/POP)$	0.39378	3.48				
$\log(AA/POP)_{-1}$	0.00786	0.20				
$\log(PF/PIM)$	0.06400	2.84				
T	0.00098	2.11				
$D691$	−0.12000	−4.43				
$D692$	0.13659	4.99				
$D714$	−0.07140	−2.60				
$D721$	0.11142	4.08				
$D20201$	−0.03674	−1.34				
$D20202$	−0.17503	−5.98				
$D20203$	0.09836	3.40				
$D20204$	0.04561	1.64				
$D20211$	0.00358	0.13				
$D20212$	0.00327	0.12				
$D20213$	0.00353	0.12				
$D20214$	0.02770	0.98				
SE	0.02665					
R^2	0.999					

χ^2 (AGE) = 23.15 (df = 3, p-value = 0.0000)

Lags test adds $\log(IM/POP)_{-2}$, $\log(Y/POP)_{-1}$, and $\log(PF/PIM)_{-1}$.
Estimation period is 1954.1–2023.2.

First-Stage Regressors

$cnst$, $\log(IM/POP)_{-1}$, $\log(AA/POP)_{-2}$, $\log(Y/POP)_{-1}$, $\log(PF/PIM)_{-1}$, $D691$, $D692$, $D714$, $D721$, $AG1$, $AG2$, $AG3$, $\log[(COG+COS)/POP]_{-1}$, $\log[(TRGH+TRSH)/(POP \cdot PH)]_{-1}$, $\log(EX/POP)_{-1}$, T, $\log POP$, $\log POP_{-1}$, $\log PIM_{-1}$, $\log(IM/POP)$)−2, $D20201$, $D20202$, $D20203$, $D20204$, $D20211$, $D20212$, $D20213$, $D20214$

4.9 Government Sectors

4.9.1 Equation 28. *UB*, Unemployment Insurance Benefits

Equation 28 in table A28 explains unemployment insurance benefits, *UB*. It is in log form and contains as explanatory variables the level of unemployment, the nominal wage rate, and the lagged dependent variable. The inclusion of the nominal wage rate is designed to pick up the effects of increases in wages on legislated benefits per unemployed worker. The equation is estimated under the assumption of first-order serial correlation of the error term.

The equation is only estimated through 2000.4. After that, when unemployment rose, the government passed temporary legislation to increase unemployment benefits. The past relationship between unemployment and unemployment benefits essentially broke down. Equation 28 is thus relevant before 2001, but after that, *UB* has been taken to be exogenous.

For the tests, the added lagged values are not significant and the time trend is significant at the five percent level but not the one percent level.

Table A28: Equation 28
LHS Variable Is log *UB*

Equation			χ^2 Tests			
RHS Variable	Coef.	*t*-stat.	Test	χ^2	df	*p*-value
cnst	0.30996	0.62	Lags	2.21	3	0.5296
$\log UB_{-1}$	0.12976	1.30	*T*	5.60	1	0.0180
$\log U$	1.47623	5.67				
$\log WF$	0.43629	5.50				
RHO1	0.89661	22.08				
SE	0.06393					
R^2	0.996					

Lags test adds $\log UB_{-2}$, $\log U_{-1}$, and $\log WF_{-1}$.
Estimation period is 1954.1–2000.4.

First-Stage Regressors

$cnst$, $\log UB_{-1}$, $\log U_{-1}$, $\log WF_{-1}$, $\log UB_{-2}$, $\log(PIM/PF)_{-1}$, $100[(PD/PD_{-1})^4 - 1]_{-1}$, $\log[(COG + COS)/POP]_{-1}$, $\log[(TRGH + TRSH)/(POP \cdot PH)]_{-1}$, $\log(EX/POP)_{-1}$, T

4.9.2 Equation 29. *INTG*, Interest Payments of the Federal Government

INTG is the level of net interest payments of the federal government. Data on this variable are NIPA data. *AG* is the level of net financial assets of the federal government. Data on this variable are FFA data. *AG* is negative because the federal government is a net debtor. It consists of both short-term and long-term securities.

The current level of interest payments of the federal government depends on the amount of existing securities issued at each date in the past and on the relevant interest rate prevailing at each date. The link from *AG* to *INTG* is thus complicated. It depends on past issues and the interest rates paid on these issues. A number of approximations have to be made in trying to model this link, and the procedure used here is as follows.

Let *RQG* denote a weighted average of the current value of the short-term interest rate, *RS*, and current and past values of 0.75 times the long-term bond rate, *RB*, with weights of .4 and .6.[6] *RB* is multiplied by 0.75, since the federal government pays a lower interest rate than the AAA corporate bond rate, which is *RB*. *RQG* is

$$\begin{aligned} RQG = [&.4RS + .75(.6)(RB + RB_{-1} + RB_{-2} + RB_{-3} \\ &+ RB_{-4} + RB_{-5} + RB_{-6} + RB_{-7})/8]/400. \end{aligned} \tag{4.32}$$

In this equation *RS* and *RB* are divided by 400 to put *RQG* at a quarterly rate in percent units. The variable $INTG/(-AG)$ is the ratio of interest payments of the federal government to the net financial debt of the federal government. This ratio is a function of current and past interest rates, among other things. In the empirical specification $INTG/(-AG)$ is taken to depend on a constant term, *RQG*, and $INTG_{-1}/(-AG_{-1})$. This equation, which is equation 29 in table A29, is estimated under the assumption of first-order serial correlation of the error term.

The results are in table A29. The coefficient estimate for *RQG* is positive and significant, and so there is an estimated link between interest rates and interest payments. Perhaps not suprisingly given the approximate nature of the equation, the equation is not robust to the addition of the lagged values for the first test. The time trend is significant at the 95 but not 99 percent confidence level.

Equation 29 is important in the model because when interest rates change or when the federal government deficit and thus debt changes,

Table A29: Equation 29
LHS Variable Is $INTG/(-AG)$

Equation			χ^2 Tests			
RHS Variable	Coef.	*t*-stat.	Test	χ^2	df	*p*-value
cnst	0.00076	7.04	Lags	123.89	2	0.0000
$(INTG/(-AG))_{-1}$	0.83241	48.03	T	3.99	1	0.0457
a	0.14741	9.72				
$D20201$	0.00015	0.53				
$D20202$	−0.00077	−2.46				
$D20203$	−0.00035	−1.11				
$D20204$	0.00005	0.14				
$D20211$	0.00033	1.05				
$D20212$	0.00000	−0.01				
$D20213$	0.00022	0.69				
$D20214$	0.00000	−0.01				
RHO1	0.37564	6.21				
SE	0.00029					
R^2	0.997					

[a]Variable is $(.4 \cdot (RS/400) + .75 \cdot .6 \cdot (1/8) \cdot (1/400) \cdot (RB + RB_{-1} + RB_{-2} + RB_{-3} + RB_{-4} + RB_{-5} + RB_{-6} + RB_{-7}))$
Lags test adds $[INTG/(-AG)]_{-1}$ and [a] lagged once.
Estimation period is 1954.1–2023.2.
OLS estimation.

federal interest payments change, which changes household interest income and adds to the deficit and debt of the federal government.

4.9.3 Equation 30. *RS*, Three-Month Treasury Bill Rate

A key question in any macro model is what one assumes about monetary policy. In the theoretical model, monetary policy is determined by an interest rate reaction function or rule, and in the empirical work, an equation like this is estimated. This equation is interpreted as an equation explaining the behavior of the Fed.

In one respect, trying to explain Fed behavior is more difficult than, say, trying to explain the behavior of the household or firm sectors. Since the Fed is run by a relatively small number of people, there can be fairly abrupt changes in behavior if the people with influence change their minds or are replaced by others with different views. Abrupt changes are less likely to happen for the household and firm sectors because of the large number of decision makers in each sector. Having said this, however, only one abrupt change in behavior appears evident in the data before 2008, which is between 1979.4 and 1982.3. This period, 1979.4–1982.3, will be called the "early Volcker" period.[7] The stated policy of the Fed during this period was that it was focusing more on monetary aggregates than it had done before.

Equation 30 in table A30 is the estimated interest rate reaction function. It has on the left-hand side *RS*. This treatment is based on the assumption that the Fed has a target bill rate each quarter and achieves this target through manipulation of its policy instruments. Although in practice the Fed controls the federal funds rate, the quarterly average of the federal funds rate and the quarterly average of the three-month Treasury bill rate are so highly correlated that it makes little difference which rate is used in estimated interest rate rules using quarterly data. The RHS variables in the equation are variables that seem likely to affect the target rate. The variables that were chosen are (1) the rate of inflation, (2) the unemployment rate, (3) the change in the unemployment rate, and (4) the percentage change in the money supply lagged one quarter, $PCM1_{-1}$. The break between 1979.4 and 1982.3 is modeled by adding the variable $D794823 \cdot PCM1_{-1}$ to the equation, where *D*794823 is a dummy variable that is 1 between 1979.4 and 1982.3 and 0 otherwise. The estimated equation also includes the lagged dependent variable and two lagged bill rate changes to pick up the dynamics.

Beginning in 2008.4 and continuing for many years, *RS* was at the zero lower bound. Equation 30 was simply not relevant for this period. The equation is thus estimated only through 2008.3. After that, *RS* is taken to be exogenous—zero for many years.

The coefficient estimates in equation 30 are all significant. Equation 30 is a "leaning against the wind" equation. *RS* is estimated to depend positively on the inflation rate and the lagged growth of the money supply and negatively on the unemployment rate and the change in the unemployment rate. Adjustment and smoothing effects are captured by the lagged values of *RS*. The coefficient on lagged money supply growth is nearly 20 times larger for the early Volcker period than either before or after, which is consistent with the Fed's stated policy of focusing more on monetary aggregates during this period. This way of accounting for the Fed policy

Table A30: Equation 30
LHS Variable Is RS

Equation			χ^2 Tests			
RHS Variable	Coef.	t-stat.	Test	χ^2	df	p-value
cnst	0.69910	4.55	Lags	2.60	3	0.4569
RS_{-1}	0.91555	49.15	RHO	3.14	1	0.0762
$100 \cdot [(PD/PD_{-1})^4 - 1]$	0.07508	3.98	T	0.87	1	0.3505
UR	−11.08222	−3.53	^{a}	0.28	1	0.5949
ΔUR	−74.03467	−4.85	^{b}	1.92	1	0.1655
$D20083 \cdot PCM1_{-1}$	0.01195	2.41				
$D794823 \cdot PCM1_{-1}$	0.21236	9.32				
ΔRS_{-1}	0.23363	4.09				
ΔRS_{-2}	−0.31145	−6.18				
SE	0.48626					
R^2	0.971					

Stability test (1954.1–1979.3 versus 1982.4–2008.3): Wald statistic is 12.521 (8 degrees of freedom, p-value = .1294)

$^a 100 \cdot (PD/PD(-4) - 1)$
$^b 100 \cdot [(PD/PD(-8))^{.5} - 1]$
Lags test adds $RS_{-4}, 100 \cdot [(PD_{-1}/PD_{-2})^4 - 1]$, and UR_{-2}
Estimation period is 1954.1–2008.3.

First-Stage Regressors
$cnst$, RS_{-1}, $100[(PD/PD_{-1})^4 - 1]_{-1}$, UR_{-1}, ΔUR_{-1}, $D20083 \cdot PCM1_{-1}$, $D794823 \cdot PCM1_{-1}$, ΔRS_{-1}, ΔRS_{-2}, $\log[(COG + COS)/POP]_{-1}$, $\log[(TRGH + TRSH)/(POP \cdot PH)]_{-1}$, $\log(EX/POP)_{-1}$

shift does not, of course, capture the richness of the change in behavior, but at least it seems to capture some of the change.

The equation does well in the tests. The added lagged values are not significant, nor is the estimate of the serial correlation coefficient and the coefficient estimate of the time trend. Two inflation expectations variables, $100 \cdot (PD/PD(-4) - 1)$ and $100 \cdot [(PD/PD(-8))^{.5} - 1]$, were added to see if they might be significant, and they are not.

A stability test was also performed for equation 30. The test excludes the early Volcker period since any hypothesis of stability that includes it is likely to be rejected. The Fed announced that its behavior was different during this period. An obvious hypothesis to test is that the equation's coefficients are the same before 1979.4 as they are after 1982.3. This was done using a Wald test. The Wald statistic is presented in equation 3.6 in Andrews and Fair (1988). It has the advantage that it works under very general assumptions about the properties of the error terms and can be used when the estimator is NL2SLS, which it is here. The Wald statistic is distributed as χ^2 with (in the present case) 8 degrees of freedom. The hypothesis of stability is not rejected. As reported in table A30, the Wald statistic is 12.52, which has a *p*-value of .1294.

It is informative to examine the long-run properties of the estimated rule. If there is a sustained decrease in the unemployment rate of, say, 1.0 percentage points, how much does *RS* rise in the long run according to the rule? This can be calculated by first solving the equation dynamically using the actual values inflation and unemployment to get a base run. Then solve again with the unemployment rate 1.0 higher for each quarter. The difference for a given quarter between the predicted value from the new run and the predicted value from the base run is the effect on the interest rate. In this case, *RS* is 1.255 percentage points higher in the long run.

A similar calculation can be done for inflation. If there is a sustained increase in the inflation variable in equation 30, *RS* is 0.992 percentage points higher in the long run, so almost exactly one for one. The long-run property of the rule is that this is a constant real rate. This property comes out of the estimates; no restrictions were placed on the estimation for this to happen.

This analysis is, of course, only to see the dynamic properties of the rule by itself. Changes in *RS* affect both unemployment and inflation, and so in practice neither variable is unchanged when *RS* changes.

Regarding the history of interest rate rules, estimated interest rate rules go back at least to Dewald and Johnson (1963), who regressed the Treasury bill rate on a constant, the Treasury bill rate lagged once, real GNP, the unemployment rate, the balance-of-payments deficit, and the consumer price index. The next example can be found in Christian (1968). I added an estimated interest rate rule to my US model in Fair (1978).[8]

After this, McNees (1986, 1992) estimated rules in which some of the explanatory variables were the Fed's internal forecasts of various variables.

Khoury (1990) provides an extensive list of estimated rules through 1986. This work all preceded Taylor's (1993) well-known paper, which proposed an interest rate policy rule, since called the "Taylor rule." With hindsight, interest rate rules should probably be called Dewald–Johnson rules, since Dewald and Johnson preceded Taylor by about 30 years!

There seems to be a general view in the literature that estimated interest rate rules do not have stable coefficient estimates over time. For example, Judd and Rudebusch (1998, p. 3) state "Overall, it appears that there have not been any great successes in modeling Fed behavior with a single, stable reaction function." The passing of the stability test for equation 30 is thus contrary this view. One likely reason that the stability hypothesis has generally been rejected in the literature is that most tests have included the early Volcker period, which is clearly different from the periods both before and after. The tests in Judd and Rudebusch (1998), for example, include the early Volcker period.

4.10 Summary

This is the key chapter of the book since the core of a model is its stochastic equations. I have tried to discuss both the strengths and weaknesses of the estimated equations. In some cases, equations are used that are not robust to the χ^2 tests. This is done for lack of a better alternative and is scope for future research. The most fragile of the main equations is the import equation 27. There is also the question whether the unemployment rate should be added to the wage equation 16. Two important results regarding the price equation 10 is that the data strongly support the level specification, and the rolling regressions show that the coefficient estimate of $1/UR$ is fairly stable.

5 Constructed Variables

A "raw data" variable is a variable obtained directly from a data source, such as consumption of services from the NIPA data. In some cases, an endogenous or exogenous variable in the model, such as consumption of services, is simply the raw data variable. In many cases, however, a variable in the model is constructed from more than one raw data variable. Most of the construction is straightforward, but in a few cases, more explanation is needed. This chapter discusses the construction of some of these variables.

Some of the variables discussed in this chapter are constructed from a peak-to-peak interpolation. For the values before the first peak, sometimes the line between the first two peaks is extended back to the first observation (1952.1) and sometimes the values are taken to be the value at the first peak. If the latter, this is denoted as "flat beginning." For the values after the last peak, sometimes the line between the last two peaks is extended forward to the last observation (2013.1) and sometimes the values are taken to be the value at the last peak. If the latter, this is denoted as "flat end."

5.1 *KD*: Stock of Durable Goods

KD is an estimate of the stock of durable goods. It is defined as

$$KD = (1 - DELD)KD_{-1} + CD, \tag{5.1}$$

where *CD* is consumer expenditures on durable goods and *DELD* is a depreciation rate. Given quarterly observations for *CD*, which are available from the NIPA, quarterly observations for *KD* can be constructed once a base quarter value and values for the depreciation rate are chosen. End of year estimates of the stock of durable goods are available from the BEA Fixed Assets tables. Given the value of *KD* at the end of 1952 and given quarterly values of *CD* for 1953.1–1953.4, a value of *DELD* can be computed such that the predicted value from equation (5.1) for 1953.4 matches within a prescribed tolerance level, the published BEA value for the end of 1953. This value of *DELD* can then be used to compute quarterly values of *KD* for 1953.1, 1953.2, and 1953.3. This process can be repeated for each year, which results in a quarterly series for *KD*. The quarterly values of *DELD* are the same for a given year, but they vary slightly across years since there is a different depreciation rate computed each year.

5.2 *KH*: Stock of Housing

KH is an estimate of the stock of housing of the household sector. It is defined as

$$KH = (1 - DELH)KH_{-1} + IHH, \tag{5.2}$$

where *IHH* is residential investment of the household sector and *DELH* is a depreciation rate. The same procedure was followed for estimating *DELH* as was followed for estimating *DELD*. The housing stock data are available from the above BEA reference for the durable goods stock data. The BEA residential stock data is for total residential investment, whereas equation (5.2) pertains only to the residential investment of the household sector. The procedure that was used for dealing with this difference is as follows. First, the values for *DELH* were chosen using total residential investment as the investment series, since this series matched the published stock data. Second, once the values of *DELH* were chosen, *KH* was constructed using *IHH* (not total residential investment). A base quarter value of *KH* of 2587.6 in 1952.1 was used. This value is .80605 times the computed value for the total housing stock for 1952.1. The value .80605 is the average of the ratio of household residential investment to total residential investment over the sample period.

5.3 *KK*: Stock of Capital

KK is an estimate of the stock of capital of the firm sector. It is defined as

$$KK = (1 - DELK)KK_{-1} + IKF, \tag{5.3}$$

where *IKF* is fixed nonresidential investment of the firm sector and *DELK* is a depreciation rate. The same procedure was followed for estimating *DELK* as was followed for estimating *DELD* and *DELH*. The capital stock data are available from the above BEA reference for the durable goods stock data. The BEA capital stock data is for total fixed nonresidential investment, whereas equation (5.3) pertains only to the fixed nonresidential investment of the firm sector. A similar procedure for dealing with this was followed here as was followed above for residential investment. First, the values for *DELK* were chosen using total fixed nonresidential investment as the investment series, since this series matched the published stock data. Second, once the values of *DELK* were chosen, *KK* was constructed using *IKF* (not total fixed nonresidential investment). A base quarter value of *KK* of 2619.8 in 1952.1 was used. This value is .85855 times the computed value for total stock of fixed nonresidential capital for 1952.1. The value .85855 is the average of the ratio of firm fixed nonresidential investment to total fixed nonresidential investment over the sample period.

5.4 *V*: Stock of Inventories

V is the stock of inventories of the firm sector. By definition, inventory investment of the firm sector, *IVF*, is equal to the change in the stock:

$$IVF = V - V_{-1}. \tag{5.4}$$

The stock data on *V* are in BEA Fixed Assets table 5.8.6A. *V* was constructed from the formula $V = V_{-1} + IVF$ using NIPA data for *IVF* and using a base quarter value of 1781.1 in 1996.4 for *V*. This is the value in NIPA table 5.8.6A.

5.5 *LAM* and *MUH*: Excess Labor and Excess Capital

The production technology of the firm sector in the US model is assumed to be one of fixed proportions. The labor coefficient per quarter, *LAM*, is constructed from a peak-to-peak interpolation of output per paid worker hour. The capital coefficient per quarter, *MUH*, is constructed from a peak-to-peak interpolation of output per capital stock. Write the production function as

$$Y = \min[LAM(JF \cdot HF^a), MU(KK \cdot HK^a)], \tag{5.5}$$

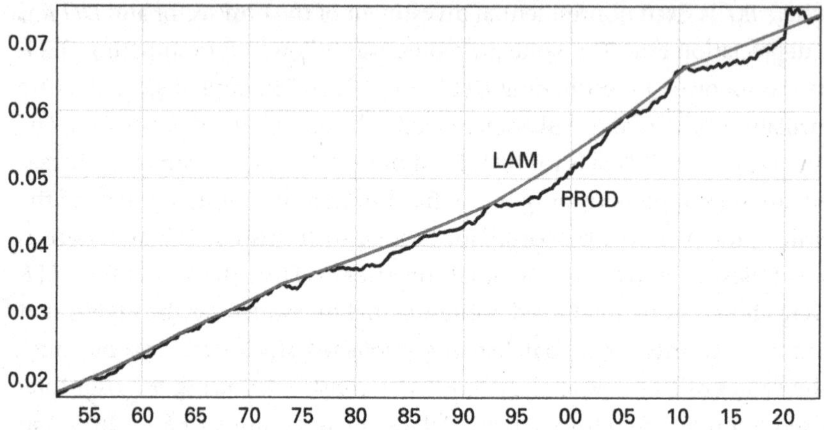

Figure 5.1
PROD and LAM 1952.1–2023.2

where Y is the output, JF is the number of workers employed (jobs), HF^a is the number of hours worked per worker, KK is the capital stock discussed above, HK^a is the number of hours each unit of KK is utilized, and LAM and MU are coefficients that may change over time due to technical progress. The variables Y, JF, and KK are observed; the others are not. For example, data on the number of hours paid for per worker exist, HF in the model, but not on the number of hours actually worked per worker, HF^a.

Figure 5.1 plots $Y/(JF \cdot HF)$ for the 1952.1–2023.2 period. Also drawn in this figure is a peak-to-peak interpolation, with peaks at 1955:2, 1963:3, 1966:1, 1973:1, 1992.4, 2010.4, and 2023.2. It is assumed that at the peaks $HF^a = HF$, so LAM is observed at the peaks. The interpolation fills in the other values of LAM. Figure 5.1 shows the well-known fact that labor productivity growth was higher before the 1970s than after.

Given an estimate of LAM for a particular quarter, the number of worker hours required to produce the output of the quarter is simply Y/LAM, which is denoted $JHMIN$. The difference between total worker hours paid for, $JF \cdot HF$, and $JHMIN$ is an estimate of the amount of excess labor on hand.

Regarding excess capital, figure 5.2 plots Y/KK for the 1952.1–2023.2 period. Also drawn in the figure is a peak-to-peak interpolation, with peaks at 1953:2, 1955:3, 1959:2, 1962:3, 1965:4, 1969:1, 1973:1, 1977:3, 1981:1,

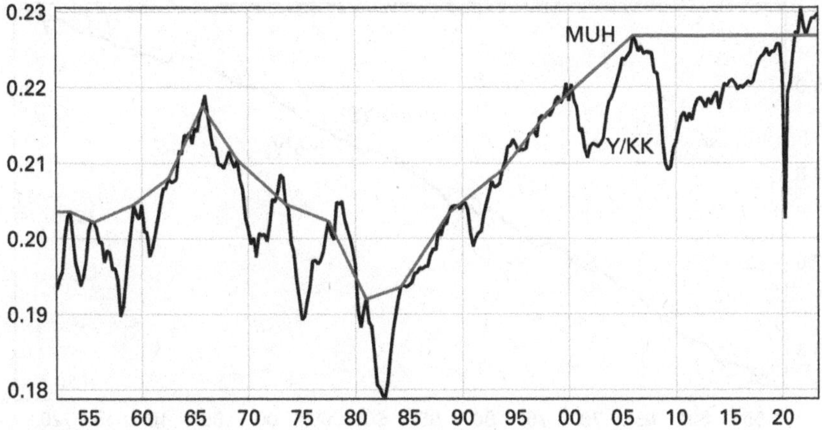

Figure 5.2
Y/KK and MUH 1952.1–2023.2

1984:2, 1988:4, 1993:4, 1998:1, 2006:1, and 2019:1. There are no data on hours paid for per unit of *KK*, and so only Y/KK can be plotted. It is assumed at the peaks that the capital stock is fully utilized, so $MU \cdot HK^a$, which is denoted *MUH*, is observed at the peaks. The interpolation fills in the other values of *MUH*.

Given an estimate of *MUH* for a particular quarter, the amount of capital required to produce the output of the quarter is simply Y/MUH, which is denoted *KKMIN*. The difference between *KK* and *KKMIN* is an estimate of the amount of excess capital on hand.

5.6 *YS*: Potential Output of the Firm Sector

YS is a measure of the potential output of the firm sector. It is computed from a peak-to-peak interpolation of $\log Y$, with peaks at 1953:2, 1966:1, 1973:2, 1999:4, 2006:4, and 2023.2. $\log Y$ and $\log YS$ are plotted in figure 5.3 for the 1952.1–2023.2 period. *YS* is not an important variable in the model; it is simply used as a scaling variable in a few cases. The demand variable in the price equation 10 is the unemployment rate, not the output gap, where *YS* would have been needed. A gap variable has been tested in a few cases, where the gap is defined as $(YS - Y)/YS$.

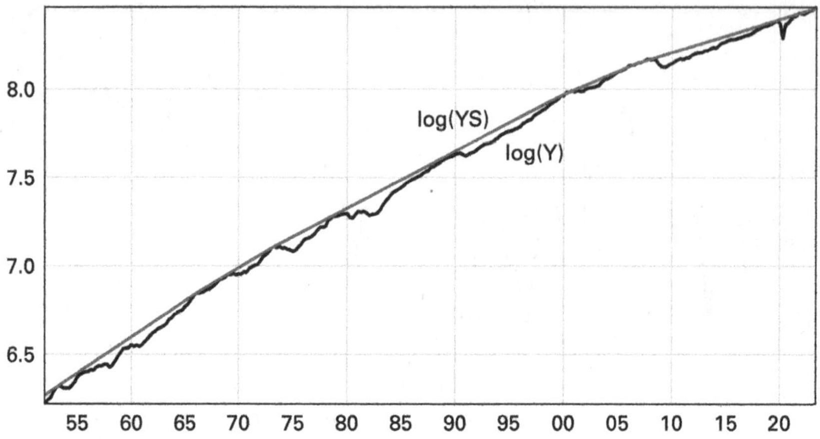

Figure 5.3
log(Y) and log(YS) 1952.1–2023.2

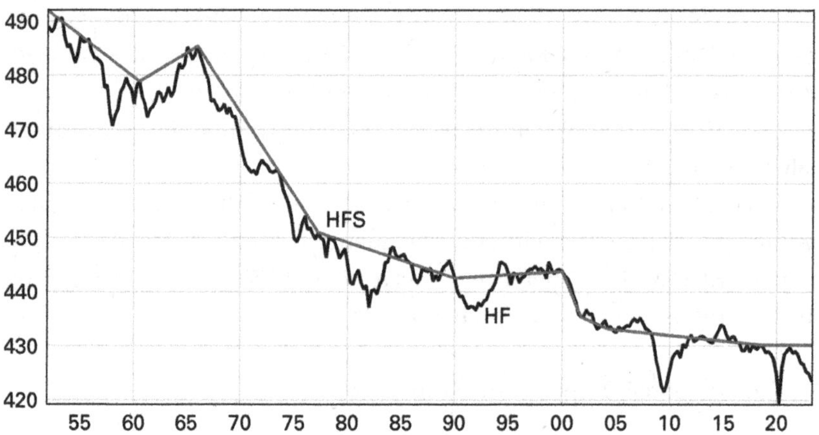

Figure 5.4
HF and HFS 1952.1–2023.2

5.7 *HFS*: Peak-to-Peak Interpolation of *HF*

HFS is a peak-to-peak interpolation of *HF*, hours paid per worker. The peaks are 1952:4, 1960.3, 1966:1, 1977:2, 1990:1, 2000:1, 2001:4, 2004:2, and 2018.3. *HF* and *HFS* are plotted in figure 5.4 for the 1952.1–2023.2 period. *HFS* is a measure of potential hours paid per worker.

5.8 *HO*: Overtime Hours

Data are not available for overtime hours, *HO*, for the first 16 quarters of the sample period—1952.1–1955.4. The equation that determines *HO*, equation 15, is estimated for the sample period beginning in 1956.1. Values of *HO* before 1956.1 were constructed by solving the equation backward. They are rarely needed.

6 Identities

As noted in section 4.1, there are about 140 identities in the US model, depending on how many variables are added for display purposes. The identities are of two types. One simply defines one variable in terms of others.

Many of the identities of this type are concerned with linking the FFA data to the NIPA data. Consider variable *SH*, which is the financial saving of the household sector. It is determined by an identity: it is equal to the total income of the household sector minus total expenditures. These are NIPA data. If *SH* is nonzero, net assets of the household sector are affected. Net assets are FFA data. Identity 66 links *SH* to the change in net assets:

$$0 = SH - \Delta AH - \Delta MH + CG - DISH, \tag{6.1}$$

where *AH* is the value of net financial assets of the household sector not counting money supply holdings, *MH* is the value of money supply holdings, *CG* is the capital gain or loss on equity held by the household sector, and *DISH* is a discrepancy variable that reconciles the NIPA and FFA data. There are six equations like this, one for each sector. The sum of the financial saving variables across the six sectors is zero, which is a redundant identity in the model.

Another example pertains to the unemployment rate. The total number of people employed is equal to the total number of jobs minus the number of moonlighters, which is identity 85:

$$E = JF + JG + JM + JS - LM, \tag{6.2}$$

where *E* is the number of people employed according to the household survey. *JF* is determined by equation 13, and *LM* is determined by equation 8. *JG*, *JM*, and *JS* are exogenous, civilian federal government jobs, military jobs, and state and local government jobs, respectively. The total number of people unemployed is equal to the total labor force minus the number of people employed, which is identity 86:

$$U = L1 + L2 + L3 - E, \tag{6.3}$$

where U is the number of people unemployed. $L1$, $L2$, and $L3$ are determined by equations 5, 6, and 7, respectively. Finally, the unemployment rate, UR, is equal to the number of people unemployed divided by the civilian labor force, which is identity 87:

$$UR = U/(L1 + L2 + L3 - AFT), \tag{6.4}$$

where AFT, the total armed forces, is exogenous.

The other type of identity defines one variable as a rate or ratio times another variable or set of variables, where the rate or ratio has been constructed to have the identity hold. Consider, for example, variable TFS, which is the value of corporate profit taxes paid by the firm sector to the state and local government sector. This variable is affected by the profits of the firm sector, $PIEF$, but also by profit tax rates in the states. It is not feasible to deal with all the tax rates. Instead, a single tax rate, denoted $D2S$, is constructed as $TFS/PIEF$. This rate is the aggregate tax rate for the quarter, and it is taken to be exogenous. The identity is thus:

$$TFS = D2S \cdot PIEF. \tag{6.5}$$

TFS is endogenous because $PIEF$ is, but not $D2S$. ($PIEF$ itself is determined by an identity.) This same procedure was followed for the other tax rates.

A similar procedure was followed to handle relative prices. The key price variable in the model is PF, the private nonfarm price deflator, which is determined by equation 10. All other price variables run off of PF. Consider the price deflator for exports, PEX. It is determined by identity 32:

$$PEX = PSI1 \cdot PF, \tag{6.6}$$

where $PSI1$ is constructed as PEX/PF and is taken to be exogenous. The relationship between PEX and PF is thus exogenous; no attempt is made to explain relative prices. PEX is endogenous because PF is, but the ratio is not.

Continuing with price deflators, PIM is the price deflator for imports and is taken to be exogenous. Given PIM and PEX, it is possible to compute the price deflator for domestic sales, PD, which is an identity in the model. Now consider the price deflator for residential investment, PIH. It is determined by identity 38:

$$PIH = PSI5 \cdot PD, \tag{6.7}$$

where *PSI5* is constructed as *PIH*/*PD* and is taken to be exogenous. The relationship between *PIH* and *PD* is thus exogenous. Again, there is no attempt to explain relative prices; in this case, the relative price of residential investment. This procedure was followed for the other prices and wage rates in the model. The wage rates run off the key wage rate, *WF*, which is determined by equation 16.

7 Exogenous Variables

7.1 The Key Exogenous Variables

There are about 150 exogenous variables in the US model, but many of these are small in magnitude and not important. Many also don't change much over time, like the aggregate tax rates and the relative price ratios. Some change but smoothly, like population. This chapter discusses the most important exogenous variables.

7.1.1 Real Government Purchases of Goods

Real federal government expenditure on goods is variable *COG* and real state and local government expenditure on goods is variable *COS*. These two variables have the same effect in the US model. The sum divided by potential output, *YS*, is plotted in figure 7.1 for the 1952.1–2023.2 period. *YS* is used as a scaling variable; it has the advantage of not being affected by business cycles. The ratio has varied considerably over time. It is clear from the figure that government expenditures are not easy to predict. They reflect the decisions of many legislatures, and the timing from passage to implementation can be erratic. No attempt is made to model these decisions. They are assumed to be political decisions not affected by economic variables. For future reference—in chapter 15—note the large fall in the ratio between 2009 and 2014.

7.1.2 Real Government Transfer Payments

Real federal government transfer payments to households is variable *TRGHQ*, and real state and local government transfer payments to households is variable *TRGSQ*. These two variables have the same effect in the US model. The sum of the two divided by potential output is plotted in

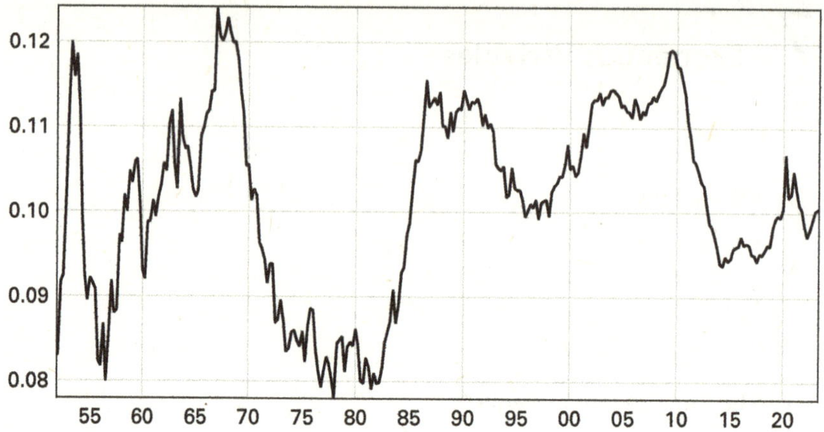

Figure 7.1
(COG + COS)/YS 1952.1–2023.2

figure 7.2 for the 1952.1–2023.2 period. This ratio has also varied considerably over time and is not easy to predict. The large increase in 2020 and 2021 is from the government response to the pandemic.

7.1.3 Government Jobs

The number of federal government civilian jobs is variable *JG*, the number of military jobs is variable *JM*, and the number of state and local government jobs is variable *JS*. The sum of the three divided by the total population 16+ is plotted in figure 7.3 for the 1952.1–2023.2 period. This ratio rose substantially in the 1960s and has gradually fallen since. Real spending on these jobs plus real government expenditures on goods is the "G" in the textbook identity "Y = C + I + G + Net Exports."

7.1.4 Real Exports

Real exports is variable *EX*. *EX*/*YS* is plotted in figure 7.4 for the 1952.1–2023.2 period. This ratio has generally risen over time. It fell in the recessions of 2001 and 2008 and during the pandemic period.

7.1.5 Price of Imports

The other key exogenous variable relating to the foreign sector is the price deflator for imports, variable *PIM*. The ratio of *PIM* to *PF* is plotted in

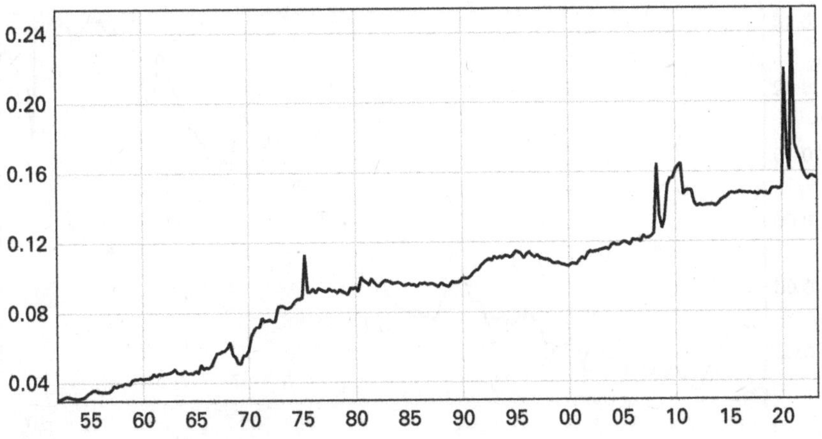

Figure 7.2
(TRGHQ + TRSHQ)/YS 1952.1–2023.2

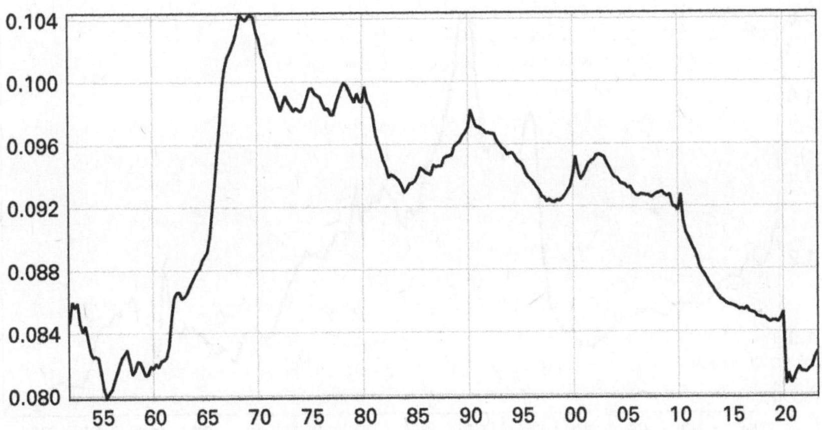

Figure 7.3
(JG + JM + JS)/POP 1952.1–2023.2

figure 7.5 for the 1952.1–2023.2 period. This ratio rose substantially in the early 1970s and the late 1970s because of the oil price increases, and it fell substantial in the 1980s. It has been fairly flat since the 1990s. As discussed in chapter 4 regarding the price equation 10, *PIM* is a key variable explaining the stagflation of the 1970s and the decrease in inflation in the 1980s.

Both *EX* and *PIM* are endogenous variables in my multicountry econometric model. US exports depend on other countries' imports, which are

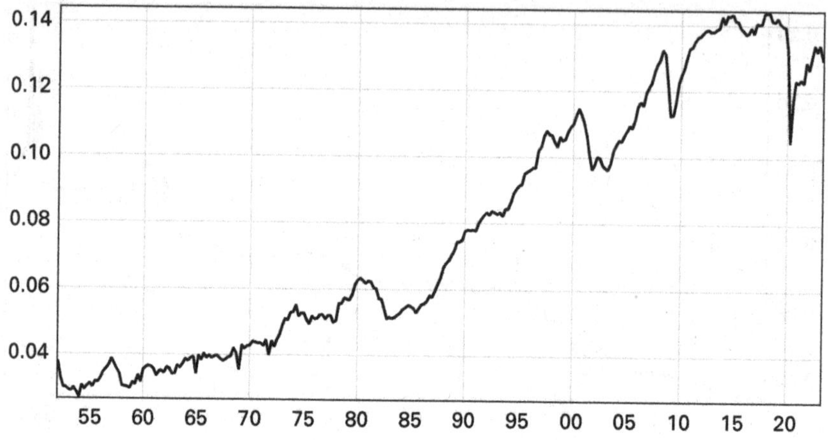

Figure 7.4
EX/YS 1952.1–2023.2

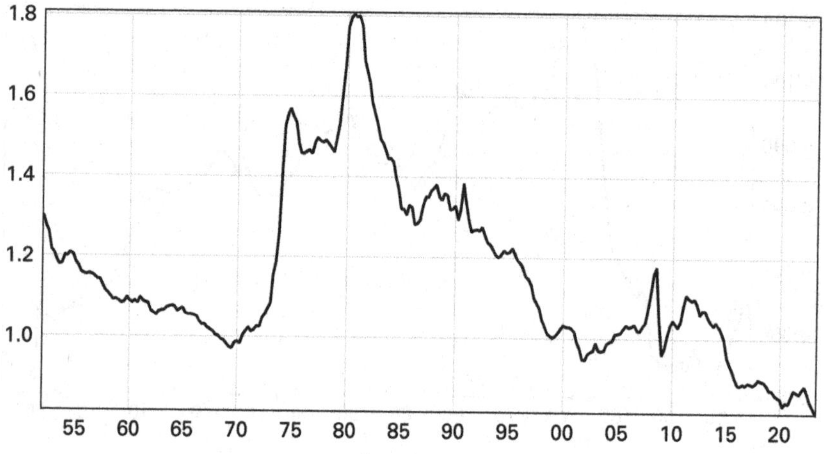

Figure 7.5
PIM/PF 1952.1–2023.2

endogenous. The import price deflator depends on other countries' export prices, which are endogenous. Both depend on exchange rates, where changes in the rates are largely unpredictable. It is the case, however, that US variables have modest effects on other countries' imports and prices of exports. The properties of the US model are not sensitive to whether or not it is embedded in the multicountry model. Therefore, as an approximation, *EX* and *PIM* are taken to be exogenous.

7.1.6 Asset Prices

The effect of asset prices on consumption expenditures is discussed in chapter 4 regarding equations 1, 2, and 3. Variable $AA1$ is the real value of financial wealth, and variable $AA2$ is the real value of housing wealth:

$$AA1 = (AH + MH)/PH \tag{7.1}$$

$$AA2 = (PKH \cdot KH)/PH, \tag{7.2}$$

where AH is the nominal value of net financial assets of the household sector excluding demand deposits and currency, MH is the nominal value of demand deposits and currency held by the household sector, KH is the real stock of housing, PKH is the market price of KH, and PH is a price deflator relevant to household spending.

Most of the variation in AH is from the change in stock prices. This is discussed more in chapter 9. It will be seen that the change in the S&P 500 stock price index, denoted here as SP, is highly correlated with variable CG in the model, which is capital gains or losses on equity held by the household sector (FFA data). Although SP is not a variable in the model, it is useful for plotting purposes. SP divided by nominal potential output, $PX \cdot YS$, is plotted in figure 7.6 for the 1952.1–2023.2 period. This figure shows that the variation in stock prices increased beginning about 1995. It will be seen in chapter 15 that fluctuations in stock prices since 1995 are important in explaining business cycles since 1995.

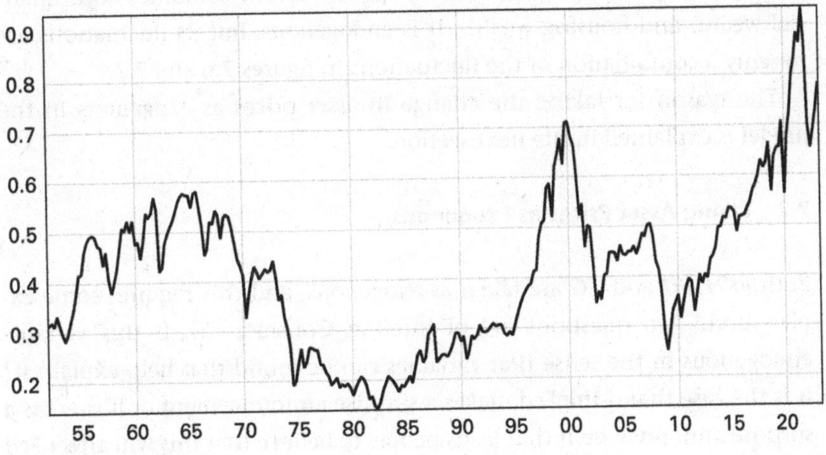

Figure 7.6
SP/(PX*YS) 1952.1–2023.2

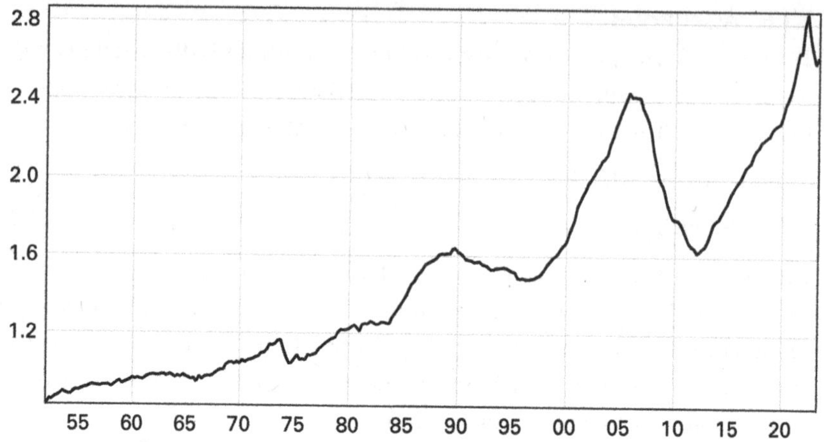

Figure 7.7
PKH/PD 1952.1–2023.2

The main fluctuations in housing wealth are from changes in *PKH*. The ratio of *PKH* to *PD*, the price deflator for domestic sales, is plotted in figure 7.7 for the 1952.1–2023.2 period. This ratio reflects the housing boom and bust. It rose substantially from 2000 to 2006, fell substantially to 2012, and then rose substantially again. These are large changes in housing wealth, which like financial wealth affect business cycles.

For completeness, the total real net wealth of households divided by real potential output, *AA*/*YS*, is plotted in figure 7.8. *AA* combines both financial wealth and housing wealth. It is endogenous, but its fluctuations are roughly a combination of the fluctuations in figures 7.6 and 7.7.

The reason for taking the change in asset prices as exogenous in the model is explained in the next section.

7.2 Taking Asset Prices as Exogenous

Both *PKH*/*PD* and *CG* are taken as exogenous, and this requires some explanation. Two questions are of interest. Consider *CG*. Is this variable endogenous in the sense that variables can be found that help explain it? It is the case that if the Fed makes a surprise announcement or if there is a surprise announcement that leads people to believe that this will affect Fed behavior, there will essentially be an immediate change in stock prices (and

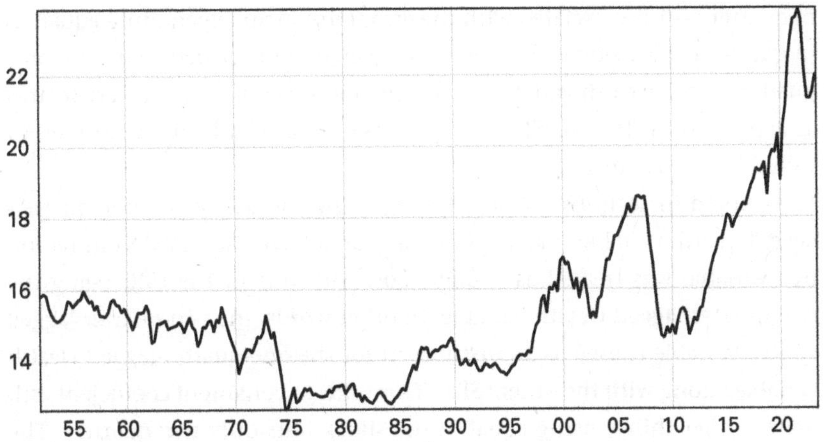

Figure 7.8
AA/YS 1952.1–2023.2

bond prices). But on a quarterly basis there is little evidence that changes in stock prices can be explained by interest rates or any other variables. Rossi (2021), section 2.3, has a review of attempts to explain asset-price changes, and there is no systematic positive evidence.[1] The argument here is that while there are clearly immediate effects on stock prices from surprise announcements, the cumulation of these effects is not large enough to show up in quarterly data. Changes in stock prices are largely unpredictable. If an equation could be found that explained stock-price changes—i.e,, systematic macroeconomic effects on stock prices—it could be added to the model and stock prices taken to be endogenous. But, as just argued, this is not the case.

Regarding *PKH*/*PD* in figure 7.7, it seems unlikely that a model could be developed that would explain the change in this ratio over the sample period—the huge rise between 2000 and 2006 and the huge fall between 2007 and 2012, and then the large rise after that.

The second question of interest is whether there are unobserved forces that affect, say, both stock prices and household expenditures. Say there is a change in consumer mood (a shock) in quarter t − 1 that negatively affects both stock prices and household expenditures in quarter t − 1. And say this change persists for a number of quarters, thus affecting both stock prices and expenditures for quarters t, t + 1, t + 2, . . . This would mean that wealth in quarter t – 1 is correlated with the error term in an expenditure equation in quarter t. This would then bias the estimate of the coefficient of a one-quarter-lagged wealth variable in an expenditure equation if it were treated as exogenous in the NL2SLS estimation. In other words, the wealth effect would be overestimated.

At noted in sections 3.2 and 4.5 regarding the use of the one-quarter-lagged wealth variable as an explanatory variable, in the NL2SLS estimation this variable was treated as endogenous, with one of the FSRs being the two-quarter-lagged wealth variable. In other words, the two-quarter-lagged wealth variable is used as an instrument for the one-quarter-lagged wealth variable (along with the other FSRs). This leads to consistent coefficient estimates, other things being equal, if the shock lasts only two quarters. The implicit assumption is thus that shocks from unobserved forces that affect both stock prices and household expenditures last no more than half a year. One justification for this assumption is that if the shocks were large and persistent for many quarters, one should be able to find this effect in the quarterly data, which is not the case. One-quarter-lagged stock prices and current household expenditures are, of course, positively correlated because one-quarter-lagged wealth affects household expenditures.

8 Solution

8.1 Deterministic Simulation

Once the α_i coefficients in the model in (3.1) have been estimated, the model can be solved. For a deterministic simulation, the error terms u_{it} are set to their expected values, usually zero. A solution requires values of the exogenous variables for the entire solution period. For, say, a quarterly model, a *static* simulation is one in which the actual values of the predetermined variables are used for each quarter. A *dynamic* simulation is one in which the predicted values of the endogenous variables for past quarters are used as values for the lagged endogenous variables when solving for the current quarter. A dynamic simulation only requires actual values of the lagged endogenous variables up to the first quarter of the overall solution period.

It is easy to solve a macroeconometric model using the Gauss–Seidel technique. The technique is easiest to describe by means of an example. Assume that the model (3.1) consists of three equations, and let x_{it} denote the vector of predetermined variables in equation i:

$$f_1(y_{1t}, y_{2t}, y_{3t}, x_{1t}, \alpha_1) = u_{1t}, \tag{8.1}$$

$$f_2(y_{1t}, y_{2t}, y_{3t}, x_{2t}, \alpha_2) = u_{2t}, \tag{8.2}$$

$$f_3(y_{1t}, y_{2t}, y_{3t}, x_{3t}, \alpha_3) = u_{3t}, \tag{8.3}$$

where y_{1t}, y_{2t}, and y_{3t} are scalars. (The model is assumed to be identified.) The technique requires that the equations be rewritten with each endogenous variable on the LHS of one equation. This is usually quite easy for macroeconometric models, since most equations have an obvious LHS variable. If, say, the LHS variable for (8.2) is $\log(y_{2t}/y_{3t})$, then y_{2t} can be written on the LHS by taking exponents and multiplying the resulting expression by y_{3t}. The technique does not require that each endogenous variable be isolated on the LHS; the LHS variable can also appear on the RHS. It is almost always possible in macroeconometric work, however, to isolate the variable, and this will be assumed in the following example.

The model (8.1)–(8.3) will be written as

$$y_{1t} = g_1(y_{2t}, y_{3t}, x_{1t}, \alpha_1, u_{1t}), \tag{8.1'}$$

$$y_{2t} = g_2(y_{1t}, y_{3t}, x_{2t}, \alpha_2, u_{2t}), \tag{8.2'}$$

$$y_{3t} = g_3(y_{1t}, y_{2t}, x_{3t}, \alpha_3, u_{3t}). \tag{8.3'}$$

Given values of the coefficients, the error terms (usually zero), and the predetermined variables and given initial guesses of the endogenous variables on the RHS, one can solve for the endogenous variables on the LHS. The initial guesses, for example, can be values of the previous quarter. These computations require one "pass" or "iteration" through the model: each equation is solved once. Given this new set of values, the model can be solved again to get another set, and so on. Convergence is reached if for each endogenous variable the values on successive iterations are within some prescribed tolerance level.

There is no guarantee that this procedure converges, and it is easy to construct examples where it does not. My experience with macroeconometric models, however, is that convergence is almost always reached. If not, the technique has the advantage that it can usually be made to converge (assuming an actual solution exists) with sufficient damping. "Damping" means changing the value for the next iteration by only a fraction of the difference between the computed value on the iteration and the previously used value.

8.2 Stochastic Simulation

Setting the error terms equal to their expected values and solving a nonlinear model does not yield expected values of the endogeneous variables. The expected value of a variable that is a nonlinear function of other variables is not the nonlinear function of the expected values of the other variables. Expected values can be computed using stochastic simulation, which also has many other uses.

Stochastic simulation can be done by drawing only error terms or also both error terms and coefficients. From the estimation of a complete model, one can get an estimate of the covariance matrix of the error terms and the covariance matrix of the coefficient estimates. Error terms and coefficients can then be drawn from these matrices. Another method, which I prefer, is to draw error terms from the historical errors, which will now be explained.

Consider doing stochastic simulation for the US model. If equation 28 is dropped, the model has 23 stochastic equations. (Equation 28, which explains *UB*, unemployment benefits, is dropped because it ends in 2000.4.) Given the coefficient estimates and the actual data, residuals can be computed. Assume that these have been computed for the 1954.1–2023.2 period, 278 observations. There are thus 278 23-dimensional error vectors. Consider solving the model for the eight-quarter period, 2018.1–2019.4. Draw randomly eight error vectors with replacement from the 278 error vectors, Using these errors (instead of zero errors), solve the model dynamically for the eight-quarter period. Record the solution values. This is one trial. Repeat this procedure, say, *N* times. This gives *N* solution values of each endogenous variable for each quarter. An estimate of the expected value of a variable is the average of these values. One can also compute various measures of dispersion, like estimated variances.

Drawing coefficients requires more work. First, draw with replacement 278 error vectors. Given these errors and the NL2SLS coefficient estimates, solve the model dynamically for the 1954.1–2023.2 period. Using the solution values as the new data set, reestimate the model using NL2SLS. Given the new coefficient estimates and the drawn error terms for the 2018.1–2019.4 period, solve the model for this period. Record the values. This is one trial. (Note that each trial requires reestimation of the entire model.) Repeat this process *N* times to compute the expected values and measures of dispersion.

The advantage of drawing from historical error vectors is that no assumptions have to be made about probability distributions. One is just drawing from the actual error vectors that occured. In addition, covariance matrices do not have to be estimated. The covariance matrix of the coefficient estimates can be quite large.

An example of using stochastic simulation to compute standard errors of multipliers is presented in chapter 13. One result I have found in performing many stochastic simulations is that for macroeconometric models, the expected values computed via stochastic simulation are quite close to the values computed from a deterministic simulation using zero errors. Stochastic simulation is important for computing variances, but not means.

8.3 Performing Experiments

Coming back to deterministic simulations, a common procedure when performing an experiment with a model for a given period is to add the actual residuals to the estimated equations and take them to be exogenous. This means that when the model is solved with no changes in the exogenous variables, a perfect tracking solution results. The base solution values are thus just the actual values. When one then changes one or more exogenous variables and solves the model with the actual residuals continued to be added, the difference between the solution value for a given endogenous variable and quarter and the actual value is an estimate of the effect of the change in the exogenous variable or variables on the endogenous variable. This procedure will be called the "perfect tracking solution" procedure.

III Analysis of the US Model

9 Size of Wealth Effects

9.1 Analysis of *CG*

The variable AH in the US model is the nominal value of net financial assets of the household sector. It is determined by identity 66. This identity was presented in chapter 6, and it is repeated here:

$$AH = AH_{-1} + SH - \Delta MH + CG - DISH, \quad 66$$

where SH is the financial saving of the household sector, MH is its holdings of demand deposits and currency, CG is the value of capital gains or losses on the financial assets held by the household sector (almost all of which is the change in the market value of equity held by the household sector), and $DISH$ is a discrepancy term.

A change in stock prices affects AH through CG. The variable CG is constructed from data from the FFA. Not surprisingly, it is highly correlated with the change in the S&P 500 stock price index. When $CG/(PX \cdot YS)$ is regressed on $(SP - SP_{-1})/(PX \cdot YS)$, where SP is the value of the S&P 500 index at the end of the quarter and $PX \cdot YS$ is the value of potential nominal output, the results are:

$$\frac{CG}{PX \cdot YS} = \underset{(6.50)}{.0548} + \underset{(38.25)}{9.22} \frac{SP - SP_{-1}}{PX \cdot YS},$$

$$R^2 = .841, 1954.1\text{–}2023.2 \quad (9.1)$$

$PX \cdot YS$ is used for scale purposes in this regression to lessen the chances of heteroskedasticity. The fit of this equation is very good, reflecting the high correlation of CG and the change in the S&P 500 index. A coefficient of 9.22 means that a 100-point change in the S&P 500 index results in a $922 billion change in the value of stocks held by the household sector.

Although *SP* is not a variable in the US model, the above analysis is useful for showing the high correlation between *CG* and the change in *SP*.

9.2 Estimated Effects of Changes in Financial and Housing Wealth

It was seen in chapter 4 that $AA1$, real financial wealth, and $AA2$, real housing wealth, have similar effects in the three consumer expenditure equations, and this restriction was imposed. This means that only AA, which equals $AA1 + AA2$, needs to be considered. The question of interest is how much do household expenditures change when AA changes? (Wealth does not appear in the housing investment equation, and so it can be ignored.) The size of this wealth effect depends on what is held constant. If the complete US model is used, then an increase in AA increases consumption expenditures, which affects other endogenous variables, which in turn affects consumption expenditures, and so on. The size of the wealth effect with nothing held constant thus depends on many features of the model, not just the properties of the consumption expenditure equations.

One can focus solely on the properties of the consumption expenditure equations by taking income and interest rates to be exogenous. Taking the four variables $YD/(POP \cdot PH)$, RSA, RMA, and AA as exogenous isolates the three consumption expenditure equations from the rest of the model. This was done, and the following experiment was performed. First, the estimated residuals were added to the three equations and taken to be exogenous—the perfect tracking solution procedure discussed in section 8.3. Second, AA was increased by \$1,000 billion in each quarter from its actual value, and the three equations were solved for the 2012.1–2019.4 period. The difference for a given quarter between the predicted value of a variable and the actual value is the estimated effect of the AA change on that variable for that quarter.

The effects on total consumption expenditures ($CS + CN + CD$) by quarter are presented in table 9.1. After four quarters, expenditures have risen \$17.4 billion, and after eight quarters, they have risen \$29.0 billion. The increases then level off at about \$38 billion. The long-run effect of a sustained increase in wealth on consumption expenditures is thus estimated to be about 4 percent per year ignoring any feedback effects.

The 4 percent estimate in table 9.1 is roughly in line with results from other approaches. The size of the wealth effect is discussed in Ludvigson and

Table 9.1
Effects on $CS+CN+CD$ of a Change in AA of 1,000

	Year							
Quarter	2012	2013	2014	2015	2016	2017	2018	2019
1	0.0	21.3	30.6	35.0	36.9	37.7	37.9	37.7
2	6.9	24.3	32.1	35.6	37.2	37.8	37.9	37.7
3	12.6	26.9	33.2	36.1	37.4	37.8	37.9	37.7
4	17.4	29.0	34.3	36.5	37.5	38.0	37.8	37.7

• Units are billions of 2012 dollars

Steindel (1999), where they conclude that "a dollar increase in wealth likely leads to a three-to-four-cent increase in consumption in today's economy" (p. 30), although they argue that there is considerable uncertainty regarding this estimate. Their approach is simpler and less structural than the present one, but the size of their estimate is similar. Starr-McCluer (1998) uses survey data to examine the wealth effect, and she concludes that her results are broadly consistent with a modest wealth effect.

Mian, Rao, and Sufi (2013, p. 30) (MRS) find 5 to 7 percent effects of housing wealth on consumption, although these effects vary considerably across zip codes. Zhou and Carroll (2012, p. 18) find 5 percent effects of housing wealth on consumption.

Case, Quigley, and Shiller (2012) (CQS) test for asymmetrical effects and find that the housing wealth elasticity is estimated to be larger in falling markets than in rising markets.[1] Their estimated elasticities are 0.10 and 0.032, respectively. How do these compare with the present results? At the beginning of 2012, $CS+CN+CD$ was about \$11 trillion. Housing wealth, $AA2$, was about \$18 trillion. If one takes the change in consumption expenditures to be \$42 billion, then the housing wealth elasticity is (42/11000)/(1000/18000) = 0.07. So this elasticity is a little lower than the CQS elasticity of 0.10 in falling markets.

10 Size of Fed's Effect on Output, Unemployment, and Inflation

When inflation picked up in 2021, there was much discussion of how high the Fed had to raise the interest rate to get inflation back down to 2 percent. In the US model, when the Fed raises the short-term interest rate, variable *RS*, the long-term rates, *RB* and *RM* increase, and the general increase in interest rates has a negative effect on household expenditures—a decrease in aggregate demand. This lowers output and employment. The unemployment rate rises, which has a negative effect on the nonfarm price deflator, variable *PF* in equation 10, and thus lowers inflation. In the discussion of equation 10 in chapter 4, it was argued that this is the only way that the Fed influences *PF*. There are no additional announcement or expectational effects.

The model can be used to estimate the size of the effect of a change in *RS* on *PF*. Consider the 16-quarter period 2016.1–2019.4. Take the error terms to be the estimated residuals—the perfect tracking solution procedure. Then increase *RS* by 1 percentage point for each quarter of the simulation period. (Equation 30 is dropped, and thus *RS* is exogenous.) For each endogenous variable for each quarter, the difference between the solution value and the base (actual) value is the estimated effect of the change. The results are in table 10.1.

Consider in table 10.1 the effects after eight quarters: *GDPR* is down 0.50 percent; *JF* is down 0.42 percent; *UR* is up 0.23 percentage points; and *PCPF* is down 0.26 percentage points. There is leakage from changes in *GDPR* to changes in *UR* because of the excess labor response in going from output to jobs and because of the discouraged worker effects on the labor force and the number of moonlighters. Thus, a rough rule of thumb is that a 1 percentage point increase in the short-term interest rate results in a 0.25

Table 10.1
Effects of a 1.0 Increase in *RS* from Baseline

GDPR and _JF_: Percent Change from Baseline
_UR_ and _PCPF_: Change from Baseline
Percentage Points

Qtr.	*GDPR*	*JF*	*UR*	*PCPF*
2016.1	−0.05	−0.01	0.01	0.00
2016.2	−0.14	−0.05	0.04	−0.03
2016.3	−0.24	−0.16	0.07	−0.07
2016.4	−0.32	−0.17	0.11	−0.11
2017.1	−0.38	−0.24	0.15	−0.16
2017.2	−0.43	−0.30	0.19	−0.21
2017.3	−0.46	−0.36	0.21	−0.23
2017.4	−0.50	−0.42	0.23	−0.26
2018.1	−0.52	−0.46	0.24	−0.28
2018.2	−0.53	−0.50	0.25	−0.29
2018.3	−0.55	−0.54	0.25	−0.30
2018.4	−0.55	−0.57	0.25	−0.26
2019.1	−0.56	−0.59	0.25	−0.24
2019.2	−0.56	−0.60	0.25	−0.26
2019.3	−0.57	−0.62	0.24	−0.23
2019.4	−0.57	−0.63	0.24	−0.22

GDPR = real GDP.
JF = number of jobs in the firm sector.
UR = unemployment rate.
PF = private nonfarm price deflator.
$PCPF = 100 \cdot [(PF/PF_{-1})^4 - 1]$

increase in the unemployment rate and a 0.25 decrease in inflation. If, for example, the Fed wanted to lower the inflation rate by 1 percentage points after eight quarters, this would require a 4 percentage point increase in *RS*, which would also increase the unemployment by 1 percentage point.

This result is pessimistic regarding the power of the Fed to lower inflation because everything has to work through aggregate demand changes. As noted above, there are no announcement or expectation effects. Because $1/UR$ is the explanatory variable in equation 10, there is an important nonlinear response in the model. The lower the unemployment rate, the larger the effect of a change in *RS* on inflation.

Table 10.2
Effects of a 1.0 Increase in *RS* from Baseline $5 Trillion Fall in Wealth in 2016.1

GDPR and JF: Percent Change from Baseline
UR and PCPF: Change from Baseline
Percentage Points

Qtr.	*GDPR*	*JF*	*UR*	*PCPF*
2016.1	−0.05	−0.01	0.01	0.00
2016.2	−0.26	−0.09	0.11	−0.11
2016.3	−0.62	−0.25	0.27	−0.26
2016.4	−0.99	−0.49	0.46	−0.44
2017.1	−1.29	−0.76	0.65	−0.63
2017.2	−1.44	−1.01	0.80	−0.79
2017.3	−1.50	−1.20	0.90	−0.84
2017.4	−1.51	−1.35	0.94	−0.89
2018.1	−1.51	−1.45	0.96	−0.91
2018.2	−1.50	−1.53	0.95	−0.90
2018.3	−1.49	−1.58	0.93	−0.88
2018.4	−1.46	−1.61	0.91	−0.75
2019.1	−1.44	−1.62	0.89	−0.67
2019.2	−1.41	−1.62	0.85	−0.70
2019.3	−1.39	−1.62	0.81	−0.61
2019.4	−1.37	−1.61	0.80	−0.55

See notes to table 10.1.

Because *CG* is exogenous, there is no stock price reaction to the increase in *RS*. Even though one can't pick this up in the data, it could be that there would be a reaction. The results in table 10.2 give an estimate of the potential size of this effect. The experiment is the same as in table 10.1 except that in the first quarter, *CG* was decreased by $5 trillion from baseline. This decrease was then sustained for the rest of the simulation period. This is a fall in the S&P 500 stock price index of about 500 points. It is a fairly large reaction to a 1 percentage point increase in *RS*.

The effects are much larger in table 10.2. After eight quarters, the unemployment is up about 0.95 percentage points and inflation is down about this amount. So instead of 4 to 1, the effect is about 1 to 1. To lower inflation by 1 percentage point would require about a 1 percentage point increase in *RS*, which would also increase the unemployment rate about 1 percentage point. The bottom line is that if the Fed can affect stock prices, this adds considerably to its ability to affect unemployment and inflation because of the wealth effect on consumption expenditures. The $5 trillion stock price change in table 10.2 is likely extreme, but it gives a sense of wealth effects in the model. It is also made up in the sense that there is no estimated relationship between Fed behavior and the change in stock prices in the model.

The overall results using the US model show that the Fed's power to control inflation is modest and takes time. The Fed is helped if there is a large stock price response to its policy changes, but there is no empirical evidence to support this on a quarterly basis.

11 Changes in Fed's Behavior since 2008

11.1 Behavioral Change

Equation 30, the Fed rule, is only estimated through 2008.3 because the zero lower bound was hit in the next quarter. If one uses the rule beyond 2008.3, it sometimes calls for a negative nominal interest rate, and so it became inoperative. The Fed kept the interest rate at roughly zero through 2015. The Fed also kept the interest rate at zero during the pandemic, from 2020.2 through all of 2021. It began raising interest rates in 2022.1 in response to rising inflation and falling unemployment.

Has the Fed's behavior since 2009 been consistent with the estimated rule except for the zero lower bound problem, or has there been a structural change in Fed behavior since then? This question can be analyzed using the US model and equation 30. It will be seen that there appears to have been a large structural change.

It will be convenient for the analysis in this chapter to drop variable $D20083 \cdot PCM1_{-1}$ as an explanatory variable from the equation and reestimate. Except for the early Volcker period, the lagged growth of the money supply has a small effect on *RS* in the equation. The reestimated equation is in table 11.1. The FSRs are the same as in table A30 except that $D20083 \cdot PCM1_{-1}$ has been dropped. The coefficient estimates in table 11.1 are very close to those in table A30.

Although the estimation period for the rule ends in 2008.3, the equation can be solved beyond this period. The experiment in this chapter is to solve the rule dynamically for the entire 1954.1–2023.1 period and examine the differences between the predicted values from the rule and the actual values, values assumed to be set by the Fed. Solving dynamically means that after

Table 11.1
Estimated Interest Rate Rule LHS Variable Is RS_t

RHS Variable	Coefficient	t-statistic
cnst	0.700	4.49
RS_{t-1}	0.916	48.43
$100 \cdot [(PD/PD_{-1})^4 - 1]$	0.0836	4.45
UR_t	−10.58	−3.34
ΔUR_t	−82.23	−5.38
$D794823_t \cdot \dot{M}1_{t-1}$	0.213	9.21
ΔRS_{t-1}	0.208	3.63
ΔRS_{t-2}	−0.335	−6.68
SE	0.493	
R^2	0.969	

Estimation method: NL2SLS.
Estimation period: 1954.1 2008.3.

a few quarters, the initial dynamic effects subside and one is observing the long-run effects.

In running this experiment, account must be taken of the fact that when the Fed changes *RS*, this affects inflation and unemployment. In the estimation of the rule in table 11.1, the endogeneity of inflation and unemployment is taken into account using NL2SLS. The coefficient estimates are consistent assuming that the FSRs are uncorrelated with the equation's error term. In the experiment, on the other hand, the rule needs to be embedded in a model that accounts for the effect of *RS* on inflation and unemployment. The US model is used for this purpose.

Equation 28, explaining unemployment insurance benefits, *UB*, was dropped from the experiment because it ends in 2000.4. *UB* was taken to be exogenous. The model thus consists of 23 estimated equations counting the rule. Remember that in the NL2SLS estimation of the equations, account has been taken of any serial correlation of the error terms by jointly estimating the serial correlation coefficients and the structural coefficients. The error terms after this estimation are taken to be shocks that are uncorrelated with the exogenous and lagged endogenous variables. In the dynamic solution, these shocks are taken to be equal to their actual (estimated) values except for the shocks to the rule, which are assumed to be zero. In other words, the

Table 11.2
Average Values for Three Subperiods

Period	*RS*	$\hat{RS}$	π	*UR*	# obs.
A: 1954.1–1979.3	4.41	4.31	8.85	5.39	103
B: 1979.4–1982.3	12.35	13.24	7.79	7.78	12
C: 1982.4–2008.3	4.97	4.64	2.49	5.89	104

- *RS* = actual value of *RS*.
- $\hat{RS}$ = predicted value of *RS*.
- π = actual value of $100 \cdot [(PD/PD_{-1})^4 - 1]$.
- *UR* = actual value of *UR*.

shocks are assumed to be what they were historically except for the shocks to the rule. The shocks to the rule are estimates of how the Fed deviated each quarter from the values predicted by the rule. The predicted values from the rule are thus what the Fed would have done had it followed the rule exactly. As noted above, the rule unconstrained sometimes calls for negative rates. In the solution, *RS* was set to zero if the rule called for a negative value.

- A: 1954.1–1979.3. Pre early Volcker.
- B: 1979.4–1982.3. Early Volcker.
- C: 1982.4–2008.3. Post early Volcker to beginning of Great Recession.
- D: 2008.4–2010.4. Great Recession to 2010.
- E: 2011.1–2019.4. 2011 to Pandemic.
- F: 2020.1–2023.1. Pandemic and Beyond.

There are six subperiods of interest. Table 11.2 presents for each of the first three subperiods the average actual value of *RS*, the average predicted value of *RS*, the average value of the actual inflation rate, and the average value of the actual unemployment rate. The table shows that the actual and predicted values of *RS* are close. This is to be expected since the equation is estimated through this period. The equation predicts well within the sample.

The nine quarterly values for subperiod D are presented in table 11.3. This is the period in which the rule generally called for *RS* less than zero, and so the predicted value was set to zero. Inflation was low and the unemployment rate was high, which is the reason for the negative predicted rates. The Fed also set the interest rate to essentially zero during this period.

Table 11.3
Values for Subperiod D

Quarter	*RS*	$\hat{RS}$	π	*UR*
2008.4	0.30	1.95	−5.53	6.90
2009.1	0.21	0.00	−3.47	8.32
2009.2	0.17	0.00	−0.25	9.31
2009.3	0.16	0.21	1.54	9.63
2009.4	0.06	0.00	2.09	9.94
2010.1	0.11	0.00	1.43	9.86
2010.2	0.15	0.00	0.58	9.68
2010.3	0.16	0.00	0.73	9.50
2010.4	0.14	0.00	2.91	9.55

• See table 11.2 for notation.

One could say that the Fed was using the rule, but with the restriction of a zero lower bound.

The 36 quarterly values for subperiod E, 2011 to Pandemic, are presented in table 11.4. Here is where the Fed began to deviate from the rule. By 2011, inflation was rising, and by the end of 2011, unemployment began to fall. The rule called for a gradual increase in rates, but the Fed kept the interest rate at essentially zero through 2015. The Fed then began raising the rate slightly, but the rates through 2019 were always lower than the rates predicted by the rule. The rule was responding to the large fall in the unemployment rate, down to 3.60 percent in 2019.4. By this quarter, the rule called for a 4.13 percent interest rate, which compares to the actual rate of 1.58 percent. These results suggest a fairly large structural change in Fed behavior relative to the pre-2008 period.

The 13 quarterly values for subperiod F, Pandemic and Beyond, are presented in table 11.5. In this pandemic period, the Fed kept the interest rate at essentially zero through 2021. The rule, on the other hand, called for a zero interest rate in 2020.2, but then large values after that. The rule is responding to the increase in inflation and decrease in the unemployment rate. For example, in 2021.4, when the Fed was still keeping the interest rate at zero, inflation was 7.21 percent and the unemployment rate was 4.22 percent. With these values, the rules calls for an interest rate value of 7.00 percent. The Fed began raising rates in 2022, and by 2023.2, the rate

Table 11.4
Values for Subperiod E

Quarter	*RS*	$\hat{RS}$	π	*UR*
2011.1	0.13	0.45	3.28	9.05
2011.2	0.05	0.57	3.94	9.09
2011.3	0.02	0.38	2.05	9.02
2011.4	0.01	0.44	1.19	8.67
2012.1	0.07	0.85	2.76	8.27
2012.2	0.09	0.81	0.99	8.18
2012.3	0.10	0.69	1.44	8.01
2012.4	0.09	0.77	1.70	7.81
2013.1	0.09	0.74	0.78	7.75
2013.2	0.05	0.73	0.39	7.54
2013.3	0.03	0.93	1.50	7.26
2013.4	0.06	1.25	1.97	6.96
2014.1	0.05	1.53	2.01	6.63
2014.2	0.03	1.82	1.75	6.23
2014.3	0.03	1.85	1.49	6.09
2014.4	0.02	1.90	−0.34	5.72
2015.1	0.03	1.78	−1.69	5.53
2015.2	0.02	1.85	1.67	5.44
2015.3	0.04	2.17	1.00	5.12
2015.4	0.12	2.09	−0.96	5.05
2016.1	0.29	1.97	−0.45	4.90
2016.2	0.26	2.12	2.67	4.93
2016.3	0.30	2.25	1.10	4.89
2016.4	0.43	2.43	2.14	4.79
2017.1	0.59	2.74	2.56	4.58
2017.2	0.89	2.93	0.94	4.37
2017.3	1.04	2.93	1.32	4.33
2017.4	1.21	3.14	2.35	4.19
2018.1	1.56	3.48	2.74	4.04
2018.2	1.84	3.71	2.49	3.94
2018.3	2.04	3.80	1.28	3.80
2018.4	2.32	3.73	0.83	3.84
2019.1	2.39	3.74	1.21	3.84
2019.2	2.30	4.13	2.56	3.65
2019.3	1.98	4.20	0.34	3.63
2019.4	1.58	4.13	1.30	3.60

• See table 11.2 for notation.

Table 11.5
Values for Subperiod F

Quarter	*RS*	$\hat{RS}$	π	*UR*
2020.1	1.11	3.85	0.59	3.82
2020.2	0.14	0.00	−2.91	13.00
2020.3	0.11	2.67	2.70	8.83
2020.4	0.09	6.09	2.74	6.78
2021.1	0.05	6.15	4.83	6.23
2021.2	0.03	5.10	5.48	5.92
2021.3	0.05	5.68	7.65	5.12
2021.4	0.05	7.00	7.21	4.22
2022.1	0.31	7.56	8.49	3.83
2022.2	1.08	7.57	9.20	3.65
2022.3	2.66	7.36	4.77	3.57
2022.4	4.04	7.20	3.89	3.62
2023.1	4.63	7.34	3.92	3.50
2023.2	5.07	7.28	2.01	3.54

• See table 11.2 for notation.

was 5.07. This, however, is still lower than the rule's value of 7.28 percent. This period is another example of the Fed's change in behavior. Had it been behaving as it did before 2008, it would have not kept the interest rate at essentially zero until 2022, given what was happening to inflation and unemployment.

Although the above results are dramatic, there is no obvious statistical test of the hypothesis that Fed behavior changed beginning in 2011. For example, the end-of-sample instability test of Andrews (2003) cannot be used. There was a structural break during the early Volcker period, for example, and for much of the 2009–2010 period, the Fed could not follow the rule because of the zero lower bound constraint. One cannot assume, for example, that the Fed followed the same rule between 1954.1 and 2010.4 and then test the hypothesis that it changed behavior after that, which is what the Andrews test requires. However, the difference between the predicted values from the historically estimated rule and the actual values are large enough after 2011 to suggest a change of behavior.

An explanation of the low interest rates since the Great Recession is thus a change in Fed behavior beginning about 2011, beginning under Ben Bernanke and continuing under Janet Yellen and Jerome Powell. Prior to this, interest rates were either as expected or zero because of the zero lower bound.

11.2 Why Did the Fed Change Its Behavior?

An interesting question is why the Fed became so much more expansive after the Great Recession. Laubach and Williams (2003) wrote an influential paper using Wicksell's (1936) concept of the "natural" rate of interest, denoted r^*. Their and subsequent estimates showed r^* falling. Larry Summers gave an influential speech on November 8, 2013, at the IMF Economic Forum arguing that the US economy was in a period of secular stagnation. This work may have led the Fed to be less inclined than it had in the past to raise rates.

There also seemed in this period to be a general view that the Fed could control inflation through its announcements by directly controlling inflation expectations. Inflation was low during subperiod E, and if inflation can be controlled through announcements, there is no need to move early even with low and falling unemployment.[1]

The deviation of Fed behavior from the historical experience is most extreme during the COVID-19 period. The view of the Fed up until about the beginning of 2022 was that almost all of the inflation that began in 2020.3 was due to supply and other transitory issues and that once these were over, the Fed's influence on inflation expectations—its credibility—would be enough to lower inflation back down to around 2.0 percent. This turned out, of course, not to be the case. As noted in the discussion of equation 10 in chapter 4, survey evidence suggests that the Fed has almost no influence on the inflation expectations of agents who are setting prices.

11.3 Literature on Low Interest Rates

There is some discussion in the literature about why interest rates have been historically low worldwide in the last two or three decades. Rachel and Smith (2017) argue that the decrease in interest rates is due to a decline in future trend growth and shifts in saving and investment preferences. Caballero, Farhi, and Gourinchas (2017) and Gourinchas (2017) develop an accounting framework and argue that there has been a secular increase in capital and equity risk premia, driving down safe real rates. Mankiw

(2022) uses insights from neoclassical growth theory to explain the decline. Blanchard (2019) discusses the implications of low interest rates for macro policy, as do Brumm et al. (2021).

The results in this chapter suggest that the answer may be the structural change in Fed behavior. The low nominal interest rates during the Great Recession and a few years after that can be explained by the Fed reacting to the sluggish economy. If there were no zero lower bound, it would have reacted even more. This behavior is consistent with historical experience. Beginning in 2011, however, under Ben Bernanke and continuing under Janet Yellen and Jerome Powell, the Fed kept the interest rate lower than the rule called for. It did not respond much to the falling unemployment rates, contrary to what it had done historically. Interest rates were thus lower than one would have expected historically. Similar considerations may also apply to other monetary authorities, since many are influenced by what the Fed does.

12 Effects of Inflation Shocks

It is the case that a positive inflation shock is contractionary in the US model, and it is informative to see why. This property is contrary to that of a class of models in the literature, where a positive price shock is expansionary, sometimes explosive. As a rough approximation, models in this class include the following three equations:

1. Interest Rate Rule: The Fed adjusts the nominal interest rate in response to inflation and the output gap (deviation of output from potential). The nominal interest rate responds positively to inflation and the output gap. The coefficient on inflation is greater than one, and so the real interest rate rises when inflation rises.

2. Price Equation: Inflation depends on the output gap, cost shocks, and expected future inflation.

3. Aggregate Demand Equation: Aggregate demand (real) depends on the real interest rate, expected future demand, and exogenous shocks. The real interest rate effect is negative.

Models in this class are nicely summarized in Clarida, Galí, and Gertler (1999), and they are used in Clarida, Galí, and Gertler (2000) to examine monetary policy rules. Taylor (1999b, p. 91) points out that virtually all the papers in Taylor (1999c) use these models and that the models are widely used for policy evaluation in many central banks. In both the backward-looking model and the forward-looking model in Svensson (2003), aggregate demand depends negatively on the real interest rate, as in the aggregate demand equation above. Romer (2000) proposes a way of teaching these models at the introductory level.

The effects of an inflation shock in this basic model are easy to see. The aggregate demand equation implies that an increase in inflation *with the nominal interest rate held constant* is expansionary (because the real interest rate falls). The model is in fact not stable in this case because an increase in output increases inflation through the price equation, which further increases output through the aggregate demand equation, and so on. In order for the model to be stable, the nominal interest rate must rise more than inflation, which means that the coefficient on inflation in the interest rate rule must be greater than one. Because of this feature, some have criticized Fed behavior in the 1960s and 1970s as following in effect a rule with a coefficient on inflation less than one—see, for example, Clarida, Galí, and Gertler (1999) and Taylor (1999a).

The properties of the US model tell a much different story. There are three main reasons positive inflation shocks are contractionary. First, as tested in chapter 4, nominal interest rates rather than real interest rates affect household expenditures. Second, the percentage increase in nominal household wealth from a positive inflation shock is less than the percentage increase in the price level, and so there is a fall in real household wealth from a positive inflation shock. This has, other things being equal, a negative effect on real household expenditures. Third, in the price and wage equations, 10 and 16, nominal wages lag prices, and so a positive inflation shock results in an initial fall in the real wage rate, which has a negative effect on real labor income.

If these three features are true, they imply that a positive inflation shock has a negative effect on aggregate demand even if the nominal interest rate is held constant. The fall in real wealth and real labor income is contractionary, and there is no offsetting rise in demand from the fall in the real interest rate. Not only does the Fed not have to increase the nominal interest rate more than the increase in inflation for there to be a contraction, it does not have to increase the nominal rate at all! The inflation shock itself will contract the economy through the real wealth and real income effects.

A simple experiment can be performed to show the effects in the US model. Consider the 16-quarter period 2016.1–2019.4. Add the estimated residuals to the stochastic equations and take them to be exogenous—the perfect tracking solution procedure. Then increase the constant term in equation 10 so that the shock to *PF* in the first quarter is about 0.5 percent.[1] There is no estimated interest rate rule for this period, and so *RS* is exogenous. Solve the model with this coefficient change. The difference

Table 12.1
Effects of a Positive Shock to the Price Equation 10 Nominal Interest Rate, *RS*, Unchanged from Base Values

	Variable	Changes from Base Values Quarters Ahead 1	2	3	4	8	12	16
1	*PF*	0.54	1.17	1.80	2.39	4.27	5.43	6.17
2	*GDPR*	0.00	−0.01	−0.04	−0.08	−0.30	−0.50	−0.61
3	*UR*	0.00	0.00	0.01	0.02	0.16	0.30	0.37
4	*WR*	−0.04	−0.09	−0.15	−0.19	−0.34	−0.45	−0.55
5	*PIEF*	1.29	3.00	4.41	4.86	7.74	9.46	10.06
6	*YD/PH*	0.02	0.03	0.07	0.06	0.04	0.02	−0.02
7	*AA*	−0.30	−0.66	−0.99	−1.30	−2.25	−2.68	−3.09
8	*CS* + *CN* + *CD*	0.00	0.00	−0.03	−0.05	−0.21	−0.38	−0.50

PF = private nonfarm price deflator.
GDPR = real GDP.
UR = unemployment rate.
WR = real wage rate, *WF*/*PF*.
PIEF = corporate profits.
YD/*PH* = real disposable income.
AA = real wealth.
CS + *CN* + *CD* = total consumption expernditures.
Percent changes except for *UR*, which is absolute change.
Simulation period: 2016.1–2019.4.

between the predicted value for each variable and quarter, the base (actual) value, is the estimated effect of the price-equation shock.

Selected results from this experiment are presented in table 12.1. Row 1 shows the effects of the change in the constant term in the price equation on the price level. The price level is .54 percent higher than its base value in the first quarter, 1.17 percent higher in the second quarter, and so on through the sixteenth quarter, where it is 6.17 percent higher. (The shock to the price equation accumulates over time because of the lagged dependent variable in the equation.)

The main point for present purposes is in row 2, which shows that real GDP falls: the inflation shock is contractionary. Real GDP is 0.61 percent lower by the sixteenth quarter. Row 3 shows that the unemployment rate is higher, by 0.37 percentage points by the sixteenth quarter.

Row 4 shows that the real wage is lower, which is because the nominal wage rate lags the price level in equations 10 and 16. Corporate profits are higher in row 5 because of the lower real wage. Real disposable income in row 6 is about unchanged. The negative effect from the fall in the real wage is roughly offset by an increase in corporate dividends because of the increase in profits (equation 18) and because of an increase in nominal transfer payments from the federal and state and local governments because of the increased inflation.

Row 7 shows that real wealth is down. This is the driving force of the contraction. Row 8 shows that household consumption expenditures are down, which is mostly caused by the fall in real wealth.

The FRB/US Model

The FRB/US model—Federal Reserve Board (2000)—is sometimes cited as a macroeconometric model that is consistent with the class of models discussed above (see, for example, Taylor, 1999b, p. 91). This model has strong real interest rate effects. In fact, if government spending is increased in the FRB/US model with the nominal interest rate held constant, real output eventually expands so much that the model will no longer solve.[2] The increase in government spending raises inflation, which with nominal interest rates held constant lowers real interest rates, which leads to an unlimited expansion. The model is not stable unless there is a nominal interest rate rule that leads to an increase in the real interest rate when inflation increases.

It may seem puzzling that two macroeconometric models could have such different properties. How can it be that the FRB/US model finds such strong real interest rate effects? The answer is that many restrictions have been imposed on the model that have the effect of imposing large real interest rate effects. In most of the expenditure equations, real interest rate effects are imposed rather than estimated. Direct tests of nominal versus real interest rates like those in section 4.5.5 are not done, and so there is no way of knowing what the data actually support in the FRB/US expenditure equations.

Large effects on stock prices are also imposed in the FRB/US model. A one percentage point decrease in the real interest rate leads to a 20 percent increase in the value of corporate equity (Reifschneider, Tetlow, and Williams, 1999, p. 5). At the end of 1999, the value of corporate equity was about $20 trillion (using data from the US Flow of Funds accounts), and 20 percent of this is $4 trillion. There is thus a huge increase in nominal household wealth for just a one percentage point decrease in the real interest rate. A positive inflation shock with the nominal interest rate held constant, which lowers the real interest rate, thus results in a large increase in both nominal and real wealth in the model. The increase in real wealth then leads through the wealth effect in the household expenditure equations to a large increase in real expenditures. This channel is an important contributor to the model not being stable when there is an increase in inflation greater than the nominal interest rate. Again, this effect on stock prices is imposed rather than estimated, and so it is not necessarily the case that the data are consistent with this restriction.

There is thus no puzzle about the vastly different properties of the two models. It is simply that important real interest rate restrictions have been imposed in the FRB/US model and not in the US model.

Conclusion

If a positive inflation shock with the nominal interest rate held constant is in fact contractionary, this has important implications for monetary policy. The coefficient on inflation in the nominal interest rate rule need not be greater than one for the economy to be stable. Also, if one is concerned with optimal policies, the optimal response by the Fed to an inflation shock is likely to be much smaller if inflation shocks are contractionary than if they are expansionary. The use of the above class of models for monetary policy is thus risky. If the models are wrong about the effects of inflation shocks, they may lead to poor monetary policy recommendations.

13 Size of Government Spending Multipliers

13.1 The Size of the Multipliers

It is straightforward using the CC approach to examine government multiplier effects. Estimating reduced-form equations to get multipliers, which is common in the literature, is not needed. Reduced-form equations are implicit in the model, with many nonlinear restrictions, and they are not directly estimated. There is thus no worry that variables have been omitted from reduced-form equations. What is required is that the structural equations be consistently estimated. Take, for example, a consumption or investment equation. If there are RHS endogenous variables, like current income or a current interest rate, and thus correlation between these variables and the error term in the equation, this has to be accounted for. NL2SLS is used for the US model. FSRs must be found that are correlated with the endogenous variables and uncorrelated with the error term. If one suspects that a current government spending or tax rate variable depends on current endogenous variables, the variable needs to be lagged one period before being used as an FSR. The aim in structural modeling is to find good structural equations—good approximations to reality—and to estimate them consistently.

This structural approach uses much more information on the economy than estimating reduced-form equations. For example, the implicit reduced-form equation for output in the US model is nonlinear and includes hundreds of exogenous and lagged endogenous variables. There are also hundreds of nonlinear restrictions on the reduced-form coefficients. Given the complexity of the economy, it seems unlikely that estimating reduced-form equations with many omitted variables and no restrictions from theory on the coefficients will produce trustworthy results even if an attempt is made to account for omitted variable bias.

There are three main government spending variables for which multiplier estimates are useful: purchases of goods, purchases of labor, and transfer payments. These variables are discussed in chapter 7. The two variables examined in this chapter are federal government purchases of goods, *COG*, and federal real transfer payments to households, *TRGHQ*. When *COG* increases, this is an increase in aggregate demand. When *TRGHQ* increases, this is an increase in income to households, who will save some and spend some. The spending part is an increase in aggregate demand. The multiplier is larger for *COG* than for *TRGHQ* because some of *TRGHQ* is saved. This is standard textbook modeling.

The effects of increasing *COG* and *TRGHQ* are examined here. Both multipliers and standard errors are computed, and the stochasic simulation procedure discussed in section 8.2 is used. The simulation period is 2016.1–2019.4, 16 quarters. The procedure used for the present experiment requires a few more details than given in section 8.2. First, as noted in section 8.2, equation 28 explaining unemployment benefits *UB* is dropped and *UB* is taken to be exogenouos. No errors from this equation are used. Second, although the main estimation period is 1954.1–2023.2, 278 observations, errors are computed only for the 1954.1–2019.4 period, 264 observations. This avoids drawing errors for the pandemic period. The errors are in fact zero in the model for the 2020.1–2021.4 period because of the use of the pandemic dummy variables. Third, errors are computed for equation 15 explaining *HO* for 1954.1–1955.4 even though the equation is only estimated beginning in 1956.1. Similarly, errors are computed for equation 30, the Fed rule explaining *RS*, for 2008.4–2019.4 even though the equation is only estimated through 2008.3.

There are thus 264 23-dimensional error vectors to draw from. Each trial is as follows. First, 278 error vectors are drawn with replacement from the 264 estimated error vectors. These errors are added to the equations and taken to be exogenous. Given these errors and the coefficient estimates based on the actual data (the coefficient estimates in tables A1–A30), the model is solved dynamically for the 1954.1–2023.2 period. These solution values are then treated as the new data set, and the 23 equations are reestimated using these data. In other words, the model is completely reestimated. Equation 15 is estimated beginning in 1956.1, and equation 30 is estimated ending in 2008.3. The other equations are estimated for the entire 1954.1–2023.2 period.

Given the new coefficient estimates and the new data, the multiplier experiment is performed for the 2016:1–2019:4 period, 16 observations. First, 16 error vectors are drawn with replacement from the 264 error vectors. They are added to the equations and taken to be exogenous.[1] The model is then solved dynamically for this period using the new data, the new coefficient estimates, and the actual values of all the exogenous variables including the government spending variable. This is the base run. Now keep everything the same but change the government spending variable and resolve the model. The difference between this solution value for a given endogenous variable and quarter and the base solution value is the estimated effect of the change in the government spending variable—the multiplier. The model is thus solved twice for the 2016.1–2019.4 period to get the estimated differences. This is one trial.

This procedure is then repeated, say, *N* times. The coefficient estimates that are used to generate the new data on each trial are the original estimates based on the actual data, not estimates based on any constructed data. The *N* trials give *N* values of each multiplier, from which measures of dispersion can be computed.

There are a variety of measures of dispersion that can be used. The ones in table 13.1 are computed as follows. Rank the *N* values of a given multiplier by size. Let m_r denote the value below which *r* percent of the values lie. The measure of dispersion is $(m_{.8413} - m_{.1587})/2$. For a normal distribution, this is one standard error. For ease of discussion, this measure will be called "a standard error." The multiplier is the median of the *N* values. The results in table 13.1 are based on 984 trials for each of the two government spending variables. The program was coded to do 1,000 trials, but 16 of these resulted in a solution failure in generating the new data set; therefore, these trials were skipped. This means that the true measures of dispersion in table 13.1 are underestimated because the extreme draws are ignored.

For *COG*, the *GDPR* multiplier peaks at 1.26 after three quarters in table 13.1. The *UR* change peaks after five quarters at a fall of 0.56 percentage points. The *PF* change is gradually increasing. After 16 quarters, *PF* is 1.19 percent higher. The *RS* change peaks after four quarters at an increase of

Table 13.1
Multipliers and Standard Errors: Deviations from Baseline in Percentage Points

qtr	*GDPR*		*UR*		*PF*		*RS*	
Spending on Goods (*COG*)								
2016.1	0.87	(0.07)	−0.20	(0.05)	0.05	(0.02)	0.16	(0.11)
2016.2	1.21	(0.09)	−0.39	(0.09)	0.14	(0.05)	0.32	(0.21)
2016.3	1.26	(0.10)	−0.51	(0.10)	0.26	(0.08)	0.42	(0.24)
2016.4	1.20	(0.10)	−0.55	(0.09)	0.37	(0.12)	0.45	(0.25)
2017.1	1.14	(0.11)	−0.56	(0.08)	0.49	(0.15)	0.46	(0.22)
2017.2	1.09	(0.12)	−0.54	(0.07)	0.58	(0.18)	0.46	(0.19)
2017.3	1.06	(0.12)	−0.51	(0.07)	0.66	(0.20)	0.45	(0.19)
2017.4	1.04	(0.13)	−0.47	(0.07)	0.74	(0.22)	0.44	(0.18)
2018.1	1.03	(0.13)	−0.45	(0.07)	0.81	(0.24)	0.44	(0.17)
2018.2	1.02	(0.13)	−0.42	(0.07)	0.88	(0.25)	0.44	(0.16)
2018.3	1.01	(0.13)	−0.40	(0.07)	0.94	(0.28)	0.42	(0.14)
2018.4	1.00	(0.13)	−0.38	(0.07)	0.99	(0.28)	0.42	(0.14)
2019.1	0.99	(0.13)	−0.36	(0.07)	1.05	(0.29)	0.41	(0.13)
2019.2	0.98	(0.13)	−0.34	(0.07)	1.10	(0.30)	0.41	(0.13)
2019.3	0.98	(0.12)	−0.33	(0.06)	1.14	(0.31)	0.40	(0.12)
2019.4	0.97	(0.13)	−0.32	(0.06)	1.19	(0.33)	0.40	(0.12)
Transfer Payments (*TRGHQ*)								
2016.1	0.09	(0.02)	0.01	(0.01)	0.00	(0.00)	0.00	(0.01)
2016.2	0.20	(0.04)	−0.04	(0.03)	0.01	(0.01)	0.02	(0.03)
2016.3	0.30	(0.06)	−0.08	(0.04)	0.03	(0.02)	0.06	(0.06)
2016.4	0.38	(0.07)	−0.12	(0.05)	0.05	(0.03)	0.10	(0.08)
2017.1	0.43	(0.08)	−0.16	(0.05)	0.088	(0.05)	0.13	(0.08)
2017.2	0.48	(0.09)	−0.20	(0.05)	0.13	(0.06)	0.16	(0.08)
2017.3	0.51	(0.09)	−0.22	(0.05)	0.17	(0.08)	0.19	(0.08)
2017.4	0.54	(0.09)	−0.24	(0.05)	0.21	(0.09)	0.23	(0.08)
2018.1	0.57	(0.09)	−0.25	(0.05)	0.26	(0.11)	0.24	(0.08)
2018.2	0.58	(0.10)	−0.25	(0.05)	0.32	(0.12)	0.25	(0.08)
2018.3	0.60	(0.10)	−0.26	(0.05)	0.38	(0.14)	0.27	(0.08)
2018.4	0.61	(0.10)	−0.26	(0.05)	0.44	(0.16)	0.28	(0.08)
2019.1	0.62	(0.10)	−0.26	(0.05)	0.49	(0.18)	0.29	(0.08)
2019.2	0.62	(0.10)	−0.26	(0.05)	0.55	(0.20)	0.30	(0.08)
2019.3	0.63	(0.10)	−0.25	(0.05)	0.63	(0.21)	0.31	(0.08)
2019.4	0.63	(0.11)	−0.25	(0.04)	0.66	(0.24)	0.32	(0.08)

0.25 percentage points. This is the estimated response of the Fed to the government spending increase. Note that equation 30 is used even though the simulation period is outside the estimation period for equation 30. The simulation period is not a period of the zero lower bound and the changes are positive, so there is no constraint. The assumption for this experiment is that the Fed follows the estimated rule for this period.

The estimated standard errors in table 13.1 are fairly small: the multipliers are estimated with a fair amount of precision. This result is consisgent with the above discussion emphasizing that all the nonlinar restrictions on the (implicit) reduced-form equations are taken into account. The standard error for 1.26, the real GDP change after three quarters, is just 0.09. Remember that the standard errors reflect the uncertainty of the coefficient estimates since the model is reestimated on each trial.

The multipliers for *TRGHQ* in table 13.1 are smaller than those for *COG* for standard textbook reasons. They also rise more slowly, and they are also precisely estimated.

The federal personal income tax rate in the model is *D1G*. Although not shown here, the multiplier effects of changing *D1G* are similar to those of changing *TRGHQ* (with the opposite sign), where *D1G* is changed to lead roughly to the change in real taxes equal to the change in *TRGHQ*. Taxes and transfer payments both affect disposable income *YD*, and so both have similar effects. The effects are not identical because *D1G* also affects the after-tax interest rates, *RSA* and *RMA*, and the after-tax wage rate, *WA*.

13.2 Multipliers in the Literature

Ramey (2011) reviews the literature on estimating the size of the government spending multiplier, where government spending is purchases of goods. She concludes that the multiplier is probably between 0.8 and 1.5, although the range is considerably higher than this.

Fair (2010) also compares multipliers from a few studies, both regarding an increase in government purchases of goods and an increase in transfer payments. After four quarters for an increase in purchases of goods, the multiplier is 1.44 for Romer and Bernstein (2009), 0.44 for Barro and Redlick (2011), 0.55 for Hall (2009), and a range of 1.0 to 2.5 for the Congressional Budget Office (CBO) (2010). After four quarters for an increase in transfer payments, the multiplier is 0.66 for Romer and Bernstein (2009), 1.10 for Romer and Romer (2010), 1.1 for Barro and Redlick (2011), and a range of 0.8 to 2.1 for the CBO (2010). The Romer and Bernstein multiplier peaks at 0.99 after 8 quarters, and the Romer and Romer multiplier peaks at 3.08 after 10 quarters.

The CBO (2010) uses results from two commercial forecasting models and the FRB-US model of the Federal Reserve Board to choose ranges for a number of government spending multipliers on output. Romer and Bernstein (2009) follow a similar methodology. They use a commercial forecasting model and the FRB-US model to choose government spending and tax multipliers on output.[2]

Hall (2009), Barro and Redlick (2011), and Romer and Romer (2010) follow a reduced-form approach. The change in real GDP is regressed on the change in the policy variable of interest and a number of other variables. The equation estimated is not, however, a true reduced-form equation because many variables are omitted, and so the coefficient estimate of the policy variable will be biased if the policy variable is correlated with omitted variables. The aim of using this approach is to choose a policy variable that seems unlikely to be correlated with the omitted variables. Hall (2009) and Barro and Redlick (2011) are concerned with government spending multipliers and focus on defense spending during wars.[3] Romer and Romer (2010) are concerned with tax multipliers and use narrative records to choose what they consider exogenous tax policy actions, i.e, actions that are uncorrelated with the omitted variables.

Auerbach and Gorodnichenko (2012) use a structural VAR approach that allows for different multipliers in expansions and recessions to estimate government spending (on goods and services) multipliers. Their general result is that multipliers are larger in recessions than in expansions.

Coenen et al. (2012) estimate government spending multipliers for nine DSGE models. The experiments consist of government spending or tax shocks from a steady state, where each model has a fiscal-policy rule that eventually returns the economy to the steady state, so there is no long-run increase in the debt/GDP ratio. The models have rational expectations, and so everyone knows that the initial increase in debt will be paid off eventually. The experiments are run under various assumptions about monetary accommodation. The experiments with these models differ from those reported above in that the debt/GDP ratio is forced back to the baseline (the steady state) in the long run. One might think that the fiscal multipliers would be small in these models because agents know that the extra spending will eventually be paid for. In fact, the short-run multipliers are fairly large in most cases and the sums of the output gaps over the entire period are generally positive. For government purchases of goods, the short-run multipliers are between about 0.7 and 1.0 with no monetary accommodation and between about 1.2 and 2.2 with two years of monetary accommodation. The short-run multipliers are also fairly large for increases in transfer payments that are targeted to liquidity-constrained households, ranging from about 1.0 to 1.5 with two years of monetary accommodation. The tone of the Coenen et al. (2012) article is that temporary fiscal stimulus can be very helpful, especially if there is monetary accommodation.

The general features of the DSGE models that lead to the above conclusion are the following. A government spending shock (or decrease in taxes) stimulates liquidity-constrained households to consume more. Given this increased demand, firms that are allowed to change their prices raise them, but firms that are not allowed to change their prices are committed to sell all that is demanded at their current (unchanged) prices. The overall price level goes up, but there is also an output effect. All this happens even though agents in the model know that the increased government debt will eventually be paid back through lower future government spending or higher taxes. The initial (essentially constrained) output effect dominates. It is also the case that the mark-up falls for those firms that cannot change their prices. The increased inflation that is generated may lead the monetary authority to raise the interest rate, and so the results are sensitive to what is assumed about monetary policy.

Finally, there is a paper by DeLong and Summers (2012), which argues that there may be times in which fiscal expansions are self-financing—no long-run increase in the debt/GDP ratio. There are no estimated equations in this paper, no lagged effects of government spending on output, and some calibrated parameters that seem unrealistic or for which there is little empirical support. For example, the marginal tax-and-transfer rate is taken to be 0.33, which seems too high. In 2011, the ratio of federal government tax receipts (including social security taxes) and unemployment benefits to GDP was 0.17. This is an average rate and the marginal rate may be higher, but 37 percent of tax receipts are social security taxes, where the tax rate is flat and then zero at some income level. There is also a key hysteresis parameter in the model, also calibrated, which reflects the assumption that potential output depends on current output in depressed states of the economy. If current fiscal stimulus increases future potential output, there is obviously some effect large enough to generate enough extra future government revenue to pay for the stimulus.

The ranges of the multipliers just discussed are much larger than the ranges implied by the estimated standard errors in table 13.1. This high precision is likely due to the fact that all the nonlinear restrictions on the reduced form are taken into account. In this sense, the theoreticdal structure is tight. For example, all the information in the identities is being used.

14 Okun's Law

The main point about Okun's law is that, for example, a 1 percent increase in real output does not result in a 1 percentage point decrease in the unemployment rate. In the US model this is easily explained. When real output increases by 1 percent, there is a less than 1 percent increase in jobs because part of the increase in labor that is needed is from drawing down excess labor (equation 13). An increase in jobs of a certain amount results in a smaller increase in the number of people employed because the number of moonlighters increases (equation 8). A given increase in the number of people employed results in a smaller decrease in unemployment because the labor force increases (equations 5–7). There are thus three main slippages from output to unemployment.

The following experiment estimates the size of these effects in the US model. Consider the period 2018.1–2019.4. Add the estimated errors to the equations and take then as exogenous—the perfect tracking solution procedure. Drop every stochastic equation in the model except the jobs equation 13, the moonlighters equation 8, and the three labor force equations 5–7. Keep the identities in. Then increase real output Y by one percent of the baseline for each of the eight quarters and solve the model. Dropping the stochastic equations isolates the equations of interest. Results are presented in table 14.1.

The percentage increase in jobs is less than 1.0 percent in each quarter. It rises from 0.28 percent in the first quarter to 0.94 percent in the eighth quarter. This is the excess labor effect. The next three columns in the table show the increase in jobs, the increase in moonlighters, and the increase in people employed. By definition, $\Delta E = \Delta JF - \Delta LM$. For example, the increase in jobs is 136,000 in the eighth quarter and the increase in moonlighters is 20,000. So the increase in people employed is 116,000. The next column

Table 14.1
Effects Behind Okun's Law Effects of a One Percent Increase in Y

qtr	$\%JF$	ΔJF	ΔLM	ΔE	ΔL	ΔU	ΔUR
2018.1	0.28	40	2	37	3	−34	−0.21
2018.2	0.49	69	5	64	9	−55	−0.34
2018.3	0.63	90	9	82	15	−67	−0.41
2018.4	0.74	106	12	94	22	−72	−0.45
2019.1	0.82	117	15	103	28	−73	−0.46
2019.2	0.87	125	18	108	33	−75	−0.46
2019.3	0.91	132	20	112	38	−74	−0.45
2019.4	0.94	136	20	116	43	−73	−0.45

$\%Y$ = output of the firm sector.
$\%JF$ = percentage change in jobs.
ΔJF = absolute change in jobs in thousands.
ΔLM = absolute change in moonlighters in thousands.
ΔE = absolute change in people employed in thousands.
ΔL = absolute change in total labor force in thousands.
ΔU = absolute change in unemployment in thousands.
ΔUR = change in the unemployment rate in percentage points.
$L = L1 + L2 + L3$.
$\Delta E = \Delta JF - \Delta LM$.
$\Delta U = \Delta L - \Delta E$.

shows the increase in the labor force from the (lessening of) discouraged worker effect. By the eighth quarter, the increase is 43,000. By definition, $\Delta U = \Delta L - \Delta E$. By the eighth quarter, the number of people unemployed is down 73,000. The last column is the change in the unemployment rate. By the eighth quarter, it is down by 0.45 percentage points, much less than 1.0 percentage point.

The size of the effects in table 14.1 vary somewhat by the business cycle, and in this sense Okun's Law is not stable. For example, at the top of a boom, there is little excess labor being held, and so jobs responds more to output than would be the case if there were more excess labor being held. At the top of a boom, there is more of a response of the unemployment rate to a change in output than otherwise.

15 Explaining Contractions and Expansions

15.1 Introduction

Since 1954, there have been nine NBER US recessions, not counting the pandemic recession, and a number of expansions. This chapter uses the US model to analyze the nine recessions and three expansions. The main question considered is how much of each episode can be explained by the model, conditional on the actual values of the exogenous variables in the model. The amount not explained is due to shocks to the stochastic equations—the error terms. If a stochastic equation is correctly specified, a shock is random unexplained behavior. If there is misspecification, at least part of the shock is due to the misspecification.

Figures 15.1 and 15.2 plot the episodes of interest, one for the unemployment rate *UR* and one for the Treasury bill rate *RS*. The period examined here ends in 2019.4; the pandemic period is excluded.[1] A solid vertical line indicates the quarter before the recession started, and a dotted vertical line indicates the quarter before the expansion started. An episode is denoted by the year in which it began, "R" for recession and "E" for expansion. As will be seen, the first two recessions, R1954 and R1960, are not well explained, although R1960 was a very mild recession. R1974 is partly explained. Otherwise, the episodes are mostly driven by fluctuations in the exogenous variables as filtered through the US model. Conditional on using the actual values of the exogenous variables, there are not many puzzles. It will be seen that asset price fluctuations are important drivers of output fluctuations.

The variables labeled "exog" in table A.2 in the appendix are taken to be exogenous. The main exogenous variables are discussed in chapter 7. The most controversial for the present analysis are the changes in asset prices—stock prices and housing prices. The choice of these variables is

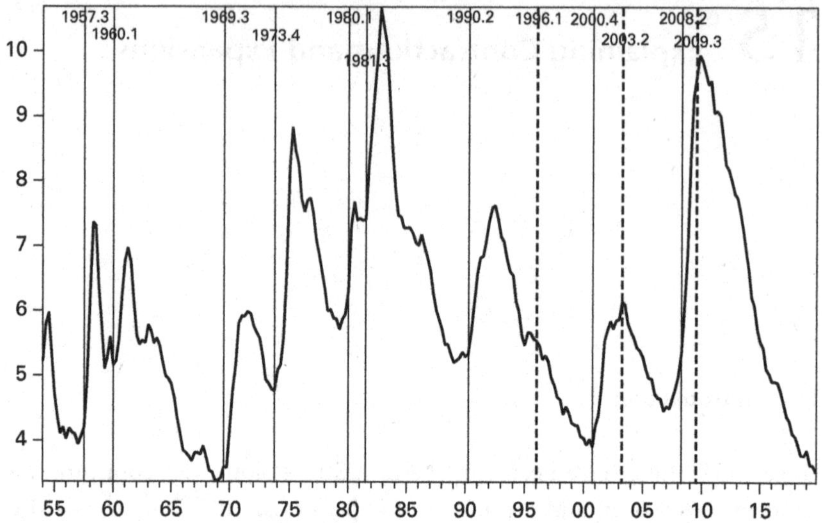

Figure 15.1
Unemployment rate 1954.1–2019.4

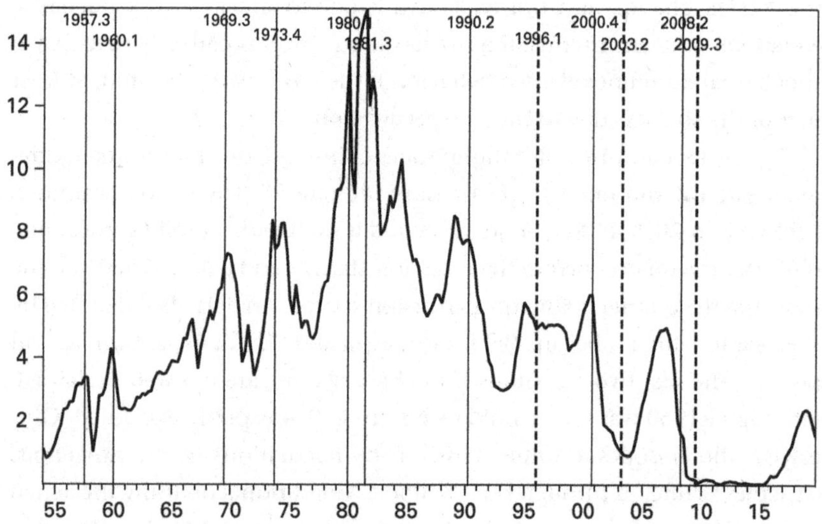

Figure 15.2
Three-month treasury bill rate 1954.1–2019.4

defended in chapter 7. Regarding monetary policy, equation 30 is used for all but the expansion E2009, where *RS* is taken to be exogenous.

The fact that the model does well in predicting the episodes does not mean it can forecast well, since the exogenous variables cannot necessarily be forecast well. The change in asset prices cannot, and even some government variables are not easy to forecast. Nor necessarily are exports and the import price deflator. This is discussed in chapter 7. In earlier work using my multicountry model, Fair (2012), I have shown that between about 25 and 37 percent of the forecast error variance of output growth over eight quarters is due to asset price changes, which are unpredictable. The present analysis is not an exercise in forecasting recessions and expansions, but in explaining them conditional on the exogenous variables.

The closest research to the present analysis is the research examining the effects of oil prices on the economy. Hamilton (1983) examined the period 1948–1972 and found for all but one of the recessions in this period, oil price increases preceded the recession with a lag of about three quarters. He argues that at least some of this was causal. In a later paper, Hamilton (2009) argues that oil price increases contributed to the contraction in 2008. This work does not use structural models; the focus is on whether oil prices help explain output contractions. It will be seen that the US model is consistent with Hamilton's story. Oil prices have a positive effect on *PIM*, especially in the first half of the sample period, and an increase in *PIM* is contractionary in the model, other things being equal.

Beginning with Mitchell (1927), there is a large literature examining whether contractions are briefer and sharper than expansions. See, for example, McKay and Reis (2008). No restrictions on recessions and expansions are used here. Each episode is unique, and each is examined separately. Angeletos, Collard, and Dellas (2020) argue for the existence of one main business-cycle driver. They use 10 macroeconomic variables in a VAR model. They do not examine individual contractions and expansions, and none of the 10 variables are the exogenous variables stressed in this paper. Given Tolstoy's famous quote, their business cycles are like happy families, whereas in this chapter each episode is an unhappy family. ("All happy families are alike; each unhappy family is unhappy in its own way.") Given the differences in the episodes analyzed here, it does not seem likely that each episode is a happy family.

The results have other implications for the literature. First, aggregate wealth, financial plus housing, appears to be enough to explain most of the 2008–2009 recession. As discussed below, credit constraints and other measures of financial distress do not appear to add much. Mian and Sufi (2015) stress the household-side credit channel, and Kehoe et al. (2020) examine both the household-side and firm-side credit channels. See the latter for a review of this large literature. Again, what the present results suggest is that analysis of credit channels does not add much to explaining the recession. Aggregate wealth declines are enough.

Second, the slow growth after the 2008–2009 recession is mostly explained by sluggish government spending. Conditional on government spending, there is no puzzle. Related to this is the question of whether the US economy is in a period of secular stagnation, as argued by Summers (2020). There is no evidence of this in the present results, although direct tests of this hypothesis have not been made.

15.2 Large Errors in the Expenditure Equations

Before presenting the prediction results, it will be useful to examine the quarters in which there were large residuals in the expenditure equations. These are equations 1, 2, 3, 4, 11, 12, and 27. To examine the large residuals, the following was done. For each equation and quarter, the predicted value of the level of the variable was computed, which was then subtracted from the actual value. This is the estimated residual in levels (not logs). For each quarter, there are seven residuals. Summing the first six residuals and subtracting the import residual gives the error in predicting GDP. (The other variables that make up GDP are exogenous and so have zero residuals.) If the absolute value of the GDP error was greater than 1 percent of the actual value of GDP for the quarter, the quarter was flagged.

Table 15.1 presents values for the flagged quarters. For each component of GDP, the level residual divided by the actual value of GDP is presented. Also presented is the GDP error divided by the actual value of GDP. There are 14 quarters out of 264 that are flagged. The largest GDP error in absolute value is in 1958.1, which is −3.58, followed by 1965.1, 1978.2, and 1980.2. Six of the 14 errors are positive, which means that GDP was larger than predicted. Most of the quarters are before 1990. There are only four

Table 15.1
Quarters With Large Residuals Errors as a Percent of Real GDP

Qtr.	*CS*	*CN*	*CD*	*IHH*	*IKF*	*IVF*	*IM*	*GDPR*
1958.1	−0.38	−0.28	−0.18	−0.37	−0.89	−1.42	0.07	−3.58
1958.3	0.10	0.21	0.00	0.24	0.59	0.42	−0.06	1.62
1965.1	0.00	0.02	0.17	0.05	0.80	0.78	−0.32	2.15
1970.3	0.11	0.13	−0.04	0.26	0.42	0.06	−0.06	1.00
1974.1	−0.35	−0.35	−0.12	−0.12	−0.08	−0.17	−0.18	−1.01
1978.2	0.19	0.03	0.22	0.27	0.63	0.81	0.02	2.13
1980.2	−0.56	−0.27	−0.37	−0.50	−0.20	−0.59	−0.37	−2.13
1980.4	0.38	−0.01	0.07	0.17	0.48	0.63	0.16	1.56
1982.1	−0.06	−0.02	0.08	0.06	−0.72	−0.91	−0.20	−1.36
1984.2	0.02	0.35	0.09	0.04	0.49	0.41	0.25	1.14
1990.4	−0.30	−0.23	−0.17	−0.14	−0.54	−0.16	−0.38	−1.15
2001.1	−0.06	−0.18	0.01	0.01	−0.82	−0.37	−0.13	−1.28
2008.1	0.10	−0.15	−0.26	−0.14	−0.40	−0.25	−0.03	−1.07
2008.4	0.00	−0.12	−0.55	−0.17	−0.70	−0.65	−0.65	−1.55

CS = service consumption, *CN* = nondurable consumption,
CD = durable consumption, *IHH* = housing investment,
IKF = plant and equipment investment, *IVF* = inventory investment,
IM = imports, *GDPR* = real GDP,
all in 2012 dollars.

quarters from 1990 onward. This table will be used in the discussion of the predictions.

15.3 Predicting the Nine Recessions

Results for the nine recessions are in table 15.2. For each recession, the errors in the stochastic equations were set to zero and the model was solved for the relevant period. This is a dynamic simulation. Differences between the actual values and the predicted values are errors. Results for real GDP, *GDPR*, the unemployment rate, *UR*, and the three-month Treasury bill rate, *RS*, are presented in the tables. For each variable and quarter, the actual and predicted values are presented and the error. The error is in percent for *GDPR* and absolute for *UR* and *RS*. The total change from the quarter before the recession to the last quarter of the recession is presented, again percent for *GDPR* and absolute for *UR* and *RS*. The following discussion will focus on the totals.

Table 15.2
Predictions of the Nine Recessions

	GDPR			*UR*			*RS*		
Qtr.	Act.	Pred.	%Err.	Act.	Pred.	Err.	Act.	Pred.	Err.
R1957									
1957.3	3017.			4.2			3.4		
1957.4	2986.	3016.	1.0	4.9	4.5	−0.5	3.3	3.3	0.0
1958.1	2908.	3015.	3.7	6.3	4.5	−1.8	1.8	3.4	1.7
1958.2	2927.	3032.	3.6	7.4	4.4	−3.0	1.0	3.7	2.8
total change	−3.0%	0.5%		3.2	0.2		−2.4	0.4	
R1960									
1960.1	3278.			5.2			3.9		
1960.2	3260.	3284.	0.7	5.2	5.2	0.0	3.0	3.5	0.6
1960.3	3276.	3310.	1.0	5.5	5.2	−0.4	2.4	3.5	1.2
1960.4	3234.	3317.	2.6	6.3	5.1	−1.1	2.3	3.8	1.5
1961.1	3256.	3338.	2.5	6.8	5.0	−1.7	2.4	3.9	1.5
total change	−0.7%	1.8%		1.6	−0.1		−1.5	0.0	
R1969									
1969.3	4971.			3.6			7.0		
1969.4	4947.	4950.	0.1	3.6	4.1	0.5	7.4	6.8	−0.6
1970.1	4940.	4949.	0.2	4.2	4.6	0.5	7.2	5.9	−1.3
1970.2	4947.	4966.	0.4	4.7	5.1	0.3	6.7	5.2	−1.4
1970.3	4992.	4983.	−0.2	5.2	5.5	0.4	6.3	4.9	−1.4
1970.4	4939.	4978.	0.8	5.8	5.8	0.0	5.4	4.8	−0.6
total change	−0.7%	0.1%		2.2	2.2		−1.7	−2.2	
R1974									
1973.4	5732.			4.8			7.5		
1974.1	5682.	5746.	1.1	5.1	5.0	0.0	7.6	6.9	−0.7
1974.2	5696.	5773.	1.3	5.2	5.3	0.2	8.2	7.3	−0.9
1974.3	5642.	5756.	2.0	5.6	5.8	0.2	8.2	7.7	−0.4
1974.4	5620.	5733.	2.0	6.6	6.3	−0.2	7.4	7.5	0.1
1975.1	5552.	5737.	3.3	8.2	6.7	−1.5	5.8	7.1	1.3
1975.2	5591.	5752.	2.9	8.8	7.1	−1.7	5.4	6.9	1.5
total change	−2.4%	0.4%		4.1	2.3		−2.1	−0.6	
R1980									
1980.1	6842.			6.3			13.4		
1980.2	6701.	6797.	1.4	7.3	6.7	−0.6	9.6	12.2	2.6
1980.3	6693.	6778.	1.3	7.7	7.5	−0.2	9.2	12.1	2.9
total change	−2.2%	−0.9%		1.4	1.2		−4.2	−1.3	

Table 15.2
(continued)

	GDPR			*UR*			*RS*		
Qtr.	Act.	Pred.	%Err.	Act.	Pred.	Err.	Act.	Pred.	Err.
R1981									
1981.3	6983.			7.4			15.1		
1981.4	6906.	6921.	0.2	8.2	8.0	−0.3	11.8	14.1	2.3
1982.1	6799.	6879.	1.2	8.8	8.7	−0.2	12.8	16.3	3.5
1982.2	6830.	6860.	0.4	9.4	9.4	0.0	12.4	15.0	2.6
1982.3	6804.	6815.	0.2	9.9	10.2	0.2	9.3	11.4	2.1
1982.4	6807.	6810.	0.0	10.7	10.6	−0.1	7.9	9.6	1.7
total change	−2.5%	−2.5%		3.3	3.2		−7.1	−5.4	
R1990									
1990.2	9398.			5.3			7.7		
1990.3	9405.	9402.	0.0	5.7	5.7	0.0	7.5	7.3	−0.2
1990.4	9319.	9403.	0.9	6.1	6.2	0.1	7.0	6.7	−0.3
1991.1	9275.	9435.	1.7	6.6	6.4	−0.2	6.0	6.1	0.1
total change	−1.3%	0.4%		1.2	1.1		−1.7	−1.6	
R2001									
2000.4	13262.			3.9			6.0		
2001.1	13219.	13385.	1.3	4.2	4.0	−0.3	4.8	5.9	1.1
2001.2	13302.	13364.	0.5	4.4	4.1	−0.3	3.7	5.9	2.3
2001.3	13248.	13282.	0.3	4.8	4.5	−0.4	3.2	5.5	2.4
2001.4	13285.	13228.	−0.4	5.5	4.9	−0.6	1.9	4.9	3.0
total change	0.2%	−0.3%		1.6	1.0		−4.1	−1.1	
R2008									
2008.2	15793.			5.3			1.6		
2008.3	15710.	15818.	0.7	6.0	5.6	−0.4	1.5	2.1	0.6
2008.4	15367.	15633.	1.7	6.9	6.2	−0.7	0.3	1.4	1.1
2009.1	15188.	15425.	1.6	8.3	6.9	−1.5	0.2	0.0	−0.2
2009.2	15162.	15384.	1.5	9.3	7.5	−1.9	0.2	0.0	−0.2
total change	−4.0%	−2.6%		4.0	2.1		−1.5	−1.6	

R1957

For this recession, real GDP was predicted to rise by 0.5 percent when it in fact fell by 3.0 percent. The unemployment rate rose by 3.2 percentage points, but was predicted to rise by only 0.2 perecentage points. The period was thus predicted to be sluggish, but not a recession. Given that the actual values of the exogenous variables were used, this says that the information in the exogenous variables (as filtered through the model) do not suggest negative growth. The recession is thus primarily due to shocks to the stochastic equations, which are unexplained. Table 15.1 shows that the main shocks were in 1958.1. There were negative and fairly large shocks to the seven consumption and investment equations (and essentially a zero shock to the import equation). If the actual errors are used in the stochastic equations for 1958.1, but zero errors otherwise, the predictions are much better. Real GDP is predicted to fall by 2.9 percent over the period (versus −3.0 actual), and the unemployment rate is predicted to fall by 1.5 percentage points (versus 3.2 actual). This is thus a fairly accurate prediction, and so it can be said that much of the recession was due to unexplained aggregate demand shocks in 1958.1.

R1960

R1960 was a fairly mild recession, with real GDP falling by 0.7 percent over the four quarters. It was predicted to rise by 1.8 percent, again sluggish but not a recession. There are no large residuals in this period in table 15.1. It is thus not possible to pinpoint any particular reason for the prediction error. The error is fairly small and there is no smoking gun.

R1969

R1969 was also mild, and in this case it was predicted well. When a recession is predicted well, one can ask whether there are large fluctuations in any of the key exogenous variables that contributed to the contraction. As can be seen in figure 7.1, in this case it is government spending on goods, $COG+COS$, which fell as a fraction of GDP during this period. This mild recession is thus at least partly due to falling government purchases of goods.

R1974

R1974 is a stagflation recession. Table 15.2 shows that over the six quarters, real GDP fell by 2.4 percent. The model predicted a sluggish period with real

GDP rising only 0.4 percent. The unemployment rate rose 4.1 percentage points and was predicted to rise by 2.3 points. Some of this recession was thus predicted, but not all. Figure 7.5 shows that the import price deflator, *PIM*, was high during this period, which in the model is inflationary and contractionary. Although not shown in the table, the actual percentage change in the GDP deflator over the six quarters was 14.7 percent. The prediction from the model was close at 16.8 percent, driven by the high values of *PIM*. Regarding interest rates, in this case of high inflation and rising unemployment, the Fed's response could go either way. Table 15.2 shows that the Fed initially increased the interest rate (through 1974.3) and then began lowering it. The predicted values from the estimated Fed rule captured this pattern. The Fed thus initially contributed to the contraction. So part of this recession is explained by the high values of *PIM* and the Fed's response. Regarding unexplained shocks, table 15.1 shows that there was one quarter of large negative shocks, 1974.1. If the actual errors are used for this quarter, but zero errors otherwise, the predicted GDP growth is −0.5 percent versus 0.4 percent in table 15.2 with zero errors. UR rises by 2.8 points rather than 2.3 points in table 15.2. Part of this recession is thus also due to unexplained negative errors in 1974.1 and part by the high values of *PIM*.

R1980

The next four recessions are predicted fairly well. For R1980, the main culprit is the high values of *PIM* (figure 7.5), which are contractionary. In the three quarters, real GDP fell by 2.2 percent and was predicted to fall by 0.9 percent. The unemployment rate rose by 1.4 percentage points and was predicted to rise by 1.2 points. The Fed kept the interest rate high and was predicted to do so because of the high inflation (not shown).

R1981

R1981 was predicted well. An actual real GDP fall of 2.5 percent, with the prediction being the same, and an actual rise in the unemployment rate of 3.3 percentage points versus 3.2 predicted. The values of *PIM* are also high during this period, although falling, which led to high inflation values and high values of the interest rate set by the Fed.[2]

R1990

R1990 was a mild recession and it was predicted fairly well. Real GDP fell by 1.3 percent versus a predicted rise of 0.4 percent, and the unemployment rate rose by 1.2 percentage points versus 1.1 predicted. There are no large changes in the exogenous variables in this period and so no one main cause.

R2001

R2001 was also mild and predicted well. Real GDP rose by 0.2 percent versus −0.3 predicted. The unemployment rate rose by 1.6 percentage points versus 1.0 predicted. The Fed lowered the interest rate more than predicted: 4.1 percentage points versus 1.1 predicted. Stock prices fell during this period (figure 7.6), and so there was a negative wealth effect. This was only a financial wealth effect, as housing prices fell (figure 7.7). Exports also fell (figure 7.4). This recession is thus explained by a fall in stock prices and exports.

R2008

R2008 is sometimes called the "Great Recession." It was predicted fairly well. Real GDP fell by 4.0 percent versus 2.8 predicted, and the unemployment rate rose by 4.0 percentage points versus 2.1 predicted. The Fed lowered the interest rate to essentially zero, which was predicted. There are three exogenous variables that stand out in this period: stock prices, housing prices, and exports (figures 7.6, 7.7, and 7.4). These three fell substantially. The wealth effect was large because both financial and housing wealth fell. This conclusion is the same as that in Fair (2017) using my multicountry model, namely that wealth effects and export effects dominate this period.

Note that in predicting R2008, no use has been made of credit constraint variables and the like. In Fair (2017), I have added the corporate AAA/BBB spread and the 10-year government/corporate AAA spread to the four household expenditure equations, and none of the spreads tried were significant. I also tried two variables from Carroll, Slacalek, and Sommer (2013), one measuring credit constraints and one measuring labor income uncertainty, and these were not significant. I also tried the excess bond premium (EBP) variable from Gilchrist and Zakrajšek (2012). This variable has a large spike in the 2008–2009 recession. It is not significant when the estimation period ends in 2007.4, but it is for the period ending in 2010.3. The evidence for EBP is thus mixed, depending on how much weight one puts on possible data mining, since it was created after the recession was known. In general, there appears to be little independent information in spreads and other measures of financial difficulties not in the wealth variable *AA* in the model.

15.4 Predicting the Three Expansions

E1996, E2000, E2009

The predictions for the three expansions are presented in table 15.3. All three are predicted well. The growth rate at an annual rate over each period is presented. For E1996, it is 4.7 percent versus 4.1 predicted; for E2003, it is 3.8 percent versus 2.9 predicted; and for E2009, it is 2.3 percent versus 2.2 predicted. For E1996 and E2003, the story is mostly asset price increases; for E1996, it is financial wealth (figure 7.6); and for E2003, it is both financial wealth and housing wealth (figures 7.6 and 7.7). These two expansions were thus driven by wealth effects. This conclusion regarding E1996 is the same as that in Fair (2004) using my multicountry model.

The expansion E2009 has been considered a puzzle in having fairly low growth rates. The economy did not come rapidly out of the recession. In this case, it is not due to negative wealth effects, since both rose somewhat (figures 7.6 and 7.7). It is the case, however, that government purchases of goods ($COG + COS$) as a fraction of real GDP fell substantially during this period (figure 7.1). The sluggish expansion is thus explained by the contractionary fiscal policy. Much of the decline in government spending was due to the 2011 agreement between President Obama and the Republicans to lower future spending in return to raise the debt ceiling. This conclusion about government spending is the same as that in Fair (2018a).

15.5 Summary of the 12 Episodes

The following is a summary of the 12 episodes. All are fairly well predicted by the US model conditional on the exogenous variables except for R1957 and part of R1974.

1. R1957: Unexplained demand shocks in 1958.1.
2. R1960: Mild. No salient exogenous variables.
3. R1969: Mild. Falling government spending.

Table 15.3
Predictions of the Three Expansions

	GDPR			*UR*			*RS*		
Qtr.	Act.	Pred.	%Err.	Act.	Pred.	Err.	Act.	Pred.	Err.
E1996									
1996.1	10825.			5.5			4.9		
1996.2	11005.	10977.	−0.3	5.5	5.4	−0.1	5.0	4.7	−0.3
1996.3	11104.	11084.	−0.2	5.3	5.4	0.1	5.1	4.5	−0.6
1996.4	11219.	11239.	0.2	5.3	5.4	0.1	5.0	4.4	−0.6
1997.1	11292.	11389.	0.9	5.2	5.5	0.2	5.1	4.0	−1.0
1997.2	11479.	11500.	0.2	5.0	5.4	0.4	5.0	3.8	−1.3
1997.3	11623.	11649.	0.2	4.9	5.2	0.4	5.0	3.8	−1.2
1997.4	11723.	11750.	0.2	4.7	5.2	0.5	5.1	3.8	−1.3
1998.1	11840.	11832.	−0.1	4.6	5.1	0.5	5.1	3.7	−1.4
1998.2	11950.	11970.	0.2	4.4	5.0	0.6	5.0	3.6	−1.4
1998.3	12099.	12068.	−0.3	4.5	4.9	0.4	4.8	3.6	−1.3
1998.4	12295.	12213.	−0.7	4.4	4.9	0.5	4.3	3.5	−0.7
1999.1	12411.	12316.	−0.8	4.3	4.7	0.4	4.4	3.7	−0.7
1999.2	12514.	12435.	−0.6	4.2	4.7	0.4	4.5	3.8	−0.6
1999.3	12680.	12559.	−1.0	4.2	4.6	0.4	4.7	3.8	−0.8
1999.4	12888.	12666.	−1.7	4.1	4.5	0.5	5.0	3.9	−1.2
2000.1	12935.	12771.	−1.3	4.0	4.0	−0.1	5.5	4.7	−0.8
2000.2	13171.	12857.	−2.4	3.9	3.9	−0.1	5.7	4.9	−0.8
total change	21.7%	18.8%		−1.6	−1.7		0.8	0.0	
annual rate	(4.7%)	(4.1%)							
E2003									
2003.2	13741.			6.2			1.0		
2003.3	13970.	13899.	−0.5	6.1	6.1	0.0	0.9	1.3	0.4
2003.4	14131.	14044.	−0.6	5.8	5.8	0.0	0.9	1.7	0.8
2004.1	14212.	14176.	−0.3	5.7	5.4	−0.2	0.9	2.2	1.3
2004.2	14323.	14288.	−0.2	5.6	5.1	−0.5	1.1	2.6	1.5
2004.3	14458.	14355.	−0.7	5.4	4.9	−0.5	1.5	2.8	1.3
2004.4	14606.	14417.	−1.3	5.4	4.8	−0.6	2.0	3.0	1.0
2005.1	14768.	14515.	−1.7	5.3	4.7	−0.6	2.5	3.4	0.9
2005.2	14840.	14615.	−1.5	5.1	4.6	−0.5	2.9	3.6	0.8
2005.3	14956.	14675.	−1.9	5.0	4.6	−0.3	3.4	3.7	0.4
2005.4	15041.	14726.	−2.1	5.0	4.8	−0.2	3.8	3.7	0.1
2006.1	15244.	14847.	−2.6	4.7	4.7	−0.1	4.4	3.6	0.7
total change	10.9%	8.0%		−1.4	−1.5		3.4	2.6	
annual rate	(3.8%)	(2.9%)							

Table 15.3
(continued)

	GDPR			*UR*			*RS*		
Qtr.	Act.	Pred.	%Err.	Act.	Pred.	Err.	Act.	Pred.	Err.
E2009									
2009.3	15217.			9.6			0.2		
2009.4	15379.	15384.	0.0	9.9	9.6	−0.4	0.1	0.0	0.0
2010.1	15456.	15471.	0.1	9.9	9.3	−0.5	0.1	0.0	0.1
2010.2	15606.	15567.	−0.2	9.7	8.9	−0.8	0.1	0.1	0.1
2010.3	15726.	15633.	−0.6	9.5	8.9	−0.6	0.2	0.0	0.2
2010.4	15808.	15715.	−0.6	9.5	8.8	−0.7	0.1	0.0	0.1
2011.1	15770.	15773.	0.0	9.1	8.5	−0.5	0.1	0.3	0.2
2011.2	15877.	15832.	−0.3	9.1	8.4	−0.7	0.0	0.5	0.4
2011.3	15871.	15844.	−0.2	9.0	8.2	−0.9	0.0	0.6	0.5
2011.4	16049.	15877.	−1.1	8.7	8.2	−0.5	0.0	0.4	0.4
2012.1	16180.	15995.	−1.1	8.3	8.5	0.2	0.1	0.1	0.0
2012.2	16254.	16058.	−1.2	8.2	8.4	0.2	0.1	0.0	0.1
2012.3	16282.	16100.	−1.1	8.0	8.3	0.3	0.1	0.0	0.1
2012.4	16300.	16135.	−1.0	7.8	8.3	0.5	0.1	0.0	0.1
2013.1	16442.	16167.	−1.7	7.8	8.3	0.6	0.1	0.0	0.1
2013.2	16464.	16209.	−1.6	7.5	8.3	0.8	0.1	0.0	0.1
2013.3	16595.	16256.	−2.0	7.3	8.3	1.0	0.0	0.0	0.0
2013.4	16713.	16361.	−2.1	7.0	8.2	1.2	0.1	0.0	0.1
2014.1	16654.	16454.	−1.2	6.6	8.0	1.4	0.0	0.1	0.1
2014.2	16868.	16595.	−1.6	6.2	7.8	1.5	0.0	0.2	0.2
2014.3	17065.	16739.	−1.9	6.1	7.5	1.4	0.0	0.4	0.4
2014.4	17141.	16868.	−1.6	5.7	7.2	1.5	0.0	0.5	0.5
2015.1	17281.	16995.	−1.7	5.5	6.9	1.4	0.0	0.5	0.5
2015.2	17381.	17130.	−1.4	5.4	6.6	1.2	0.0	0.6	0.6
2015.3	17437.	17225.	−1.2	5.1	6.4	1.3	0.0	0.7	0.7
2015.4	17463.	17302.	−0.9	5.0	6.3	1.3	0.1	0.7	0.6
2016.1	17566.	17409.	−0.9	4.9	6.2	1.3	0.3	0.6	0.3
2016.2	17619.	17485.	−0.8	4.9	6.1	1.2	0.3	0.6	0.4
2016.3	17724.	17597.	−0.7	4.9	6.0	1.1	0.3	0.8	0.5
2016.4	17813.	17659.	−0.9	4.8	6.0	1.2	0.4	0.8	0.4
2017.1	17889.	17825.	−0.4	4.6	5.8	1.2	0.6	1.0	0.4
2017.2	17979.	17922.	−0.3	4.4	5.7	1.3	0.9	1.2	0.3
2017.3	18128.	17986.	−0.8	4.3	5.6	1.3	1.0	1.3	0.3
2017.4	18310.	18150.	−0.9	4.2	5.4	1.2	1.2	1.5	0.3
total change	20.3%	19.3%		−5.4	−4.2		1.1	1.4	
annual rate	(2.3%)	(2.2%)							

4. R1974: Partly unexplained demand shocks in 1974.1. Partly high values of the price of imports.
5. R1980: High values of the price of imports.
6. R1981: High values of the price of imports.
7. R1990: Mild. No salient exogenous variables.
8. E1996: Rising stock prices.
9. R2001: Mild. Falling stock prices and exports.
10. E2003: Rising stock prices and housing prices.
11. R2008: Falling stock prices, housing prices, and exports.
12. E2009: Sluggish expansion. Falling government spending.

It is clear that one of the main driving forces is the change in asset prices, equity prices before 1995 and both equity prices and housing prices since. More detailed financial variables are not needed for the aggregate predictions. Import prices played an important role in the 1970s and early 1980s. Export declines were also important in a number of the recessions. US exports depend on other countries' imports, which depend on other countries' economies. Changes in asset prices are positively correlated across countries, and so it could be that part of a change in US exports is from US asset price changes through wealth effects.

The effects of the exogenous variables on the economy are filtered through the US model. Misspecifications in the model will affect the accuracy of the effects. The fact that the model does well in predicting most of the episodes is support for it. If it were a poor approximation, one would expect more of a need to explain the fluctuations using the shocks to the stochastic equations.

Finally, it is clear that the pandemic recession is not due to fluctuations in the exogenous variables considered in this chapter. There were huge shocks to some of the stochastic equations, which are unexplained and just picked up by the use of dummy variables. The pandemic episode is a classic example of structural change, at least temporarily, which a macro model like the US model is not equipped to handle. There are no past pandemic observations to use.

IV Optional Material

16 Models with Rational Expectations

16.1 Introduction

This chapter discusses the extra work needed if one assumes that expectations are rational in the sense of being model consistent. I don't believe that this assumption is realistic, and so to me this chapter is a waste of time. But others may not agree, so here it is.

The general rational expectations (RE) version of the model introduced in section 3.1 is

$$f_i(y_t, y_{t-1}, \ldots, y_{t-p}, E_{t-1}y_t, E_{t-1}y_{t+1}, \ldots, E_{t-1}y_{t+h}, x_t, \alpha_i) = u_{it} \quad i=1,\ldots,n, \quad t=1,\ldots,T, \tag{16.1}$$

where E_{t-1} is the conditional expectations operator based on the model and on information through period $t-1$. The function f_i may be nonlinear in variables, parameters, and expectations. The model in (16.1) will be called the "RE model." The restriction on the expectations of the future variable values in this model is that they are rational, or "model consistent." Agents are assumed to use the model to solve for the expectations.

16.2 Single Equation Estimation of RE Models

With only slight modifications, the 2SLS estimator can be used to estimate equations that contain expectational variables in which the expectations are formed rationally.[1] It will be useful to begin with an example. Assume that the equation to be estimated is

$$y_{it} = X_{1it}\alpha_{1i} + E_{t-1}X_{2it+j}\alpha_{2i} + u_{it}, \quad t=1,\ldots,T, \tag{16.2}$$

where X_{1it} is a vector of explanatory variables and $E_{t-1}X_{2it+j}$ is the expectation of X_{2it+j} based on information through period $t-1$. j is some fixed positive integer. This example assumes that there is only one expectational variable and only one value of j, but this is only for illustration. The more general case will be considered shortly. For now, u_{it} is assumed not to be serially correlated. The serial correlation case is taken up in section 16.3.

A traditional assumption about expectations is that the expected future values of a variable are a function of its current and past values. One might postulate, for example, that $E_{t-1}X_{2it+j}$ depends on X_{2it} and X_{2it-1}, where it is assumed that X_{2it} (as well as X_{2it-1}) is known at the time the expectation is made. The equation could then be estimated with X_{2it} and X_{2it-1} replacing $E_{t-1}X_{2it+j}$ in (16.2). Note that this treatment, which is common to the CC approach, is not inconsistent with the view that agents are "forward looking." Expected future values do affect current behavior. It's just that the expectations are formed in fairly simply ways—say by looking only at the current and lagged values of the variable itself.

Assume instead that $E_{t-1}X_{2it+j}$ is rational and assume that there is an observed vector of variables (observed by the econometrician), denoted here as Z_{it}, that is used in part by agents in forming their (rational) expectations. The following method does not require for consistent estimates that Z_{it} includes all the variables used by agents in forming their expectations.

Let the expectation error for $E_{t-1}X_{2it+j}$ be

$$ {}_{t-1}\epsilon_{it+j} = X_{2it+j} - E_{t-1}X_{2it+j} \quad t = 1, \ldots, T, \tag{16.3}$$

where X_{2it+j} is the actual value of the variable. Substituting (16.3) into (16.2) yields:

$$\begin{aligned} y_{it} &= X_{1it}\alpha_{1i} + X_{2it+j}\alpha_{2i} + u_{it} - {}_{t-1}\epsilon_{it+j}\alpha_{2i} \\ &= X_{it}\alpha_i + v_{it} \end{aligned} \quad t = 1, \ldots, T, \tag{16.4}$$

where $X_{it} = (X_{1it}\ X_{2it+j})$, $\alpha_i = (\alpha_{1i}\ \alpha_{2i})'$, and $v_{it} = u_{it} - {}_{t-1}\epsilon_{it+j}\alpha_{2i}$.

Consider now the 2SLS estimation of (16.4), where the vector of FSRs is the vector Z_{it} used by agents in forming their expectations. A necessary condition for consistency is that Z_{it} and v_{it} be uncorrelated. This will be true if both u_{it} and ${}_{t-1}\epsilon_{it+j}$ are uncorrelated with Z_{it}. The assumption that Z_{it} and u_{it} are uncorrelated is the usual 2SLS assumption. The assumption that Z_{it} and ${}_{t-1}\epsilon_{it+j}$ are uncorrelated is the rational expectations assumption. If expectations are formed rationally and if the variables in Z_{it} are used (perhaps along with others) in forming the expectation of X_{2it+j}, then Z_{it} and ${}_{t-1}\epsilon_{it+j}$ are uncorrelated. Given this assumption (and the other standard assumptions that are necessary for consistency), the 2SLS estimator of α_i in equation (16.4) is consistent.

The 2SLS estimator does not, however, account for the fact that v_{it} in (16.4) is a moving average error of order $j-1$, and so it loses some efficiency for values of j greater than 1. The modification of the 2SLS estimator to account for the moving average process of v_{it} is Hansen's (1982) generalized method of moments (GMM) estimator, which will now be described.

Write (16.4) in matrix notation as

$$y_i = X_i\alpha_i + v_i, \tag{16.5}$$

where X_i is $T \times k_i$, α_i is $k_i \times 1$, and y_i and v_i are $T \times 1$. Also, let Z_i denote, as above, the $T \times K_i$ matrix of FSRs. The assumption in (16.3) that there is only one expectational variable and only one value of j can now be relaxed. The matrix X_i can include more than one expectational variable and more than one value of j per variable. In other words, there can be more than one led value in this matrix.

The 2SLS estimate of α_i in (16.5) is

$$\hat{\alpha}_i = [X_i'Z_i(Z_i'Z_i)^{-1}Z_i'X_i]^{-1}X_i'Z_i(Z_i'Z_i)^{-1}Z_i'y_i. \tag{16.6}$$

This use of the 2SLS estimator for models with rational expectations is due to McCallum (1976).

As just noted, this use of the 2SLS estimator does not account for the moving average process of v_{it}, and so it loses efficiency if there is at least one value of j greater than 1. Also, the standard formula for the covariance matrix of $\hat{\alpha}_i$ is not correct when at least one value of j is greater than 1. If, for example, j is 3 in (16.4), an unanticipated shock in period $t+1$ will affect ${}_{t-1}\epsilon_{it+3}$, ${}_{t-2}\epsilon_{it+2}$, and ${}_{t-3}\epsilon_{it+1}$, and so v_{it} will be a second-order moving average. Hansen's GMM estimator accounts for this moving average process. The GMM estimate in the present case (denoted $\tilde{\alpha}_i$) is

$$\tilde{\alpha}_i = (X_i'Z_iM_i^{-1}Z_i'X_i)^{-1}X_i'Z_iM_i^{-1}Z_i'y_i, \tag{16.7}$$

where M_i is some consistent estimate of $\lim T^{-1}E(Z_i'v_iv_i'Z_i)$. The estimated covariance matrix of $\tilde{\alpha}_i$ is

$$T(X_i'Z_iM_i^{-1}Z_i'X_i)^{-1}. \tag{16.8}$$

There are different versions of $\tilde{\alpha}_i$ depending on how M_i is computed. To compute M_i, one first needs an estimate of the residual vector v_i. The residuals can be estimated using the 2SLS estimate $\hat{\alpha}_i$

$$\hat{v}_i = y_i - X_i\hat{\alpha}_i. \tag{16.9}$$

A general way of computing M_i is as follows. Let $f_{it} = \hat{v}_{it} \otimes Z_{it}$, where $\hat{v}_{it}$ is the tth element of $\hat{v}_i$. Let $R_{ip} = (T-p)^{-1} \sum_{t=p}^{T} f_{it} f'_{it-p}$, $p = 0, 1, \ldots, P$, where P is the order of the moving average. M_i is then $(R_{i0} + R_{i1} + R'_{i1} + \ldots + R_{iP} + R'_{iP})$. In many cases, computing M_i in this way does not result in a positive definite matrix, and so $\tilde{\alpha}_i$ cannot be computed. I have never had much success in obtaining a positive definite matrix for M_i computed in this way.

There are, however, other ways of computing M_i. One way, which is discussed in Hansen (1982) and Cumby, Huizinga, and Obstfeld (1983) but is not pursued here, is to compute M_i based on an estimate of the spectral density matrix of $Z'_{it} v_{it}$ evaluated at frequency zero. An alternative way is to compute M_i under the following assumption:

$$E(v_{it} v_{is} \mid Z_{it}, Z_{it-1}, \ldots) = E(v_{is} v_{is}), \qquad t \geq s, \tag{16.10}$$

which says that the contemporaneous and serial correlations in v_i do not depend on Z_i. This assumption is implied by the assumption that $E(v_{it} v_{is}) = 0, t \geq s$, if normality is also assumed. Under this assumption, M_i can be computed as follows. Let $a_{ip} = (T-p)^{-1} \sum_{t=p}^{T} \hat{v}_{it} \hat{v}_{it-p}$ and $B_{ip} = (T-p)^{-1} \sum_{t=p}^{T} Z_{it} Z'_{it-p}$, $p = 0, 1, \ldots, P$. M_i is then $(a_{i0} B_{i0} + a_{i1} B_{i1} + a_{i1} B'_{i1} + \ldots + a_{iP} B_{iP} + a_{iP} B'_{iP})$. In practice, this way of computing M_i usually results in a positive definite matrix.

16.3 The Case of an Autoregressive Structural Error

Since many macroeconometric equations have autoregressive error terms, it is useful to consider how the above estimator is modified to cover this case. Return for the moment to the example in (16.2) and assume that the error term u_{it} in the equation follows a first-order autoregressive process:

$$u_{it} = \rho_{1i} u_{it-1} + \eta_{it}. \tag{16.11}$$

Lagging equation (16.2) one period, multiplying through by ρ_{1i}, and subtracting the resulting expression from (16.2) yields:

$$\begin{aligned} y_{it} = {} & \rho_{1i} y_{it-1} + X_{1it} \alpha_{1i} - X_{1it-1} \alpha_{1i} \rho_{1i} + E_{t-1} X_{2it+j} \alpha_{2i} \\ & - E_{t-2} X_{2it+j-1} \alpha_{2i} \rho_{1i} + \eta_{it}. \end{aligned} \tag{16.12}$$

Note that this transformation yields a new viewpoint date, $t-2$. Let the expectation error for $E_{t-2} X_{2it+j-1}$ be

$${}_{t-2}\epsilon_{it+j-1} = X_{2it+j-1} - E_{t-2} X_{2it+j-1}. \tag{16.13}$$

Substituting (16.3) and (16.13) into (16.12) yields:

$$\begin{aligned} y_{it} &= \rho_{1i}y_{it-1} + X_{1it}\alpha_{1i} - X_{1it-1}\alpha_{1i}\rho_{1i} + X_{2it+j}\alpha_{2i} - X_{2it+j-1}\alpha_{2i}\rho_{1i} \\ &\quad + \eta_{it} - {}_{t-1}\epsilon_{it+j}\alpha_{2i} + {}_{t-2}\epsilon_{it+j-1}\alpha_{2i}\rho_{1i} \\ &= \rho_{1i}y_{it-1} + X_{it}\alpha_i - X_{it-1}\alpha_i\rho_{1i} + v_{it}, \end{aligned} \tag{16.14}$$

where X_{it} and α_i are defined after (16.4) and now $v_{it} = \eta_{it} \; - {}_{t-1}\epsilon_{it+j}\alpha_{2i} + {}_{t-2}\epsilon_{it+j-1}\;\alpha_{2i}\rho_{1i}$. Equation (16.14) is nonlinear in coefficients because of the introduction of ρ_{1i}. Again, X_{it} can in general include more than one expectational variable and more than one value of j per variable.

Given a set of FSRs, equation (16.14) can be estimated by 2SLS. The estimates are obtained by minimizing

$$S_i = v_i'Z_i(Z_i'Z_i)^{-1}Z_i'v_i = v_i'D_iv_i. \tag{16.15}$$

Equation (16.15) is just equation (16.4) rewritten for the error term in (16.14). A necessary condition for consistency is that Z_{it} and v_{it} be uncorrelated, which means that Z_{it} must be uncorrelated with η_{it}, ${}_{t-1}\epsilon_{it+j}$, and ${}_{t-2}\epsilon_{it+j-1}$. In order to insure that Z_{it} and ${}_{t-2}\epsilon_{it+j-1}$ are uncorrelated, Z_{it} must not include any variables that are not known as of the beginning of period $t-1$. This is an important additional restriction in the autoregressive case.[2]

In the general nonlinear case (16.15) (or (16.4)) can be minimized using a general purpose optimization algorithm. In the particular case considered here, however, a simple iterative procedure can be used, where one iterates between estimates of α_i and ρ_{1i}. Minimizing $v_i'D_iv_i$ with respect to α_i and ρ_{1i} results in the following first-order conditions:

$$\hat{\alpha}_i = [(X_i - X_{i-1}\hat{\rho}_{1i})'D_i(X_i - X_{i-1}\hat{\rho}_{1i})]^{-1}(X_i - X_{i-1}\hat{\rho}_{1i})'D_i(y_i - y_{i-1}\hat{\rho}_{1i}), \tag{16.16}$$

$$\hat{\rho}_{1i} = \frac{(y_{i-1} - X_{i-1}\hat{\alpha}_i)'D_i(y_i - X_i\hat{\alpha}_i)}{(y_{i-1} - X_{i-1}\hat{\alpha}_i)'D_i(y_{i-1} - X_{i-1}\hat{\alpha}_i)}, \tag{16.17}$$

where the -1 subscript denotes the vector or matrix of observations lagged one period. Equations (16.16) and (16.17) can easily be solved iteratively. Given the estimates $\hat{\alpha}_i$ and $\hat{\rho}_{1i}$ that solve (16.16) and (16.17), one can compute the 2SLS estimate of v_i, which is

$$\hat{v}_i = y_i - y_{i-1}\hat{\rho}_{1i} - X_i\hat{\alpha}_i + X_{i-1}\hat{\alpha}_i\hat{\rho}_{1i}. \tag{16.18}$$

Regarding Hansen's estimator, given $\hat{v}_i$, one can compute M_i in a number of possible ways. These calculations simply involve $\hat{v}_i$ and Z_i. Given M_i, Hansen's estimates of α_i and ρ_{1i} are obtained by minimizing[3]

$$SS_i = v_i' Z_i M_i^{-1} Z_i' v_i = v_i' C_i v_i. \tag{16.19}$$

Minimizing (16.19) with respect to α_i and ρ_{1i} results in the first-order conditions (16.16) and (16.17) with C_i replacing D_i. The estimated covariance matrix is

$$T(G_i' C_i G_i)^{-1}, \tag{16.20}$$

where $G = (X_i - X_{i-1}\hat{\rho}_{1i} \quad y_{i-1} - X_{i-1}\hat{\alpha}_i)$.

To summarize, Hansen's method in the case of a first-order autoregressive structural error consists of: (1) choosing Z_{it} so that it does not include any variables not known as of the beginning of period $t-1$, (2) solving (16.16) and (16.17), (3) computing $\hat{v}_i$ from (16.18), (4) computing M_i in one of the number of possible ways using $\hat{v}_i$ and Z_i, and (5) solving (16.16) and (16.17) with C_i replacing D_i.

16.4 Solution of RE Models

The "extended path" (EP) method for solving RE models, which is discussed in this subsection, is presented in Fair and Taylor (1983).[4] It is an extension of the iterative technique used in Fair (1979) for solving a model with rational expectations in the bond and stock markets, which is itself based on an idea in Poole (1976). The EP method has come to be widely used for deterministic simulations of rational expectations models. The EP method has been programmed as part of the TROLL computer package and is routinely used to solve large-scale rational expectations models at the IMF, the Federal Reserve, the Canadian Financial Ministry, and other government agencies. It has also been used for simulation studies such as DeLong and Summers (1986) and King (1988). Other solution methods for rational expectations models are summarized in Taylor and Uhlig (1990).

The RE model (16.3) is rewritten here with first-order autoregressive errors explicitly added.

$$f_i(y_t, y_{t-1}, \ldots, y_{t-p}, E_{t-1}y_t, E_{t-1}y_{t+1}, \ldots, E_{t-1}y_{t+h}, x_t, \alpha_i) = u_{it} \tag{16.21}$$

$$u_{it} = \rho_i u_{it-1} + \epsilon_{it}, \quad (i = 1, \ldots, n). \tag{16.22}$$

The EP method will now be described.

16.4.1 Case 1: $\rho_i = 0$

Consider solving the model for period s. It is assumed that estimates of α_i are available, that current and expected future values of the exogenous variables are available, and that the current and future values of the error terms have been set to their expected values (which will always be taken to be zero here). If the expectations $E_{s-1}y_s, E_{s-1}y_{s+1}, \ldots, E_{s-1}y_{s+h}$ were known, (16.21) could be solved in the usual ways (usually by the Gauss–Seidel technique). The model would be simultaneous, but future predicted values would not affect current predicted values. The EP method iterates over solution *paths*. Values of the expectations through period $s+h+k+h$ are first guessed, where k is a fairly large number relative to h.[5] Given these guesses, the model can be solved for periods s through $s+h+k$ in the usual ways. This solution provides new values for the expectations through period $s+h+k$; the new expectations values are the solution values. Given these new values, the model can be solved again for periods s through $s+h+k$, which provides new expectations values, and so on. This process stops (if it does) when the solution values for one iteration are within a prescribed tolerance criterion of the solution values for the previous iteration for all periods s through $s+h+k$.

So far, the guessed values of the expectations for periods $s+h+k+1$ through $s+h+k+h$ (the h periods beyond the last period solved) have not been changed. If the solution values for periods s through $s+h$ depend in a nontrivial way on these guesses, then overall convergence has not been achieved. To check for this, the entire process above is repeated for k one larger. If increasing k by one has a trivial effect (based on a tolerance criterion) on the solution values for s through $s+h$, then overall convergence has been achieved; otherwise k must continue to be increased until the criterion is met. In practice what is usually done is to experiment to find the value of k that is large enough to make it likely that further increases are unnecessary for any experiment that might be run and then do no further checking using larger values of k.

The expected future values of the exogenous variables (which are needed for the solution) can either be assumed to be the actual values (if available and known by agents) or be projected from an assumed stochastic process. If the expected future values of the exogenous variables are not the actual values, one extra step is needed at the end of the overall solution. In the above process, the expected values of the exogenous variables would be used for all the solutions, the expected values of the exogenous variables being chosen ahead of time. This yields values for $E_{s-1}y_s, E_{s-1}y_{s+1}, \ldots, E_{s-1}y_{s+h}$. Given these values, (20) is then solved for period s using the *actual* value of x_s, which yields the final solution value $\hat{y}_s$. To the extent that the expected value of x_s differs from the actual value, $E_{s-1}y_s$ will differ from $\hat{y}_s$.

Two points about this method should be mentioned. First, no general convergence proofs are available. If convergence is a problem, one can sometimes "damp" the solution values to obtain convergence. In practice, convergence is usually not a problem. There may, of course, be more than one set of solution values, and so there is no guarantee that the particular set found is unique. If there is more than one set, the set that the method finds may depend on the guesses used for the expectations for the h periods beyond $s+h+k$.

Second, the method relies on the certainty equivalence assumption even though the model is nonlinear. Since expectations of functions are treated as functions of the expectations in future periods in equation (7.18), the solution is only approximate unless f_i is linear. This assumption is like the linear quadratic approximation to rational expectations models that has been proposed, for example, by Kydland and Prescott (1982). Although the certainty equivalence assumption is widely used, including in the engineering literature, it is, of course, not always a good approximation.

16.4.2 Case 2: $\rho_i \neq 0$ and Data before $s-1$ Available

The existence of serial correlation complicates the problem considerably. The error terms for period $t-1$ ($u_{it-1}, i=1,\ldots,n$) depend on expectations that were formed at the end of period $t-2$, and so a new viewpoint date is introduced. This case is discussed in section 2.2 in Fair and Taylor (1983), but an error was made in the treatment of the second viewpoint date. The following method replaces the method in section 2.2 of this paper.[6]

Consider again solving for period s. If the values of u_{is-1} were known, one could solve the model as above. The only difference is that the value of an error term like u_{is+r-1} would be $\rho_i^r u_{is-1}$ instead of zero. The overall solution method first uses the EP method to solve for period $s-j$, where $j>0$, based on the assumption that $u_{is-j-1}=0$. Once the expectations are solved for, (16.21) is used to solve for u_{is-j}. The actual values of y_{s-j} and x_{s-j} are used for this purpose (although the solution values are used for the expectations) because these are structural errors being estimated, not reduced-form errors.

Given the values for u_{is-j}, the model is solved for period $s-j+1$ using the EP method, where an error term like u_{is-j+r} is computed as $\rho_i^r u_{is-j}$. Once the expectations are solved for, (16.21) is used to solve for u_{is-j+1}, which can be used in the solution for period $s-j+2$, and so on through the solution for period s.

The solution for period s is based on the assumption that the error terms for period $s-j-1$ are zero. To see if the solution values for period s are sensitive to this assumption, the entire process is repeated with j increased by 1. If going back one more period has effects on the solution values for period s that are within a prescribed tolerance criterion, then overall convergence has been achieved; otherwise j must continue to be increased. Again, in practice, one usually finds a value of j that is large enough to make it likely that further increases are unnecessary for any experiment that might be run and then do no further checking using larger values of j.

It should be noted that once period s is solved for, period $s+1$ can be solved for without going back again. From the solution for period s, the values of u_{is} can be computed, which can then be used in the solution for period $s+1$ using the EP method.

16.4.3 Case 3: $\rho_i \neq 0$ and Data before Period $s-1$ Not Available

This case is based on the assumption that $\epsilon_{is-1}=0$ when solving for period s. This type of an assumption is usually made when estimating multiple equation models with moving average residuals. The solution problem is to find the values of u_{is-1} that are consistent with this assumption. The overall method begins by guessing values for u_{is-2}. Given these values, the model can be solved for period $s-1$ using the EP method and the fact that $u_{is+r-2}=\rho_i^r u_{is-2}$. From the solution values for the expectations, (16.21) and (16.22) can be used to solve for ϵ_{is-1}.[7] If the absolute values of these errors are within a prescribed tolerance criterion, convergence has been achieved. Otherwise, the new guess for u_{is-2} is computed as the old guess plus ϵ_{is-1}/ρ_i. The model is solved again for period $s-1$ using the new guess and the EP method, and so on until convergence is reached.

At the point of convergence, u_{is-1} can be computed as $\rho_i u_{is-2}$, where u_{is-2} is the estimated value on the last iteration (the value consistent with ϵ_{is-1} being within a prescribed tolerance criterion of zero). Given the values of u_{is-1}, one can solve for period s using the EP method, and the solution is finished.

16.5 Computational Costs of the EP Method

The easiest way to think about the computational costs of the solution method is to consider how many times the equations of a model must be "passed" through. Let N be the number of passes through the model that it takes to solve the model for one period, given the expectations. N is usually some number less than 10 when the Gauss–Seidel technique is used. The EP method requires solving the model for $h+k+1$ periods. Let M be the number of iterations it takes to achieve convergence over these periods. Then the total number of passes for convergence is $N \cdot M(h+k+1)$. If, say, h is 5, k is 30, M is 15, and N is 5, then the total number of passes needed to solve the model for one period is 11,250, which compares to only 5 when there are no expectations. If k is increased by one to check for overall convergence, the total number of passes is slightly more than doubled; although, as noted above, this check is not always done. In the discussion of computational costs in the rest of this section, it will be assumed that this check is not done.

For Case 2 above, the number of passes is increased by roughly a factor of j if overall convergence is not checked. Checking for overall convergence slightly more than doubles the number of passes. j is usually a number between 5 and 10. If q is the number of iterations it takes to achieve convergence for Case 3 above, the number of passes is increased by a factor of $q+1$. In practice q seems to be between about 5 and 10. Note for both Cases 2 and 3 that the number of passes is increased relative to the nonserial correlation case only for the solution for the first period (period s). If period $s+1$ is to be solved for, no additional passes are needed over those for the regular case.

16.6 FIML Estimation of RE Models

Assume that the estimation period is 1 through T.[8] The objective function that FIML maximizes (assuming normality) is

$$L = -\frac{T}{2}\log|\Sigma| + \sum_{t=1}^{T}\log|J_t|, \tag{16.23}$$

where Σ is the covariance matrix of the error terms and J_t is the Jacobian matrix for period t. Σ is of the dimension of the number of stochastic equations in the model, and J_t is of the dimension of the total number of equations in the model. The ij element of Σ is $(1/T)\Sigma_{t=1}^{T}\epsilon_{it}\epsilon_{jt}$. Since the expectations have viewpoint date $t-1$, they are predetermined from the point of view of taking derivatives for the Jacobian, and so no additional problems are involved for the Jacobian in the rational expectations case. In what follows, α will be used to denote the vector of all the coefficients in the model. In the serial correlation case, α also includes the ρ_i coefficients.

FIML estimation of moderate to large models is expensive even in the standard case, and some tricks are needed to make the problem computationally feasible. An algorithm that can be used for large-scale applications is discussed in Parke (1982), and this algorithm will not be discussed here. Suffice it to say that FIML estimation of large-scale models is computationally feasible—see section 3.8 and also Fair and Parke (1980). What any algorithm needs to do is to evaluate L many times for alternative values of α in the search for the value that maximizes L.

In the standard case, computing Σ for a given value of α is fairly inexpensive. One simply solves (16.21) and (16.22) for the ϵ_{it} error terms given the data and the value of α. This is only one pass through the model since it is the structural error terms that are being computed. In the rational expectations case, however, computing the error terms requires knowing the values of the expectations, which themselves depend on α. Therefore, to compute Σ for a given value of α one has to solve for the expectations for each of the T periods. If, say, 11,250 passes through the model are needed to solve the model for one period and if T is 100, then 1,125,000 passes are needed for one evaluation of Σ and thus one evaluation of L.[9]

It should be clear that the straightforward combination of the EP solution method and FIML estimation procedures is not likely to be computationally feasible for most applications. There is, however, a way of cutting the number of times the model has to be solved over the estimation period to roughly the number of estimated coefficients. The trick is to compute numerical derivatives of the expectations with respect to the parameters and use these derivatives to compute Σ (and thus L) each time the algorithm requires a value of L for a given value of α.

Consider the derivative of $E_{t-1}y_{t+r}$ with respect to the first element of α. One can first solve the model for a given value of α and then solve it again for the first element of α changed by a certain percent, both solutions using the EP method. The computed derivative is then the difference in the two solution values of $E_{t-1}y_{t+r}$ divided by the change in the first element of α. To compute all the derivatives requires $K+1$ solutions of the model over the T number of observations, where K is the dimension of α.[10] One solution is for the base values, and the K solutions are for the K changes in α, one coefficient change per solution. From these $K+1$ solutions, $K \cdot T(h+1)$ derivatives are computed and stored for each expectations variable, one derivative for each length ahead for each period for each coefficient.[11] Once these derivatives are computed, they can be used in the computation of Σ for a given change in α, and no further solutions of the model are needed. In other words, when the maximization algorithm changes α and wants the corresponding value of L, the derivatives are first used to compute the expectations, which are then used in the computation of Σ. Since one has (from the derivatives) an estimate of how the expectations change when α changes, one does not have to solve the model any more to get the expectations.

Assuming that the solution method in Case 3 above is used for the FIML estimates, derivatives of u_{it-1} with respect to the coefficients are also needed when the errors are serially correlated. These derivatives can also be computed from the $K+1$ solutions, and so no extra solutions are needed in the serial correlation case.

Once the $K+1$ solutions of the model have been done and the maximization algorithm has found what it considers to be the optimum, the model can be solved again for the T periods using the optimal coefficient values and then L computed. This value of L will in general differ from the value of L computed using the derivatives for the same coefficient values, since the derivatives are only approximations. At this point, the new solution values (not computed using the derivatives) can be used as new base values and the problem turned over to the maximization algorithm again. This is the second "iteration" of the overall process. Once the maximization algorithm has found the new optimum, new base values can be computed, a new iteration performed, and so on. Convergence is achieved when the coefficient estimates from one iteration to the next are within a prescribed tolerance criterion of each other. This procedure can be modified by recomputing the derivatives at the end of each iteration. This may improve convergence, but it obviously adds considerably to the expense. At a minimum, one might want to recompute the derivatives at the end of overall convergence and then do one more iteration. If the coefficients change substantially on this iteration, then overall convergence has not in fact been achieved.

Examples of using this method for the FIML estimation of RE models are presented in Fair and Taylor (1990), and this material is not repeated here. The reader is referred to the original paper.

16.7 Stochastic Simulation of RE Models

For models with rational expectations, one must state very carefully what is meant by a stochastic simulation of the model and what stochastic simulation is to be used for.[12] In the present case, stochastic simulation is *not* used to improve on the accuracy of the solutions of the expected values. The expected values are computed exactly as described above—using the EP method. This way of solving for the expected values can be interpreted as assuming that agents at the beginning of period s form their expectations of the endogenous variables for periods s and beyond by (1) forming expectations of the exogenous variables for periods s and beyond, (2) setting the error terms equal to their expected values (say zero) for periods s and beyond, (3) using the existing set of coefficient estimates of the model, and then (4) solving the model for periods s and beyond. These solution values are the agents' expectations.

For present purposes, stochastic simulation begins once the expected values have been solved for. Given the expected values for periods s through $s+h$, stochastic simulation is performed for period s. The problem is now no different from the problem for a standard model because the expectations are predetermined. If it is assumed that the errors are distributed $N(0, \hat{\Sigma})$, where $\hat{\Sigma}$ is the FIML estimate of Σ from the last subsection, then errors from this distribution can be drawn for period s. Alternatively, errors can be drawn from estimated (historic) residuals. Given these draws (and the expectations), the model can be solved for period s in the usual ways. This is one repetition. Another repetition can be done using a new draw of the vector of error terms, and so on. The means and variances of the forecast values can then be computed. Note in this setup that agents are assumed *not* to know the error draws when forming their expectations. Their expectations are based on the assumption that the errors for periods s and beyond are zero. Their expectations are not the same as the solution of the model with the drawn errors for period s because they used zero errors for period s. Note that if there is, say, an interest rate rule in the model—a monetary policy reaction function—agents know this rule in that it is used in the solution for their expectations. The rule is part of the structure of the model.

One can also use this approach to analyze the effects of uncertainty in the coefficients by assuming that the coefficients are distributed $N(\hat{\alpha}, \hat{V}_4)$, where $\hat{\alpha}$ is the FIML estimate of α and $\hat{V}_4$ is the estimated covariance matrix of $\hat{\alpha}$. In this case, each draw also involves the vector of coefficients.[13]

If u_{it} is serially correlated as in (16.22), then an estimate of u_{is-1} is needed for the solution for period s. This estimate is, however, available from the solution of the model to get the expectations (see Case 2 in the previous subsection), and so no further work is needed. The estimate of u_{is-1} is simply taken as predetermined for all the repetitions, and u_{is} is computed as $\rho_i u_{is-1}$ plus the draw for ϵ_{is}. (Note that the ϵ errors are drawn, not the u errors.)

Stochastic simulation is quite inexpensive if only results for period s are needed because the model only needs to be solved once using the EP method. Once the expectations are obtained, each repetition merely requires solving the model for period s. The EP method is not needed because the expectations are predetermined. If, on the other hand, results for more than one period are needed and the simulation is dynamic, the EP method must be used p times for each repetition, where p is the length of the period.

Consider the multiperiod problem. As above, the expectations with viewpoint date $s-1$ can be solved for and then a vector of error terms drawn for period s and (perhaps) a vector of coefficients also drawn to compute the predicted value of y_{is} for each i. This is the first step.

Now go to period $s+1$, where the viewpoint date is s. An agent's expectation of, say, y_{is+2} is different with viewpoint date s than with viewpoint date $s-1$. In particular, the value of y_{is} is in general different from what the agent at the end of period $s-1$ expected it to be (because of the error terms that were drawn for period s).[14] A new set of expectations must thus be computed with viewpoint date s. Agents are assumed to use the original set of coefficients (not the set that was drawn if in fact coefficients were drawn) and to set the values of the error terms for periods $s+1$ and beyond equal to zero. Then given the solution values for period s and the actual value of x_s, agents are assumed to solve the model for their expectations for periods $s+1$ and beyond. This requires a second use of the EP method. These expectations are then predetermined for viewpoint date s. Given these expectations, a vector of error terms for period $s+1$ is drawn and the model is solved for period $s+1$. If equation i has a serially correlated error, then u_{is+1} is equal to $\rho_i^2 u_{is-1}$ plus the draw for ϵ_{is+1}. Now go to period $s+2$ and repeat the process, where another use of the EP method is needed to compute the new expectations. The process is repeated through the end of the period of interest. At the end, this is one repetition. If the length of the period is p, then the EP method is used p times per repetition. The overall process is then repeated for the second repetition, and so on. Note that if coefficients are drawn, only one coefficient draw is used per repetition, i.e., per dynamic simulation. After J repetitions, one can compute means and variances just as above, where there are now means and variances for each period ahead of the prediction. Also note that agents are always assumed to use the original set of coefficients and for each viewpoint date to set the current and future error terms to zero. They do not perform stochastic simulation themselves.

Stochastic simulation results for an RE model are presented in Fair and Taylor (1990), and this material is not repeated here. The reader is again referred to the original paper. These results and others suggest that stochastic simulation as defined above is computationally feasible for models with rational expectations. Stochastic simulation is in fact likely to be cheaper than even FIML estimation using the derivatives. If, for example, the FIML estimation period is 100 observations and there are 25 coefficients to estimate, FIML estimation requires that the model be solved 2,600 times using the EP method to get the derivatives. For a stochastic simulation of 8 periods and 100 repetitions, on the other hand, the model has to be solved using the EP method only 800 times.

17 Multicountry Econometric Models

The CC approach is not restricted by the size of a model, and models of more than one country can be specified. One can specify a model for each country, like the US model for the United States, and then link them together. The main links are exports, imports, exchange rates, export and import prices, and perhaps interest rates. One needs a trade share matrix to allocate the total exports of a country to each of the other countries. There are exchange rate equations, usually specified as each country's exchange rate relative to the US dollar. These equations may depend on relative interest rates and relative prices, but for the most part changes in exchange rates are unpredictable. Regarding interest rates, many monetary authorities are influeced by what the US Federal Reserve does, and so US monetary policy may affect other countries' monetary policy. This link is easy to model and test by simply adding *RS* to other countries' estimated interest rate rules.

I have specified a multicountry econometric (MC) model. The best reference is a document on my website titled "Macroeconometric Modeling." Also, Fair (2020) discusses the estimated trade share equations. I have chosen not to include the MC model in this book. No new methodology is required, and there are many weeds. It will be useful, however, to discuss the main effects on the US model from embedding it in the MC model.

Exports *EX* are exogenous in the US model and endogenous in the MC model. The total level of imports of each country is determined by an equation like equation 27 in the US model, where the level of imports depends on output, perhaps wealth, domestic price relative to import price, and perhaps interest rates. Let α_{ijt} denote the share of *i*'s exports to *j* out of the total imports of *j* in quarter *t*. There are estimated equations for α_{ijt}, where the trade share depends on *i*'s export price index relative to the export price indices of all the other countries. The export prices are all converted to US dollars through the exchange rate equations. The exports of the United States to country *j* (where *i* is the United States) is thus equal to the respective trade share times the total imports of country *j*. Summing these export values across all the countries yields total US exports *EX*. The lower the US price of exports relative to an index of the export prices of the other countries, the larger is the share imported from the United States and so the larger is the total value of US exports. The domestic price level in local currency in each country is determined by an equation like equation 10 in the US model. These price levels are converted to export price levels in US dollars using the exchange rates.

EX will thus increase if the total imports of other countries increase unless offset by changes in the trade shares through relative export price changes. A depreciation of the dollar will lead to an increase in *EX* through larger US trade shares.

The price of imports *PIM* is exogenous in the US model and endogenous in the MC model. *PIM* depends on a weighted index of the other countries' export prices in dollars. For example, domestic price increases in other countries that are not offset by exchange rate movements will lead to an increase in *PIM*. A depreciation of the dollar will lead to a decrease in US total imports (*IM*) through an increase in *PIM* relative to the US domestic price level *PF*.

As noted in chapter 7, differences between multiplier effects in the US and MC models are small. For example, when US government spending increases, this stimulates the economies of the other countries because US imports are higher (and thus other countries' exports). This in turn increases US exports because the other countries are now importing more because of their stimulus. There is thus a "trade feedback effect." The expansions in the other countries may lead to an increase in their domestic price levels and thus their export prices in dollars unless offset by exchange rate changes. This in turn increases US import prices and thus *PIM*. The increse in *PIM* increases the domestic price level through equation 10. There is thus a "price feedback effect." In general, however, these feedback effects are modest.

If, say, the Fed increase the US interest rate, this may appreciate the dollar, which, other things being equal, stimulates imports and contracts exports. This is an added negative effect on US output. There is also an added negative effect on US inflation, other things being equal, because US import prices are lower. The appreciation of the dollar may be mitigated by the fact that other countries' interest rates may increase in response to the US increase as other countries' monetary authorities are influence by the Fed. The interest rate effects on the value of the dollar are modest, and this link is empirically small in the MC model.

18 Further Material

There are a number of applications using the CC methodology that I have omitted from this text. These applications are discussed in "Macroeconometric Modeling" (MM) mentioned in the previous chapter. Here I list them with a brief discussion. In brackets are the sections in MM where more discussion can be found.

Much more can be done with stochastic simulation and bootstrapping. This includes examining the distributions of the coefficient estimates and estimating event probabilities, like the probability that a recession will occur [2.7, 3.9]. For example, a period can be chosen, a vector of errors drawn, and the model solved dynamically. This is one trial. Do this, say, 1,000 times and record on each trial whether there were two consecutive quarters of negative real growth. The estimated probability of a recession defined this way is just the number of times out of 1,000 that this event ocurred.

More can be done in testing complete models, including evaluation predictive accuracy and examining the information content of a model's forecasts [2.9, 3.10]. It is possible to use stochastic simulation to estimate the uncertainty of forecasts from the structural errors and the coefficient estimates. The degree of misspecification of a model can also be estimated. The sources of economic fluctuations can be examined [4.8.1].

Optimal control techniques are fairly easy to apply to models in the CC tradition [2.10]. One can specify an objective function and compute policies that maximize this function. With this methodology, performance measures can be estimated: how did a particular president or Fed chair do in maximizing the function? [4.8.2]. Much optimal control work relies on the assumption of certainty equivalence, and this assumption can be tested and examined [2.11, 3.11].

Using stochastic simulation and optimal control analysis, one can examine the best way for a monetary authority to report uncertainty [4.9].

While these more advanced techniques are interesting (and easy to use), some may be too clever by half. Is an estimated model a good enough approximation to reality to allow these techniques to be applied to it? Any misspecification may lead some of the more advanced results to be unreliable.

Appendix

A.1 The US Model in Tables

The tables that pertain to the US model are presented in this appendix. Table A.1 presents the six sectors in the US model: household (*h*), firm (*f*), financial (*b*), foreign (*r*), federal government (*g*), and state and local government (*s*). In order to account for the flow of funds among these sectors and for their balance-sheet constraints, the US Flow of Funds Accounts (FFA) and the US National Income and Product Accounts (NIPA) must be linked. Many of the identities in the US model are concerned with this linkage. Table A.1 shows how the six sectors in the US model are related to the sectors in the FFA. The notation on the right side of this table (H1, FA, etc.) is used in table A.5 in the description of the FFA data.

Table A.2 lists all the variables in the US model in alphabetical order and the equations in which they appear. Table A.3 lists all the stochastic equations and identities. The coefficient estimates for the stochastic equations are presented in table A.4, where within this table the coefficient estimates and tests for equation 1 are presented in table A1, for equation 2 in table A2, and so on. Tables A1–A30 are also presented in chapter 4; they are just repeated here.

The remaining three tables provide more detailed information about the model. Tables A.5–A.7 show how the variables were constructed from the raw data.

A.2 The Raw Data

The variables from the NIPA are presented first in table A.5, in the order in which they appear in the Bureau of Economic Analysis (BEA) tables. The

BEA uses "chain-type weights" in the construction of real magnitudes, and the data based on these weights have been used here.[1] Because of the use of the chain-type weights, real GDP is not the sum of its real components. To handle this, a discrepancy variable, denoted *STATP*, was created, which is the difference between real GDP and the sum of its real components. (*STATP* is constructed using equation 83 in table A.3.) *STATP* is small in magnitude, and it is taken to be exogenous in the model.

The variables from the FFA are presented next in table A.5, ordered by their code numbers. Some of these variables are NIPA variables that are not published by the BEA but that are needed to link the two accounts. Interest rate variables are presented next in the table, followed by employment and population variables. The source for the interest rate data is the website of the Board of Governors of the Federal Reserve System (BOG) and FRED. The source for the employment and population data is the website of the Bureau of Labor Statistics (BLS). Data on the armed forces are not published by the BLS, and these data were computed from population data from the US Census Bureau.

Some adjustments that were made to the raw data are presented next in table A.5. These are explained beginning in the next paragraph. Finally, all the raw data variables are presented at the end of table A.5 in alphabetical order along with their numbers. This allows one to find a raw data variable quickly. Otherwise, one has to search through the entire table looking for the particular variable. All the raw data variables are numbered with an"R" in front of the number to distinguish them from the variables in the model.

The adjustments that were made to the raw data are as follows. The quarterly social insurance variables R200–R205 were constructed from the annual variables R89–R94 and the quarterly variables R35, R47, and R68. Only annual data are available on the breakdown of social insurance contributions between the federal and the state and local governments with respect to the categories "personal," "government employer," and "other employer." It is thus necessary to construct the quarterly variables using the annual data. It is implicitly assumed in this construction that as employers, state and local governments do not contribute to the federal government and vice versa.

The constructed tax variables R206 and R207 pertain to the breakdown of corporate profit taxes of the financial sector between federal and state and local. Data on this breakdown do not exist. It is implicitly assumed in this construction that the breakdown is the same as it is for the total corporate sector.

The tax and transfer variables *THG* (R43) and *TRGHPAY* (R57) were adjusted to account for the tax surcharge of 1968.3–1970.3 and the tax rebate of 1975.2. The increase in taxes from the tax surcharge was taken out of *TRG* and the level of transfer payments *TRGHPAY* was decreased instead. The decrease in taxes from the tax rebate was added to *THG* and the level of transfer payments *TRGHPAY* was increased instead. The tax surcharge numbers were taken from Okun (1971), table 1, p. 171. The tax rebate was $31.2 billion at an annual rate. The two variables were also adjusted in a similar way between 2008.2 and 2011.3 for the effects of the US stimulus bill. Added to *THG* and *TRGHPAY* for each of the 12 quarters (at annual rates) were $797.6, $228.0, $608.0, $956.0, $996.0, $924.0, $1,024, $1,064.0, $60.0, $212.0, $296.0, and $396.0 billion, respectively.

The employment and population data from the BLS are rebenchmarked each year, and the past data are not adjusted by the BLS to the new benchmarks. Presented next in table A.5 are the adjustments that were made to obtain consistent series. These adjustments take the form of various "multiplication factors" for the old data. For the period in question and for a particular variable the old data are multiplied by the relevant multiplication factor to create data for use in the model. The TPOP variables listed in table A.5 are used to phase out the multiplication factors. In some of the early DSGE modeling—see Fair (2020)—the rebenchmarking was not taken into account, and so there were spikes in the data each January.

For raw data variable *NILCMA*, which is the change in currency *CUR*, the values for 1999.4 and 2000.1 were extreme, one 48.072 and the other −28.673. The average of these two values, 9.699, was used instead for both quarters.

For a few quarters, the values of *DF*, net dividends paid by *f*, *DR*, net dividends paid by *r*, and *PIEFRET*, foreign earnings retained abroad by *f*, were affected by US legislation. In one quarter, *DF* was negative. Adjustments were made to undo the accounting behind the reported values. For the affected quarters a particular value was added to *DF*, subtracted from *DR*, and added to *PIEFRET*. The values were chosen to smooth out the series. Then *THETA4* was computed as *PIEFRET*/*PIEF* using the new values, and

DRQ was computed as *DR*/*GDPD* using the new values. Values for 14 quarters were changed, 2003.2, 2005.2–2005.4, 2006.4, and 2018.1–2020.1. The 14 values are (in billions of dollars at quarterly rates) −15, 7, 43, 77, −20, 224, 127, 20, 90, 29, 29, 12, 15, and 28.

Table A.6 presents the balance-sheet constraints that the data satisfy. The variables in this table are raw data variables. The equations in the table provide the main checks on the collection of the data. If any of the checks are not met, one or more errors have been made in the collection process. Although the checks in the table may look easy, considerable work is involved in having them met.

Table A.1
The Six Sectors of the US Model

Sector	Corresponding Sector(s) in the Flow of Funds Accounts
1 Household (h)	1 Households and Nonprofit Organizations (H)
2 Firm (f)	2a Nonfinancial Corporate Business (F1) 2b Nonfinancial Noncorporate Business (NN)
3 Financial (b)	3 Financial Business (B) except Government Sponsored Enterprises (CA) and Monetary Authority (MA)
4 Foreign (r)	4 Rest of the World (R)
5 Fed. Gov. (g)	5a Federal Government (US)
	5b Government-Sponsored Enterprises (CA) 5c Monetary Authority (MA)
6 S & L Gov. (s)	6 State and Local Governments (S)

- The abbreviations h, f, b, r, g, and s are used throughout this appendix.
- The abbreviations H, F1, NN, B, R, US, CA, MA, and S are used in table A.5 in the description of the flow of funds data and, when appropriate, in other tables.

Table A.2
The Variables in the US Model in Alphabetical Order

Variable	Eq.	Description	Used in Equations
AA	133	Total net wealth, h, B2012$.	1, 2, 3, 5, 6, 7, 27
*AA*1	88	Total net financial wealth, h, B2012$.	133
*AA*2	89	Total net housing wealth, h, B2012$.	133
AB	73	Net financial assets, b, B$.	none
AF	70	Net financial assets, f, B$.	none
AFT	exog	Total armed forces, g, millions	87
AG	77	Net financial assets, g, B$.	29
*AG*1	exog	Percent of 16+ population 26–55 minus percent 16–25.	1, 2, 3, 4, 27
*AG*2	exog	Percent of 16+ population 56–65 minus percent 16–25.	1, 2, 3, 4, 27
*AG*3	exog	Percent of 16+ population 66+ minus percent 16–25.	1, 2, 3, 4, 27
AH	66	Net financial assets, h, B$.	88
AR	75	Net financial assets, r, B$.	none
AS	79	Net financial assets, s, B$.	none
BO	exog	Bank borrowing from the Fed, B$.	73
BR	exog	Total bank reserves, B$.	73
*CCF*1	67	Capital consumption, F1, B$.	68
CCG	150	Capital consumption, g, B$.	68, 69, 76
CCGQ	exog	Capital consumption, g, B2012$.	150
CCH	151	Capital consumption, h, B$.	65, 68, 69
CCHQ	exog	Capital consumption, h, B2012$.	151
CCS	152	Capital consumption, s, B$.	68, 69, 78
CCSQ	exog	Capital consumption, s, B2012$.	152
CD	3	Consumer expenditures for durable goods, B2012$.	34, 51, 52, 58, 60, 61, 65, 96, 97, 116
CDH	96	Capital expenditures, consumer durable goods, h, B$.	65, 68
CG	exog	Capital gains(+) or losses(−) on the financial assets of h, B$.	12, 66
CN	2	Consumer expenditures for nondurable goods, B2012$.	34, 51, 52, 60, 61, 65, 116
cnst2cs	exog	Time-varying constant term, 1974.1–1994.3.	1
cnst2l2	exog	Time-varying constant term, 1971.3–1989.4.	6

Table A.2
(continued)

Variable	Eq.	Description	Used in Equations
cnst2kk	exog	Time-varying constant term, 1981.3–1986.2.	12
COG	exog	Purchases of consumption and investment goods, g, B2012$.	60, 61, 76, 104
COS	exog	Purchases of consumption and investment goods, s, B2012$.	60, 61, 78, 110
CS	1	Consumer expenditures for services, B2012$.	34, 51, 52, 60, 61, 65, 116
CTB	exog	Net capital transfers paid, financial corporations, B$.	72
CTF1	exog	Net capital transfers paid, nonfinancial corporations, B$.	69
CTGB	exog	Financial stabilization payments, B$.	68, 69
CTGMB	exog	Net capital transfers paid, g, less financial stabilization payments, B$.	76
CTH	exog	Net capital transfers paid, h, B$.	65
CTNN	exog	Net capital transfers paid, noncorporate business, B$.	69
CTR	exog	Net capital transfers paid, r, B$.	74
CTS	exog	Net capital transfers paid, s, B$.	78
CUR	26	Currency held outside banks, B$.	71, 77
D1G	exog	Personal income tax parameter, g.	47, 126, 127, 128
D1S	exog	Personal income tax parameter, s.	48, 126, 127, 128
D2G	exog	Profit tax rate, g.	12, 17, 49, 121
D2S	exog	Profit tax rate, s.	12, 17, 50, 121
D3G	exog	Indirect business tax rate, g.	35, 36, 37, 51
D3S	exog	Indirect business tax rate, s.	35, 36, 37, 52
D4G	exog	Employee social security tax rate, g.	53, 126
D5G	exog	Employer social security tax rate, g.	10, 54
D6G	exog	Capital consumption rate for CCF1, g.	67
D593	exog	1 in 1959:3; 0 otherwise.	11, 13
D594	exog	1 in 1959:4; 0 otherwise.	11
D601	exog	1 in 1960:1; 0 otherwise.	11
D691	exog	1 in 1969:1; 0 otherwise.	27
D692	exog	1 in 1969:2; 0 otherwise.	27

Table A.2
(continued)

Variable	Eq.	Description	Used in Equations
D714	exog	1 in 1971:4; 0 otherwise.	27
D721	exog	1 in 1972:1; 0 otherwise.	27
D794823	exog	1 in 1979:4–1982:3; 0 otherwise.	30
D20083	exog	1 in 1952.1–2008.3; 0 otherwise.	30
D20201	exog	1 in 2020.1; 0 otherwise.	1, 2, 3, 4, 5, 6, 7, 8, 10, 11, 12, 13, 14, 15, 16, 17, 18, 23, 24, 26, 27, 29
D20202	exog	1 in 2020.2; 0 otherwise.	1, 2, 3, 4, 5, 6, 7, 8, 10, 11, 12, 13, 14, 15, 16, 17, 18, 23, 24, 26, 27, 29
D20203	exog	1 in 2020.3; 0 otherwise.	1, 2, 3, 4, 5, 6, 7, 8, 10, 11, 12, 13, 14, 15, 16, 17, 18, 23, 24, 26, 27, 29
D20204	exog	1 in 2020.4; 0 otherwise.	1, 2, 3, 4, 5, 6, 7, 8, 10, 11, 12, 13, 14, 15, 16, 17, 18, 23, 24, 26, 27, 29
D20211	exog	1 in 2021.1; 0 otherwise.	1, 2, 3, 4, 5, 6, 7, 8, 10, 11, 12, 13, 14, 15, 16, 17, 18, 23, 24, 26, 27, 29
D20212	exog	1 in 2021.2; 0 otherwise.	1, 2, 3, 4, 5, 6, 7, 8, 10, 11, 12, 13, 14, 15, 16, 17, 18, 23, 24, 26, 27, 29
D20213	exog	1 in 2021.3; 0 otherwise.	1, 2, 3, 4, 5, 6, 7, 8, 10, 11, 12, 13, 14, 15, 16, 17, 18, 23, 24, 26, 27, 29
D20214	exog	1 in 2021.4; 0 otherwise.	1, 2, 3, 4, 5, 6, 7, 8, 10, 11, 12, 13, 14, 15, 16, 17, 18, 23, 24, 26, 27, 29
DB	153	Net dividends paid, b, B$.	64, 68, 69, 115
DBQ	exog	Net dividends paid, b, B2012$.	153
DELD	exog	Physical depreciation rate of the stock of durable goods, rate per quarter.	58

Table A.2
(continued)

Variable	Eq.	Description	Used in Equations
DELH	exog	Physical depreciation rate of the stock of housing, rate per quarter.	59
DELK	exog	Physical depreciation rate of the stock of capital, rate per quarter.	92
DF	18	Net dividends paid, f, B$.	64, 69, 115
DG	exog	Net dividends paid, g, B$.	64, 76, 105, 115
DISB	exog	Discrepancy for b, B$.	73
DISF	exog	Discrepancy for f, B$.	70
DISG	exog	Discrepancy for g, B$.	77
DISH	exog	Discrepancy for h, B$.	66
DISR	exog	Discrepancy for r, B$.	75
DISS	exog	Discrepancy for s, B$.	79
DR	154	Net dividends paid, r, B$.	57, 64, 115
DRQ	exog	Net dividends paid, r, B2012$.	154
DS	exog	Net dividends paid, s, B$.	64, 78, 112, 115
E	85	Total employment, civilian and military, millions.	86
EX	exog	Exports, B2012$.	33, 60, 61, 74
EXPG	106	Net expenditures, g, B$.	107
EXPS	113	Net expenditures, s, B$.	114
FA	exog	Farm gross product, B2012$.	17, 26, 31
GDP	82	Gross Domestic Product, B$.	84, 129
GDPD	84	GDP price deflator.	111, 123, 130, 150–169
GDPR	83	Gross Domestic Product, B2012$.	84, 122, 130
GNP	129	Gross National Product, B$.	131
GNPD	131	GNP price deflator.	none
GNPR	130	Gross National Product, B2012$.	131
GSB	155	Gross saving, B, B$.	68, 69, 72
GSBQ	exog	Gross saving, B, B2012$.	155
GSCA	exog	Gross saving, CA, B$.	68, 69, 76
GSMA	exog	Gross saving, MA, B$.	68, 69, 76
GSNN	156	Gross saving, NN, B$.	68
GSNNQ	exog	Gross saving, NN, B2012$.	156
HF	14	Average number of hours paid per job, f, hours per quarter.	62, 100, 118
HFF	100	Deviation of *HFF* from *HFS*.	15
HFS	exog	Potential value of *HF*.	13, 14, 100

Table A.2
(continued)

Variable	Eq.	Description	Used in Equations
HG	exog	Average number of hours paid per civilian job, g, hours per quarter.	43, 64, 76, 82, 83, 104, 115, 126
HM	exog	Average number of hours paid per military job, g, hours per quarter.	43, 64, 76, 82, 83, 104, 115, 126
HN	62	Average number of non overtime hours paid per job, f, hours per quarter.	43, 53, 54, 64, 67, 68, 115, 121, 126
HO	15	Average number of overtime hours paid per job, f, hours per quarter.	43, 53, 54, 62, 67, 68, 115, 121, 126
HS	exog	Average number of hours paid per job, s, hours per quarter.	43, 64, 78, 82, 83, 110, 115, 126
IBTG	51	Indirect business taxes, g, B$.	34, 52, 61, 76, 82, 105
IBTS	52	Indirect business taxes, s, B$.	34, 51, 61, 78, 82, 112
IGZ	157	Gross investment, g, B$.	106
IGZQ	exog	Gross investment, g, B2012$.	157
IHB	exog	Residential investment, b, B2012$.	60, 61, 72
IHF	exog	Residential investment, f, B2012$.	60, 61, 68
IHH	4	Residential investment, h, B2012$.	34, 59, 60, 61, 65
IKB	exog	Nonresidential fixed investment, b, B2012$.	60, 61, 72
IKF	92	Nonresidential fixed investment, f, B2012$.	60, 61, 67, 69
IKG	exog	Nonresidential fixed investment, g, B2012$.	60, 61, 76
IKH	exog	Nonresidential fixed investment, h, B2012$.	60, 61, 65
IM	27	Imports, B2012$.	33, 60, 61, 74
INS	exog	Insurance and pension reserves to h from g, B$.	65, 76
INTF	exog	Net interest payments, f, B$.	64, 68, 69, 115
INTG	29	Net interest payments, g, B$.	56, 64, 76, 106, 115
INTGR	56	Net interest payments, g to r, B$.	57, 64, 115
INTS	exog	Net interest payments, s, B$.	64, 78, 113, 115
INTZ	158	Net interest payments, other, B$.	64, 68, 69, 115
INTZQ	exog	Net interest payments, other, B2012$.	158

Table A.2
(continued)

Variable	Eq.	Description	Used in Equations
ISZ	159	Gross investment, s, B$.	113
ISZQ	exog	Gross investment, s, B2012$.	159
IVA	exog	Inventory valuation adjustment, B$.	68
IVF	117	Inventory investment, f, B2012$.	68
JF	13	Number of jobs, f, millions.	14, 43, 53, 54, 64, 68, 69, 85, 115, 118, 121
JG	exog	Number of civilian jobs, g, millions.	43, 64, 76, 82, 83, 85, 104, 115, 126
JHMIN	94	Number of worker hours required to produce Y, millions.	13, 14
JM	exog	Number of military jobs, g, millions.	43, 64, 76, 82, 83, 85, 104, 115
JS	exog	Number of jobs, s, millions.	43, 64, 78, 82, 83, 85, 110, 115, 126
KD	58	Stock of durable goods, B2012$.	none
KH	59	Stock of housing, h, B2012$.	89
KK	12	Stock of capital, f, B2012$.	92
KKMIN	93	Amount of capital required to produce Y, B2012$.	12
L1	5	Labor force of men 25–54, millions.	86, 87
L2	6	Labor force of women 25–54, millions.	86, 87
L3	7	Labor force of all others, 16+, millions.	86, 87
LAM	exog	Amount of output capable of being produced per worker hour.	10, 16, 94
LM	8	Number of "moonlighters": difference between the total number of jobs (establishment data) and the total number of people employed (household survey data), millions.	85
M1	81	Money supply, end of quarter, B$.	124
MB	71	Net demand deposits and currency, b, B$.	73

Table A.2
(continued)

Variable	Eq.	Description	Used in Equations
MDIF	exog	Net increase in demand deposits and currency of banks in US possessions plus change in demand deposits and currency of private nonbank financial institutions plus change in demand deposits and currency of federally sponsored credit agencies and mortgage pools minus mail float, US government, B$.	81
MF	17	Demand deposits and currency, f, B$.	70, 71, 81
MG	160	Demand deposits and currency, g, B$.	71, 77
MGQ	exog	Demand deposits and currency, g, B2012$.	160
MH	161	Demand deposits and currency, h, B$.	66, 71, 81, 88
MHQ	exog	Demand deposits and currency, h, B2012$.	161
MR	162	Demand deposits and currency, r, B$.	71, 75, 81
MRQ	exog	Demand deposits and currency, r, B2012$.	162
MS	163	Demand deposits and currency, s, B$.	71, 79, 81
MSQ	exog	Demand deposits and currency, s, B2012$.	163
MUH	exog	Amount of output capable of being produced per unit of capital.	93
NICD	97	Net investment in consumer durables, h, B$.	65, 68, 69
NNF	exog	Net acquisition of nonproduced nonfinancial assets, f, B$.	69
NNG	exog	Net acquisition of nonproduced nonfinancial assets, g, B$.	76
NNH	exog	Net acquisition of nonproduced nonfinancial assets, h, B$.	65
NNR	exog	Net acquisition of nonproduced nonfinancial assets, r, B$.	74
NNS	exog	Net acquisition of nonproduced nonfinancial assets, s, B$.	78

Table A.2
(continued)

Variable	Eq.	Description	Used in Equations
PCD	37	Price deflator for CD.	34, 51, 52, 61, 65, 96, 97, 116
PCGDPD	123	Percentage change in GDPD, annual rate, percentage points.	none
PCGDPR	122	Percentage change in GDPR, annual rate, percentage points.	none
*PCM*1	124	Percentage change in M1, annual rate, percentage points.	30
PCN	36	Price deflator for CN.	34, 51, 52, 61, 65, 116
PCS	35	Price deflator for CS.	34, 51, 52, 61, 65, 116
PD	33	Price deflator for X - EX + IM (domestic sales).	12, 30, 35, 36, 37, 38, 39, 40, 41, 42, 55
PEX	32	Price deflator for EX.	33, 61, 74
PF	10	Price deflator for nonfarm sales.	16, 17, 26, 27, 31, 119
PFA	111	Price deflator for farm sales.	31
PG	40	Price deflator for COG.	61, 76, 104
PH	34	Price deflator for CS + CN + CD + IHH inclusive of indirect business taxes.	1, 2, 3, 4, 7, 88, 89
PIEF	67	Before-tax profits, f, B$.	18, 49, 50, 121, 132
PIEFRET	132	Foreign earnings retained abroad, f, B$.	57, 69
PIH	38	Price deflator for residential investment.	34, 61, 65, 68, 72
PIK	39	Price deflator for nonresidential fixed investment.	21, 61, 65, 68, 72, 76
PIM	exog	Price deflator for IM.	10, 27, 33, 61, 74
PIV	42	Price deflator for inventory investment, adjusted.	67, 82
PKH	55	Market price of *KH*.	89
POP	120	Noninstitutional population 16+, millions.	1, 2, 3, 4, 5, 6, 7, 8, 26, 27, 47, 48
*POP*1	exog	Noninstitutional population of men 25–54, millions.	5, 120

Table A.2
(continued)

Variable	Eq.	Description	Used in Equations
*POP*2	exog	Noninstitutional population of women 25–54, millions.	6, 120
*POP*3	exog	Noninstitutional population of all others, 16+, millions.	7, 120
PROD	118	Output per paid for worker hour ("productivity").	none
PS	41	Price deflator for COS.	61, 78, 110
*PSI*1	exog	Ratio of PEX to PX.	32
*PSI*2	exog	Ratio of PCS to (1 + D3G + D3S)PD.	35
*PSI*3	exog	Ratio of PCN to (1 + D3G + D3S)PD.	36
*PSI*4	exog	Ratio of PCD to (1 + D3G + D3S)PD.	37
*PSI*5	exog	Ratio of PIH to PD.	38
*PSI*6	exog	Ratio of PIK to PD.	39
*PSI*7	exog	Ratio of PG to PD.	40
*PSI*8	exog	Ratio of PS to PD.	41
*PSI*9	exog	Ratio of PIV to PD.	42
*PSI*10	exog	Ratio of WG to WF.	44
*PSI*11	exog	Ratio of WM to WF.	45
*PSI*12	exog	Ratio of WS to WF.	46
*PSI*13	exog	Ratio of gross product of g and s to total employee hours of g and s.	83
*PSI*14	exog	Ratio of PKH to PD.	55
*PSI*15	exog	Ratio of INTGR to INTG.	56
PUG	104	Purchases of goods and services, g, B$.	106
PUS	110	Purchases of goods and services, s, B$.	113
PX	31	Price deflator for total sales.	12, 32, 33, 61, 72, 82, 119
Q	164	Gold and foreign exchange, g, B$.	75,77
QQ	exog	Gold and foreign exchange, g, B2012$.	164
RB	23	Bond rate, percentage points.	29
RECG	105	Net receipts, g, B$.	107
RECS	112	Net receipts, s, B$.	114
RM	24	Mortgage rate, percentage points.	128

Table A.2
(continued)

Variable	Eq.	Description	Used in Equations
RMA	128	After-tax mortgage rate, percentage points.	2, 3, 4
RNT	165	Rental income, h, B$.	64, 68, 69, 115
RNTQ	exog	Rental income, h, B2012$.	165
RS	30	Three-month Treasury bill rate, percentage points.	17, 23, 24, 29, 127
RSA	127	After-tax bill rate, percentage points.	1, 26
SB	72	Financial saving, b, B$.	73
SF	69	Financial saving, f, B$.	70
SG	76	Financial saving, g, B$.	77
SGP	107	NIPA surplus (+) or deficit (−), g, B$.	none
SH	65	Saving, h, B$.	66
SHRPIE	121	Ratio of after-tax profits to the wage bill net of employer social security taxes.	none
SIFG	54	Employer social insurance contributions, f to g, B$.	67, 68, 76, 103
SIFS	exog	Employer social insurance contributions, f to s, B$.	67, 68, 78, 109
SIG	103	Total employer and employee social insurance contributions to g, B$.	105
SIGG	exog	Employer social insurance contributions, g to g, B$.	64, 76, 103, 115, 126
SIHG	53	Employee social insurance contributions, h to g, B$.	65, 76, 103, 115
SIHS	exog	Employee social insurance contributions, h to s, B$.	65, 78, 109, 115
SIS	109	Total employer and employee social insurance contributions to s, B$.	112
SISS	exog	Employer social insurance contributions, s to s, B$.	64, 78, 109, 115, 126
SR	74	Financial saving, r, B$.	75
SRZ	116	Approximate NIPA saving rate, h.	none
SS	78	Financial saving, s, B$.	79
SSP	114	NIPA surplus (+) or deficit (−), s, B$.	none
STAT	exog	Statistical discrepancy, B$.	68, 69, 80

Table A.2
(continued)

Variable	Eq.	Description	Used in Equations
STATP	exog	Statistical discrepancy relating to the use of chain type price indices, B2012$.	83
SUBG	exog	Subsidies less current surplus of government enterprises, g, B$.	68, 69, 76, 106
SUBS	exog	Subsidies less current surplus of government enterprises, s, B$.	68, 69, 78, 113
T	exog	1 in 1952:1, 2 in 1952:2, etc.	3, 4, 6, 10, 14, 16
TBL2	exog	Time-varying time trend, 1971.3–1989.4.	6
TFR	exog	Taxes, f to r, B$.	18, 74, 101
TBG	166	Corporate profit taxes, b to g, B$.	68, 69, 76, 102
TBGQ	exog	Corporate profit taxes, b to g, B2012$.	166
TBS	exog	Corporate profit taxes, b to s, B$.	68, 69, 78, 108
TCG	102	Corporate profit tax receipts, g, B$.	105
TCS	108	Corporate profit tax receipts, s, B$.	112
*TF*1	101	Corporate profit tax payments, F1, B$.	69
TFG	49	Corporate profit taxes, f to g, B$.	18, 76, 101, 102
TFS	50	Corporate profit taxes, f to s, B$.	18, 49, 78, 101, 108
*THETA*1	exog	Ratio of *PFA* to *GDPD*.	111
*THETA*2	exog	Ratio of *CDH* to *PCD* · *CD*.	96
*THETA*3	exog	Ratio of *NICD* to *PCD* · *CD*.	97
*THETA*4	exog	Ratio of *PIEFRET* to *PIEF*.	132
THG	47	Personal income taxes, h to g, B$.	65, 76, 101, 115
THS	48	Personal income taxes, h to s, B$.	65, 78, 105, 112, 115
TRFG	exog	Transfer payments, f to g, B$.	68, 69, 76, 105
TRFH	exog	Transfer payments, f to h, B$.	64, 68, 69, 115
TRFR	exog	Transfer payments, f to r, B$.	68, 69, 74
*TRRG*2	exog	Taxes, r to g, B$.	74, 80
TRFS	exog	Transfer payments, f to s, B$.	68, 69, 78, 112
TRGH	167	Transfer payments (net), g to h, B$.	65, 76, 106, 115
TRGHQ	exog	Transfer payments (net), g to h, B2012$.	167
TRGR	exog	Transfer payments (net), g to r, B$.	74, 76, 106
TRGS	168	Transfer payments, g to s, B$.	76, 78, 106, 112

Table A.2
(continued)

Variable	Eq.	Description	Used in Equations
TRGSQ	exog	Transfer payments, g to s, B2012$.	168
TRHR	exog	Transfer payments, h to r, B$.	65, 74, 115
TRRS	exog	Transfer payments, r to s, B$.	74, 78
TRSH	169	Transfer payments, s to h, excluding unemployment insurance benefits, B$.	65, 78, 111, 115
TRSHQ	exog	Transfer payments, s to h, excluding unemployment insurance benefits, B2012$.	169
TTRRF	exog	Transfer payments and taxes, r to f, B$	68, 69, 74
U	86	Number of people unemployed, millions.	28, 87
UB	28	Unemployment insurance benefits, B$.	65, 78, 111, 115
UR	87	Civilian unemployment rate.	5, 6, 7, 8, 10, 30
USOTHER	exog	Net receipts of factor income from the rest of the world not counting net interest receipts, net dividend receipts, and foreign earnings retained abroad, B$.	57, 68, 69
USROW	57	Net receipts of factor income from the rest of the world, B$.	74, 129, 130
V	63	Stock of inventories, f, B2012$.	11, 82, 117
WA	126	After-tax wage rate. (Includes supplements to wages and salaries except employer contributions for social insurance.)	7
WF	16	Average hourly earnings excluding overtime of workers in f. (Includes supplements to wages and salaries except employer contributions for social insurance.)	10, 11, 28, 43, 44, 45, 46, 53, 54, 64, 68, 69, 121, 126
WG	44	Average hourly earnings of civilian workers in g. (Includes supplements to wages and salaries including employer contributions for social insurance.)	43, 64, 76, 82, 104, 115, 126

Table A.2
(continued)

Variable	Eq.	Description	Used in Equations
WH	43	Average hourly earnings excluding overtime of all workers. (Includes supplements to wages and salaries except employer contributions for social insurance.)	none
WM	45	Average hourly earnings of military workers. (Includes supplements to wages and salaries including employer contributions for social insurance.)	43, 64, 76, 82, 104, 115, 126
WR	119	Real wage rate of workers in f. (Includes supplements to wages and salaries except employer contributions for social insurance.)	none
WS	46	Average hourly earnings of workers in s. (Includes supplements to wages and salaries including employer contributions for social insurance.)	43, 64, 78, 82, 110, 115, 126
X	60	Total sales, B2012$.	11, 17, 26, 31, 33, 63
XX	61	Total sales, B$.	68, 69, 82
Y	11	Total production, B2012$.	10, 12, 13, 14, 27, 63, 83, 93, 94, 118
YD	115	Disposable income, h, B$.	1, 2, 3, 4, 116
YS	exog	Potential output, B2012$.	12
YT	64	Taxable income, h, B$.	47, 48, 65

• B$ = Billions of dollars.
• B2012$ = Billions of 2012 dollars.

Table A.3
The Equations of the US Model

Stochastic Equations		
Eq.	LHS Variable	Explanatory Variables
Household Sector		
1	$\log(CS/POP)$	$cnst2cs$, $cnst$, $AG1$, $AG2$, $AG3$, $\log(CS/POP)_{-1}$, $\log[YD/(POP \cdot PH)]$, RSA, $\log(AA/POP)_{-1}$, $D20201$, $D20202$, $D20203$, $D20204$, $D20211$, $D20212$, $D20213$, $D20214$, $RHO=1$ [Consumer expenditures: services]
2	$\log(CN/POP)$	$cnst$, $AG1$, $AG2$, $AG3$, $\log(CN/POP)_{-1}$, $\log(AA/POP)_{-1}$, $\log[YD/(POP \cdot PH)]$, RMA, $D20201$, $D20202$, $D20203$, $D20204$, $D20211$, $D20212$, $D20213$, $D20214$,$RHO=1$ [Consumer expenditures: nondurables]
3	$\log(CD/POP)$	$cnst$, $AG1$, $AG2$, $AG3$, $\log(CD/POP)_{-1}$, $\log[YD/(POP \cdot PH)]$, RMA, $\log(AA/POP)_{-1}$, $D20201$, $D20202$, $D20203$, $D20204$, $D20211$, $D20212$, $D20213$, $D20214$ [Consumer expenditures: durables]
4	$\log(IHH/POP)$	$cnst$, $AG1$, $AG2$, $AG3$, $\log(IHH/POP)_{-1}$, $\log[YD/(POP \cdot PH)]$, RMA_{-1}, $D20201$, $D20202$, $D20203$, $D20204$, $D20211$, $D20212$, $D20213$, $D20214$, $RHO=1$ [Residential investment–h]
5	$\log(L1/POP1)$	$cnst$, $\log(L1/POP1)_{-1}$, $\log(AA/POP)_{-1}$, UR, $D20201$, $D20202$, $D20203$, $D20204$, $D20211$, $D20212$, $D20213$, $D20214$ [Labor force–men 25–54]
6	$\log(L2/POP2)$	$cnst2l2$, $cnst$, $TBL2$, T, $\log(L2/POP2)_{-1}$, $\log(AA/POP)_{-1}$, UR, $D20201$, $D20202$, $D20203$, $D20204$, $D20211$, $D20212$, $D20213$, $D20214$ [Labor force–women 25–54]
7	$\log(L3/POP3)$	$cnst$, $\log(L3/POP3)_{-1})$, $\log(WA/PH)$, $\log(AA/POP)_{-1}$, UR, $D20201$, $D20202$, $D20203$, $D20204$, $D20211$, $D20212$, $D20213$, $D20214$ [Labor force–all others 16+]
8	$\log(LM/POP)$	$cnst$, $\log(LM/POP)_{-1}$, UR, $D20201$, $D20202$, $D20203$, $D20204$, $D20211$, $D20212$, $D20213$, $D20214$ [Number of moonlighters]
Firm Sector		
10	$\log PF$	$\log PF_{-1}$, $\log[WF(1+D5G)/LAM]$, $cnst$, T, $\log PIM$, $1/UR$, $D20201$, $D20202$, $D20203$, $D20204$, $D20211$, $D20212$, $D20213$, $D20214$, $RHO=1$ [Price deflator for nonfarm sales]

Table A.3
(continued)

Stochastic Equations		
Eq.	LHS Variable	Explanatory Variables
11	$\log Y$	$cnst$, $\log Y_{-1}$, $\log X$, $\log V_{-1}$, $D593$, $D594$, $D601$, $D20201$, $D20202$, $D20203$, $D20204$, $D20211$, $D20212$, $D20213$, $D20214$, $RHO = 3$ [Production–f]
12	$\Delta \log KK$	$cnst2kk$, $cnst$, $\log(KK/KKMIN)_{-1}$, $\Delta \log KK_{-1}$, $\Delta \log Y$, $\Delta \log Y_{-1}$, $\Delta \log Y_{-2}$, $\Delta \log Y_{-3}$, $\Delta \log Y_{-4}$, $\Delta \log Y_{-5}$, $(CG_{-2} + CG_{-3} + CG_{-4})/(PX_{-2}YS_{-2} + PX_{-3}YS_{-3} + PX_{-4}YS_{-4})$, $D20201$, $D20202$, $D20203$, $D20204$, $D20211$, $D20212$, $D20213$, $D20214$ [Stock of capital–f]
13	$\Delta \log JF$	$cnst$, $\log[JF/(JHMIN/HFS)]_{-1}$, $\Delta \log JF_{-1}$, $\Delta \log Y$, $D593$, $D20201$, $D20202$, $D20203$, $D20204$, $D20211$, $D20212$, $D20213$, $D20214$ [Number of jobs–f]
14	$\Delta \log HF$	$cnst$, $\log(HF/HFS)_{-1}$, $\log[JF/(JHMIN/HFS)]_{-1}$, $\Delta \log Y$, T, $D20201$, $D20202$, $D20203$, $D20204$, $D20211$, $D20212$, $D20213$, $D20214$ [Average number of hours paid per job–f]
15	$\log HO$	$cnst$, HFF, HFF_{-1}, $D20201$, $D20202$, $D20203$, $D20204$, $D20211$, $D20212$, $D20213$, $D20214$, $RHO = 1$ [Average number of overtime hours paid per job–f]
16	$\log(WF/LAM)$	$\log(WF/LAM)_{-1}$, $\log PF$, $cnst$, $D20201$, $D20202$, $\log PF_{-1}$, $D20201$, $D20202$, $D20203$, $D20204$, $D20211$, $D20212$, $D20213$, $D20214$ [Average hourly earnings excluding overtime–f]
17	$\log(MF/PF)$	$cnst$, T, $\log(MF/PF)_{-1}$, $\log(X - FA)$, $RS(1 - D2G - D2S)$, $D20201$, $D20202$, $D20203$, $D20204$, $D20211$, $D20212$, $D20213$, $D20214$ [Demand deposits and currency–f]
18	$\Delta \log DF$	$\log[(PIEF - TFG - TFS - TFR)/DF_{-1}]$, $D20201$, $D20202$, $D20203$, $D20204$, $D20211$, $D20212$, $D20213$, $D20214$ [Dividends paid–f]
Financial Sector		
23	$RB - RS_{-2}$	$cnst$, $RB_{-1} - RS_{-2}$, $RS - RS_{-2}$, $RS_{-1} - RS_{-2}$, $D20201$, $D20202$, $D20203$, $D20204$, $D20211$, $D20212$, $D20213$, $D20214$, $RHO = 1$ [Bond rate]
24	$RM - RS_{-2}$	$cnst$, $RM_{-1} - RS_{-2}$, $RS - RS_{-2}$, $RS_{-1} - RS_{-2}$, $D20201$, $D20202$, $D20203$, $D20204$, $D20211$, $D20212$, $D20213$, $D20214$ [Mortgage rate]

Table A.3
(continued)

Stochastic Equations		
Eq.	LHS Variable	Explanatory Variables
26	$\log[CUR/(POP\cdot PF)]$	$cnst$, $\log[CUR/(POP\cdot PF)]_{-1}$, $\log[(X-FA)/POP]$, RSA, $D20201$, $D20202$, $D20203$, $D20204$, $D20211$, $D20212$, $D20213$, $D20214$ [Currency held outside banks]
Import Equation		
27	$\log(IM/POP)$	$cnst$, $AG1$, $AG2$, $AG3$, $\log(IM/POP)_{-1}$, $\log[Y/(POP\cdot PH)]$, $\log(AA/POP)_{-1}$, $\log(PF/PIM)$, T, $D691$, $D692$, $D714$, $D721$, $D20201$, $D20202$, $D20203$, $D20204$, $D20211$, $D20212$, $D20213$, $D20214$ [Imports]
Government Sectors		
28	$\log UB$	$cnst$, $\log UB_{-1}$, $\log U$, $\log WF$, $RHO=1$ [Unemployment insurance benefits]
29	$INTG/(-AG)$	$cnst$, $[INTG/(-AG)]_{-1}$, $(1/400)[.4RS+.75(.6)(1/8)(RB+RB_{-1}+RB_{-2}+RB_{-3}+RB_{-4}+RB_{-5}+RB_{-6}+RB_{-7})]$, $D20201$, $D20202$, $D20203$, $D20204$, $D20211$, $D20212$, $D20213$, $D20214$, $RHO=1$ [Net interest payments–g]
30	RS	$cnst$, RS_{-1}, $100[(PD/PD_{-1})^4-1]$, UR, ΔUR, $D20083\cdot PCM1_{-1}$, $D794823\cdot PCM1_{-1}$, ΔRS_{-1}, ΔRS_{-2} [Three-month Treasury bill rate]

Identities		
Eq.	LHS Variable	Explanatory Variables
31	$PX=$	$[PF(X-FA)+PFA\cdot FA]/X$ [Price deflator for total sales]
32	$PEX=$	$PSI1\cdot PX$ [Price deflator for EX]
33	$PD=$	$(PX\cdot X-PEX\cdot EX+PIM\cdot IM)/(X-EX+IM)$ [Price deflator for domestic sales]
34	$PH=$	$(PCS\cdot CS+PCN\cdot CN+PCD\cdot CD+PIH\cdot IHH+IBTG+IBTS)/(CS+CN+CD+IHH)$ [Price deflator for (CS + CN + CD + IHH) inclusive of indirect business taxes]
35	$PCS=$	$PSI2(1+D3G+D3S)PD$ [Price deflator for CS]
36	$PCN=$	$PSI3(1+D3G+D3S)PD$ [Price deflator for CN]
37	$PCD=$	$PSI4(1+D3G+D3S)PD$ [Price deflator for CD]

Table A.3
(continued)

Identities

Eq.	LHS Variable	Explanatory Variables
38	$PIH =$	$PSI5 \cdot PD$ [Price deflator for residential investment]
39	$PIK =$	$PSI6 \cdot PD$ [Price deflator for nonresidential fixed investment]
40	$PG =$	$PSI7 \cdot PD$ [Price deflator for COG]
41	$PS =$	$PSI8 \cdot PD$ [Price deflator for COS]
42	$PIV =$	$PSI9 \cdot PD$ [Price deflator for inventory investment]
43	$WH =$	$100[(WF \cdot JF(HN + 1.5HO) + WG \cdot JG \cdot HG + WM \cdot JM \cdot HM + WS \cdot JS \cdot HS)/(JF(HN + 1.5HO) + JG \cdot HG + JM \cdot HM + JS \cdot HS)]$ [Average hourly earnings excluding overtime of all workers]
44	$WG =$	$PSI10 \cdot WF$ [Average hourly earnings of civilian workers–g]
45	$WM =$	$PSI11 \cdot WF$ [Average hourly earnings of military workers]
46	$WS =$	$PSI12 \cdot WF$ [Average hourly earnings of workers–s]
47	$THG =$	$D1G \cdot YT$ [Personal income taxes–h to g]
48	$THS =$	$D1S \cdot YT$ [Personal income taxes–h to s]
49	$TFG =$	$D2G(PIEF - TFS)$ [Corporate profits taxes–f to g]
50	$TFS =$	$D2S \cdot PIEF$ [Corporate profits taxes–f to s]
51	$IBTG =$	$[D3G/(1 + D3G)](PCS \cdot CS + PCN \cdot CN + PCD \cdot CD - IBTS)$ [Indirect business taxes–g]
52	$IBTS =$	$[D3S/(1 + D3S)](PCS \cdot CS + PCN \cdot CN + PCD \cdot CD - IBTG)$ [Indirect business taxes–s]
53	$SIHG =$	$D4G[WF \cdot JF(HN + 1.5HO)]$ [Employee social insurance contributions–h to g]
54	$SIFG =$	$D5G[WF \cdot JF(HN + 1.5HO)]$ [Employer social insurance contributions–f to g]
55	$PKH =$	$PSI14 \cdot PD$ [Market price of *KH*]

Table A.3
(continued)

Identities		
Eq.	LHS Variable	Explanatory Variables
56	$INTGR =$	$PSI15 \cdot INTG$ [Net interest payments, g to r]
57	$USROW =$	$-INTGR + DR + PIEFRET + USOTHER$ [Net receipts of factor income from the rest of the world]
58	$KD =$	$(1 - DELD)KD_{-1} + CD$ [Stock of durable goods]
59	$KH =$	$(1 - DELH)KH_{-1} + IHH$ [Stock of housing–h]
60	$X =$	$CS + CN + CD + IHH + IKF + EX - IM + COG + COS + IKH + IKB + IKG + IHF + IHB$ [Total real sales]
61	$XX =$	$PCS \cdot CS + PCN \cdot CN + PCD \cdot CD + PIH \cdot IHH + PIK \cdot IKF + PEX \cdot EX - PIM \cdot IM + PG \cdot COG + PS \cdot COS + PIK(IKH + IKB + IKG) + PIH(IHF + IHB) - IBTG - IBTS$ [Total nominal sales]
62	$HN =$	$HF - HO$ [Average number of non overtime hours paid per job–f]
63	$V =$	$V_{-1} + Y - X$ [Stock of inventories–f]
64	$YT =$	$WF \cdot JF(HN + 1.5HO) + WG \cdot JG \cdot HG + WM \cdot JM \cdot HM + WS \cdot JS \cdot HS + RNT + INTZ + INTF + INTG - INTGR + INTS + DF + DB + DR + DG + DS + TRFH - TRHR - SIGG - SISS$ [Taxable income–h]
65	$SH =$	$YT - SIHG - SIHS - THG - THS - PCS \cdot CS - PCN \cdot CN - PCD \cdot CD + TRGH + TRSH + UB + INS + NICD + CCH - CTH - PIH \cdot IHH - CDH - PIK \cdot IKH - NNH$ [Financial saving–h]
66	$0 =$	$SH - \Delta AH - \Delta MH + CG - DISH$ [Budget constraint–h; (determines AH)]
67	$CCF1 =$	$D6G(PIK \cdot IKF + PIK_{-1} \cdot IKF_{-1} + PIK_{-2} \cdot IKF_{-2} + PIK_{-3} \cdot IKF_{-3})/4$ [Capital consumption, F1]
68	$PIEF =$	$XX + PIV \cdot IVF + SUBS + SUBG + USOTHER - WF \cdot JF(HN + 1.5HO) - RNT - INTZ - INTF - TRFH - NICD - CCH + CDH - TBS - TRFS - CCS - TRFR - DB - GSB - CTGB - GSMA - GSCA - TBG - TRFG - CCG - SIFG - SIFS - GSNN - IVA - CCF1 - STAT + TTRRF$ [Before-tax profits–f]

Table A.3
(continued)

Identities		
Eq.	LHS Variable	Explanatory Variables
69	$SF =$	$XX + SUBS + SUBG + PIEFRET + USOTHER - WF \cdot JF(HN + 1.5HO) - RNT - INTZ - INTF - TRFH - NICD - CCH + CDH - TBS - TRFS - CCS - TRFR - DB - GSB - CTGB - GSMA - GSCA - TBG - TRFG - CCG - SIFG - SIFS - STAT - DF - TF1 - PIK \cdot IKF - PIH \cdot IHF - NNF - CTF1 - CTNN + TTRRF$ [Financial saving–f]
70	$0 =$	$SF - \Delta AF - \Delta MF - DISF$ [Budget constraint–f; (determines AF)]
71	$0 =$	$\Delta MB + \Delta MH + \Delta MF + \Delta MR + \Delta MG + \Delta MS - \Delta CUR$ [Demand deposit identity; (determines MB)]
72	$SB =$	$GSB - CTB - PIH \cdot IHB - PIK \cdot IKB$ [Financial saving–b]
73	$0 =$	$SB - \Delta AB - \Delta MB - \Delta(BR - BO) - DISB$ [Budget constraint–b; (determines AB)]
74	$SR =$	$-PEX \cdot EX - USROW + PIM \cdot IM + TFR + TRFR + TRHR + TRGR - CTR - NNR - TRRS - TRRG2 - TTRRF$ [Financial saving–r]
75	$0 =$	$SR - \Delta AR - \Delta MR + \Delta Q - DISR$ [Budget constraint–r; (determines AR)]
76	$SG =$	$GSMA + GSCA + THG + IBTG + TBG + TFG + SIHG + SIFG - DG + TRFG - PG \cdot COG - WG \cdot JG \cdot HG - WM \cdot JM \cdot HM - TRGH - UB - TRGR - TRGS - INTG - SUBG + CCG - INS - CTGMB - NNG - PIK \cdot IKG + SIGG + CTGB$ [Financial saving–g]
77	$0 =$	$SG - \Delta AG - \Delta MG + \Delta CUR + \Delta(BR - BO) - \Delta Q - DISG$ [Budget constraint–g; (determines AG unless AG is exogenous)]
78	$SS =$	$THS + IBTS + TBS + TFS + SIHS + SIFS - DS + TRGS + TRFS - PS \cdot COS - WS \cdot JS \cdot HS - TRSH - INTS - SUBS + CCS - CTS - NNS + SISS + TRRS$ [Financial saving–s]
79	$0 =$	$SS - \Delta AS - \Delta MS - DISS$ [Budget constraint–s; (determines AS)]
80	$0 =$	$SH + SF + SB + SR + SG + SS + STAT + TRRG2$ [Redundant equation—for checking]
81	$M1 =$	$M1_{-1} + \Delta MH + \Delta MF + \Delta MR + \Delta MS + MDIF$ [Money supply]
82	$GDP =$	$XX + PIV(V - V_{-1}) + IBTG + IBTS + WG \cdot JG \cdot HG + WM \cdot JM \cdot HM + WS \cdot JS \cdot HS$ [Nominal GDP]

Table A.3
(continued)

Identities		
Eq.	LHS Variable	Explanatory Variables
83	$GDPR =$	$Y + PSI13(JG \cdot HG + JM \cdot HM + JS \cdot HS) + STATP$ [Real GDP]
84	$GDPD =$	$GDP/GDPR$ [GDP price deflator]
85	$E =$	$JF + JG + JM + JS - LM$ [Total employment, civilian and military]
86	$U =$	$L1 + L2 + L3 - E$ [Number of people unemployed]
87	$UR =$	$U/(L1 + L2 + L3 - AFT)$ [Civilian unemployment rate]
88	$AA1 =$	$(AH + MH)/PH$ [Total net financial wealth–h]
89	$AA2 =$	$(PKH \cdot KH)/PH$ [Total net housing wealth–h]
92	$IKF =$	$KK + (1 - DELK)KK_{-1}$ [Nonresidential fixed investment–f]
93	$KKMIN =$	Y/MUH [Amount of capital required to produce Y]
94	$JHMIN =$	Y/LAM [Number of worker hours required to produce Y]
96	$CDH =$	$THETA2 \cdot PCD \cdot CD$ [Capital expenditures, consumer durable goods, h]
97	$NICD =$	$THETA3 \cdot PCD \cdot CD$ [Net investment in consumer durables, h]
100	$HFF =$	$HF - HFS$ [Deviation of *HF* from *HFS*]
101	$TF1 =$	$TFG + TFS + TFR$ [Corporate profit tax payments, F1]
102	$TCG =$	$TFG + TBG$ [Corporate profit tax receipts–g]
103	$SIG =$	$SIHG + SIFG + SIGG$ [Total social insurance contributions to g]
104	$PUG =$	$PG \cdot COG + WG \cdot JG \cdot HG + WM \cdot JM \cdot HM$ [Purchases of goods and services–g]
105	$RECG =$	$THG + TCG + IBTG + SIG + TRFG - DG$ [Net receipts–g]
106	$EXPG =$	$PUG + TRGH + TRGR + TRGS + INTG + SUBG - IGZ + UB$ [Net expenditures–g]

Table A.3
(continued)

Identities

Eq.	LHS Variable	Explanatory Variables
107	$SGP =$	$RECG - EXPG$ [NIPA surplus or deficit–g]
108	$TCS =$	$TFS + TBS$ [Corporate profit tax receipts–s]
109	$SIS =$	$SIHS + SIFS + SISS$ [Total social insurance contributions to s]
110	$PUS =$	$PS \cdot COS + WS \cdot JS \cdot HS$ [Purchases of goods and services–s]
111	$PFA =$	$THETA1 \cdot GDPD$ [Price deflator for farm sales]
112	$RECS =$	$THS + TCS + IBTS + SIS + TRGS + TRFS - DS$ [Net receipts–s]
113	$EXPS =$	$PUS + TRSH + INTS + SUBS - ISZ$ [Net expenditures–s]
114	$SSP =$	$RECS - EXPS$ [NIPA surplus or deficit–s]
115	$YD =$	$WF \cdot JF(HN + 1.5HO) + WG \cdot JG \cdot HG + WM \cdot JM \cdot HM + WS \cdot JS \cdot HS + RNT + INTZ + INTF + INTG - INTGR + INTS + DF + DB + DR + DG + DS + TRFH + TRGH + TRSH + UB - SIHG - SIHS - THG - THS - TRHR - SIGG - SISS$ [Disposable income–h]
116	$SRZ =$	$(YD - PCS \cdot CS - PCN \cdot CN - PCD \cdot CD)/YD$ [Approximate NIPA saving rate–h]
117	$IVF =$	$V - V_{-1}$ [Inventory investment–f]
118	$PROD =$	$Y/(JF \cdot HF)$ [Output per paid for worker hour:"productivity"]
119	$WR =$	WF/PF [Real wage rate of workers in f]
120	POP	$= POP1 + POP2 + POP3$ [Noninstitutional population 16 and over]
121	$SHRPIE =$	$[(1 - D2G - D2S)PIEF]/[WF \cdot JF(HN + 1.5HO)]$ [Ratio of after-tax profits to the wage bill net of employer social security taxes]
122	$PCGDPR =$	$100[(GDPR/GDPR_{-1})^4 - 1]$ [Percentage change in GDPR]
123	$PCGDPD =$	$100[(GDPD/GDPD_{-1})^4 - 1]$ [Percentage change in GDPD]

Table A.3
(continued)

Identities		
Eq.	LHS Variable	Explanatory Variables
124	$PCM1 =$	$100[(M1/M1_{-1})^4 - 1]$ [Percentage change in M1]
126	$WA =$	$100[(1 - D1G - D1S - D4G)[WF \cdot JF(HN + 1.5HO)] + (1 - D1G - D1S)(WG \cdot JG \cdot HG + WM \cdot JM \cdot HM + WS \cdot JS \cdot HS - SIGG - SISS)]/[JF(HN + 1.5HO) + JG \cdot HG + JM \cdot HM + JS \cdot HS]$ [After-tax wage rate]
127	$RSA =$	$RS(1 - D1G - D1S)$ [After-tax three-month Treasury bill rate]
128	$RMA =$	$RM(1 - D1G - D1S)$ [After-tax mortgage rate]
129	$GNP =$	$GDP + USROW$ [Nominal GNP]
130	$GNPR =$	$GDPR + USROW/GDPD$ [Real GNP]
131	$GNPD =$	$GNP/GNPR$ [GNP price deflator]
132	$PIEFRET =$	$THETA4 \cdot PIEF$ [Foreign earnings retained abroad—f]
133	$AA =$	$AA1 + AA2$ [Total net wealth–h]
Nominal Variables		
150	$CCG =$	$GDPD \cdot CCGQ$
151	$CCH =$	$GDPD \cdot CCHQ$
152	$CCS =$	$GDPD \cdot CCSQ$
153	$DB =$	$GDPD \cdot DBQ$
154	$DR =$	$GDPD \cdot DRQ$
155	$GSB =$	$GDPD \cdot GSBQ$
156	$GSNN =$	$GDPD \cdot GSNNQ$
157	$IGZ =$	$GDPD \cdot IGZQ$
158	$INTZ =$	$GDPD \cdot INTZQ$
159	$ISZ =$	$GDPD \cdot ISZQ$
160	$MG =$	$GDPD \cdot MGQ$
161	$MH =$	$GDPD \cdot MHQ$

Table A.3
(continued)

Identities		
Eq.	LHS Variable	Explanatory Variables
162	$MR =$	$GDPD \cdot MRQ$
163	$MS =$	$GDPD \cdot MSQ$
164	$Q =$	$GDPD \cdot QQ$
165	$RNT =$	$GDPD \cdot RNTQ$
166	$TBG =$	$GDPD \cdot TBGQ$
167	$TRGH =$	$GDPD \cdot TRGHQ$
168	$TRGS =$	$GDPD \cdot TRGSQ$
169	$TRSH =$	$GDPD \cdot TRSHQ$

Table A.4
Coefficient Estimates and Test Results for the Stochastic Equations

Table A1: Equation 1
LHS Variable Is log(*CS*/*POP*)

Equation			χ^2 Tests			
RHS Variable	Coef.	*t*-stat.	Test	χ^2	df	*p*-value
cnst2cs	0.05774	6.08	Lags	10.53	3	0.0146
cnst	−0.11738	−3.34	T	0.52	1	0.4730
*AG*1	−0.07410	−2.57				
*AG*2	−0.24226	−6.66				
*AG*3	−0.04431	−0.94				
$\log(CS/POP)_{-1}$	0.82165	21.03				
$\log[YD/(POP \cdot PH)]$	0.10946	2.51				
RSA	−0.00117	−4.80				
$\log(AA/POP)_{-1}$	0.03186	4.78				
*D*20201	−0.02966	−8.00				
*D*20202	−0.15101	−20.40				
*D*20203	0.03342	3.27				
*D*20204	−0.01500	−2.30				
*D*20211	−0.03045	−2.98				
*D*20212	−0.00061	−0.09				
*D*20213	−0.00183	−0.35				
*D*20214	−0.00869	−2.06				
RHO1	0.19587	3.03				
SE	0.00359					
R^2	1.000					

χ^2 (AGE) = 64.30 (df = 3, *p*-value = 0.0000)

Lags test adds $\log(CS/POP)_{-2}$, $\log[YD/(POP \cdot PH)]_{-1}$, and RSA_{-1}.
Estimation period is 1954.1–2023.2.
$T_1 = 1973.4$; $T_2 = 1994.4$.

First-Stage Regressors

cnst2cs, *cnst*, *AG*1, *AG*2, *AG*3, $\log(CS/POP)_{-1}$, $\log(AA/POP)_{-2}$, RSA_{-1}, $cnst2cs_{-1}$, $AG1_{-1}$, $AG2_{-1}$, $AG3_{-1}$, $\log(AA/POP)_{-3}$, $\log(CS/POP)_{-2}$, $\log[(COG + COS)/POP]_{-1}$, $\log[(TRGH+TRSH)/(POP \cdot PH)]_{-1}$, $\log(EX/POP)_{-1}$, $\log POP$, $\log POP_{-1}$, *D*20201, *D*20202, *D*20203, *D*20204, *D*20211, *D*20212, *D*20213, *D*20214, $D20214_{-1}$

Table A2: Equation 2
LHS Variable Is log(CS/POP)

Equation			χ^2 Tests			
RHS Variable	Coef.	t-stat.	Test	χ^2	df	p-value
cnst	−0.22546	−2.62	Lags	6.95	3	0.0736
$AG1$	0.00494	0.24	T	0.02	1	0.8963
$AG2$	−0.11311	−1.96				
$AG3$	0.00446	0.07				
$\log(CN/POP)_{-1}$	0.83507	18.98				
$\log(AA/POP)_{-1}$	0.04918	2.51				
$\log[YD/(POP \cdot PH)]$	0.04663	3.49				
RMA	−0.00109	−2.72				
$D20201$	0.00979	1.50				
$D20202$	−0.04822	−7.04				
$D20203$	0.05533	7.48				
$D20204$	−0.00487	−0.72				
$D20211$	0.02183	3.05				
$D20212$	0.02458	3.60				
$D20213$	0.00374	0.55				
$D20214$	0.00406	0.61				
RHO1	0.23187	3.53				
SE	0.00637					
R^2	0.999					

χ^2 (AGE) = 5.85 (df = 3, p-value = 0.1192)

Lags test adds $\log(CN/POP)_{-2}$, $\log[YD/(POP \cdot PH)]_{-1}$, and RMA_{-1}.
Estimation period is 1954.1–2023.2.

First-Stage Regressors

$cnst$, $AG1$, $AG2$, $AG3$, $\log(CN/POP)_{-1}$, $\log(AA/POP)_{-2}$, $\log[YD/(POP \cdot PH)]_{-1}$, RMA_{-1}, $AG1_{-1}$, $AG2_{-1}$, $AG3_{-1}$, $\log(AA/POP)_{-3}$, $\log(CN/POP)_{-2}$, $\log[(COG + COS)/POP]_{-1}$, $\log[(TRGH + TRSH)/(POP \cdot PH)]_{-1}$, $\log(EX/POP)_{-1}$, $D20201$, $D20202$, $D20203$, $D20204$, $D20211$, $D20212$, $D20213$, $D20214$, $D20214_{-1}$

Table A3: Equation 3

LHS Variable Is $\log(CD/POP)$

Equation			χ^2 Tests			
RHS Variable	Coef.	*t*-stat.	Test	χ^2	df	*p*-value
cnst	−0.48389	−2.04	Lags	6.93	3	0.0742
$AG1$	−0.08633	−1.22	RHO	14.05	1	0.0002
$AG2$	−0.10283	−0.48	T	5.16	1	0.0231
$AG3$	0.20536	0.91				
$\log(CD/POP)_{-1}$	0.90717	31.24				
$\log[YD/(POP \cdot PH)]$	0.14488	2.97				
RMA	−0.00322	−2.40				
$\log(AA/POP)_{-1}$	0.03687	0.97				
$D20201$	−0.04902	−1.67				
$D20202$	−0.03289	−1.10				
$D20203$	0.14328	4.84				
$D20204$	−0.01389	−0.47				
$D20211$	0.05931	2.00				
$D20212$	0.01285	0.44				
$D20213$	−0.07190	−2.42				
$D20214$	−0.00117	−0.04				
SE	0.02864					
R^2	0.999					

χ^2 (AGE) = 1.51 (df = 3, *p*-value = 0.6791)

Lags test adds $\log(CD/POP)_{-2}$, $\log[YD/(POP \cdot PH)]_{-1}$, and RMA_{-1}.
Estimation period is 1954.1–2023.2.

First-Stage Regressors

cnst, $AG1$, $AG2$, $AG3$, $\log(CD/POP)_{-1}$, $\log(AA/POP)_{-2}$, $\log[YD/(POP \cdot PH)]_{-1}$, RMA_{-1}, $\log[(COG+COS)/POP]_{-1}$, $\log[(TRGH+TRSH)/(POP \cdot PH)]_{-1}$, $\log(EX/POP)_{-1}$, T, $D20201$, $D20202$, $D20203$, $D20204$, $D20211$, $D20212$, $D20213$, $D20214$

Table A4: Equation 4
LHS Variable Is log(*IHH*/*POP*)

Equation			χ^2 Tests			
RHS Variable	Coef.	*t*-stat.	Test	χ^2	df	*p*-value
cnst	−1.13917	−2.23	Lags	8.94	3	0.0301
$AG1$	0.70929	1.00	T	0.03	1	0.8533
$AG2$	−5.76579	−3.26				
$AG3$	2.30981	1.19				
$\log(IHH/POP)_{-1}$	0.52439	9.23				
$\log[YD/(POP \cdot PH)]$	0.23067	1.62				
RMA_{-1}	−0.03817	−6.59				
$D20201$	0.04312	1.25				
$D20202$	−0.10445	−2.11				
$D20203$	0.05815	1.09				
$D20204$	0.07003	1.29				
$D20211$	0.02872	0.49				
$D20212$	0.00189	0.04				
$D20213$	0.00012	0.00				
$D20214$	0.00783	0.23				
RHO1	0.91093	28.72				
SE	0.03510					
R^2	0.980					

χ^2 (AGE) = 5.02 (df = 3, *p*-value = 0.1702)

Lags test adds $\log(IHH/POP)_{-2}$, $\log[YD/(POP \cdot PH)]_{-1}$, and RMA_{-2}.
Estimation period is 1954.1–2023.2.

First-Stage Regressors

$cnst$, $\log(IHH/POP)_{-1}$, RMA_{-1}, $\log[YD/(POP \cdot PH)]_{-1}$, $AG1$, $AG2$, $AG3$, $AG1_{-1}$, $AG2_{-1}$, $AG3_{-1}$, $\log(IHH/POP)_{-2}$, RMA_{-2}, $\log[(COG+COS)/POP]_{-1}$, $\log[(TRGH+TRSH)/(POP \cdot PH)]_{-1}$, $\log(EX/POP)_{-1}$, T, $D20201$, $D20202$, $D20203$, $D20204$, $D20211$, $D20212$, $D20213$, $D20214$, $D20214_{-1}$

Table A5: Equation 5

LHS Variable Is $\log(L1/POP1)$

Equation			χ^2 Tests			
RHS Variable	Coef.	*t*-stat.	Test	χ^2	df	*p*-value
cnst	0.02921	3.58	Lags	6.20	2	0.0451
$\log(L1/POP1)_{-1}$	0.90492	35.55	RHO	2.55	1	0.1101
$\log(AA/POP)_{-1}$	−0.00657	−3.58	T	3.83	1	0.0504
UR	−0.05004	−3.52				
$D20201$	0.00225	0.92				
$D20202$	−0.02223	-8.07				
$D20203$	0.01184	4.84				
$D20204$	−0.00092	−0.38				
$D20211$	0.00187	0.77				
$D20212$	0.00497	2.04				
$D20213$	0.00495	2.02				
$D20214$	−0.00005	−0.02				
SE	0.00240					
R^2	0.994					

Lags test adds $\log(L1/POP1)_{-2}$ and UR_{-1}.

Estimation period is 1954.1–2023.2.

First-Stage Regressors

cnst, $\log(L1/POP1)_{-1}$, $\log(AA/POP)_{-2}$, UR_{-1}, $\log[(COG+COS)/POP]_{-1}$, $\log[(TRGH+TRSH)/(POP \cdot PH)]_{-1}$, $\log(EX/POP)_{-1}$, $D20201$, $D20202$, $D20203$, $D20204$, $D20211$, $D20212$, $D20213$, $D20214$

Table A6: Equation 6
LHS Variable Is log(*L2*/*POP2*)

Equation			χ^2 Tests			
RHS Variable	Coef.	*t*-stat.	Test	χ^2	df	*p*-value
cnst2l2	0.09780	5.53	Lags	2.01	2	0.3666
cnst	−0.08147	−1.73	RHO	1.30	1	0.2539
TBL2	−0.00052	−6.01				
T	0.00060	7.07				
$\log(L2/POP2)_{-1}$	0.85000	32.55				
$\log(AA/POP)_{-1}$	−0.01235	−1.61				
UR	−0.14491	−4.46				
D20201	0.00013	0.03				
D20202	−0.01765	−3.19				
D20203	0.00946	1.83				
D20204	0.00167	0.33				
D20211	0.00445	0.87				
D20212	0.00441	0.86				
D20213	0.00410	0.80				
D20214	0.00496	0.98				
SE	0.00491					
R^2	1.000					

Lags test adds $\log(L2/POP2)_{-2}$ and UR_{-1}
Estimation period is 1954.1–2023.2.
$T_1 = 1971.4$; $T_2 = 1989.4$.

First-Stage Regressors

cnst2l2, *cnst*, *TBL2*, *T*, $\log(L2/POP2)_{-1})$, $\log(AA/POP)_{-2}$, UR_{-1}, $\log[(COG + COS)/POP]_{-1}$, $\log[(TRGH + TRSH)/(POP \cdot PH)]_{-1}$, $\log(EX/POP)_{-1}$, *D20201*, *D20202*, *D20203*, *D20204*, *D20211*, *D20212*, *D20213*, *D20214*

Table A7: Equation 7

LHS Variable Is $\log(L3/POP3)$

Equation			χ^2 Tests			
RHS Variable	Coef.	*t*-stat.	Test	χ^2	df	*p*-value
cnst	0.03767	2.02	Lags	3.13	3	0.3713
$\log(L3/POP3)_{-1}$	0.97257	70.63	RHO	4.15	1	0.0415
$\log(WA/PH)$	0.01612	2.18	T	2.06	1	0.1514
$\log(AA/POP)_{-1}$	−0.01207	−2.30	$\log PH$	2.20	1	0.1382
UR	−0.12130	−3.95				
$D20201$	−0.00770	−1.48				
$D20202$	−0.04469	−8.10				
$D20203$	0.02638	5.04				
$D20204$	0.00738	1.42				
$D20211$	−0.01011	−1.93				
$D20212$	0.00661	1.26				
$D20213$	0.00287	0.55				
$D20214$	0.00576	1.10				
SE	0.00512					
R^2	0.989					

Lags test adds $\log(L3/POP3)_{-2}$, $\log(WA/PH)_{-1}$, and UR_{-1}.
Estimation period is 1954.1–2023.2.

First-Stage Regressors

cnst, $\log(L3/POP3)_{-1})$, $\log(AA/POP)_{-2}$, $\log(WA/PH)_{-1}$, UR_{-1}, $\log[(COG + COS)/POP]_{-1}$, $\log[(TRGH + TRSH)/(POP \cdot PH)]_{-1}$, $\log(EX/POP)_{-1}$, *D20201*, *D20202*, *D20203*, *D20204*, *D20211*, *D20212*, *D20213*, *D20214*

Table A8: Equation 8
LHS Variable Is log(LM/POP)

Equation			χ^2 Tests			
RHS Variable	Coef.	*t*-stat.	Test	χ^2	df	*p*-value
cnst	−0.30620	−4.34	Lags	1.07	2	0.5865
log(LM/POP)$_{-1}$	0.89168	39.92	RHO	0.00	1	0.9901
UR	−1.47326	−4.42	T	1.17	1	0.2802
*D*20201	−0.16958	−2.51				
*D*20202	0.39594	5.67				
*D*20203	−0.12685	−1.88				
*D*20204	−0.33893	−5.07				
*D*20211	0.09747	1.44				
*D*20212	0.07786	1.16				
*D*20213	0.02061	0.31				
*D*20214	−0.09655	−1.43				
SE	0.06672					
R^2	0.922					

Lags test adds log(LM/POP)$_{-2}$ and UR_{-1}.
Estimation period is 1954.1–2023.2.

First-Stage Regressors

cnst, log(LM/POP)$_{-1}$, UR_{-1}, log[$(COG + COS)/POP$]$_{-1}$, log[$(TRGH + TRSH)/(POP \cdot PH)$]$_{-1}$, log($EX/POP$)$_{-1}$, *D*20201, *D*20202, *D*20203, *D*20204, *D*20211, *D*20212, *D*20213, *D*20214

Table A10: Equation 10
LHS Variable Is $\log PF$

Equation			χ^2 Tests			
RHS Variable	Coef.	t-stat.	Test	χ^2	df	p-value
$\log PF_{-1}$	0.85948	60.77	Lags	16.37	3	0.0010
$\log[WF(1+D5G)/LAM]$	0.07627	4.88	UR	1.21	1	0.2716
cnst	−0.01418	−1.08	GAP	3.58	1	0.0584
T	0.00021	7.37	$1/(GAP+.07)$	1.57	1	0.2098
$\log PIM$	0.04918	16.46				
$1/UR$	0.00059	6.96				
$D20201$	−0.00649	−1.71				
$D20202$	−0.01230	−2.81				
$D20203$	0.00317	0.75				
$D20204$	0.00068	0.16				
$D20211$	0.00418	1.02				
$D20212$	0.00187	0.46				
$D20213$	0.00760	1.88				
$D20214$	0.00453	1.18				
RHO1	0.25956	4.25				
SE	0.00372					
R^2	1.000					

Lags test adds $\log PF_{-2}$, $\log PIM_{-1}$, and $1/UR_{-1}$.
Estimation period is 1954.1–2023.2.

First-Stage Regressors

$\log PF_{-1}$, $\log[[WF(1+D5G)/LAM]_{-1}$, $cnst$, T, $\log PIM_{-1}$, $1/UR_{-1}$, UR_{-1}, $\log[(COG+COS)/POP]_{-1}$, $\log[(TRGH+TRSH)/(POP{\cdot}PH)]_{-1}$, $\log(EX/POP)_{-1}$, $\log PF_{-2}$, $D20201$, $D20202$, $D20203$, $D20204$, $D20211$, $D20212$, $D20213$, $D20214$

Table A11: Equation 11
LHS Variable Is $\log Y$

Equation			χ^2 Tests			
RHS Variable	Coef.	*t*-stat.	Test	χ^2	df	*p*-value
cnst	0.29989	4.55	Lags	3.67	2	0.1595
$\log Y_{-1}$	0.31759	6.58	T	1.69	1	0.1939
$\log X$	0.85539	15.60				
$\log V_{-1}$	−0.21962	−8.55				
$D593$	−0.00966	−2.61				
$D594$	−0.00375	−1.03				
$D601$	0.00953	2.58				
$D20201$	−0.00640	−1.59				
$D20202$	−0.02745	−4.70				
$D20203$	0.02451	4.21				
$D20204$	0.00222	0.49				
$D20211$	−0.00298	−0.63				
$D20212$	−0.00993	−2.12				
$D20213$	−0.01258	−2.97				
$D20214$	−0.00012	−0.03				
RHO1	0.40195	5.27				
RHO2	0.37467	5.85				
RHO3	0.16696	2.44				
SE	0.00406					
R^2	1.000					

Lags test adds $\log Y_{-2}$ and $\log X_{-1}$.
Estimation period is 1954.1–2023.2.

First-Stage Regressors

cnst, $\log Y_{-1}$, $\log V_{-1}$, $D593$, $D594$, $D601$, $\log Y_{-2}$, $\log Y_{-3}$, $\log Y_{-4}$, $\log V_{-2}$, $\log V_{-3}$, $\log V_{-4}$, $D601_{-1}$, $D601_{-2}$, $D601_{-3}$, $\log[(COG+COS)/POP]_{-1}$, $\log[(TRGH+TRSH)/(POP\cdot PH)]_{-1}$, $\log(EX/POP)_{-1}$, $D20201$, $D20202$, $D20203$, $D20204$, $D20211$, $D20212$, $D20213$, $D20214$, $D20214_{-1}$, $D20214_{-2}$, $D20214_{-3}$

Table A12: Equation 12
LHS Variable Is $\Delta \log KK$

Equation			χ^2 Tests			
RHS Variable	Coef.	t-stat.	Test	χ^2	df	p-value
cnst2kk	−0.00043	−3.82	Lags	5.15	3	0.1614
cnst	0.00094	3.60	T	3.41	1	0.0648
$\log(KK/KKMIN)_{-1}$	−0.00836	−3.43				
$\Delta \log KK_{-1}$	0.87323	42.07				
$\Delta \log Y$	0.01366	1.53				
$\Delta \log Y_{-1}$	0.00867	2.20				
$\Delta \log Y_{-2}$	0.00332	0.82				
$\Delta \log Y_{-3}$	0.00406	1.12				
$\Delta \log Y_{-4}$	0.00686	1.94				
^{a}	0.00074	4.08				
$D20201$	−0.00092	−1.94				
$D20202$	−0.00117	−1.23				
$D20203$	0.00137	1.50				
$D20204$	0.00013	0.20				
$D20211$	−0.00051	−0.84				
$D20212$	−0.00021	−0.35				
$D20213$	−0.00159	−2.97				
$D20214$	−0.00122	−2.67				
RHO1	0.15657	2.27				
SE	0.00043					
R^2	0.977					

^{a}Variable is $(CG_{-2}+CG_{-3}+CG_{-4})/(PX_{-2}YS_{-2}+PX_{-3}YS_{-3}+PX_{-4}YS_{-4})$
Lags test adds $\log(KK/KKMIN)_{-2}$, $\Delta \log Y_{-5}$, and ^{a} lagged once.
Estimation period is 1954.1–2023.2.
$T_1 = 1978.4$; $T_2 = 1987.4$.

First-Stage Regressors

cnst2kk, *cnst*, $\log KK_{-1}$, $\log KK_{-2}$, $\log Y_{-1}$, $\log Y_{-2}$, $\log Y_{-3}$, $\log Y_{-4}$, $\log Y_{-5}$, $\log(KK/KKMIN)_{-1}$, $\Delta \log Y_{-5}$, ^{a} lagged twice, $\log[(COG+COS)/POP]_{-1}$, $\log[(TRGH+TRSH)/(POP\cdot PH)]_{-1}$, $\log(EX/POP)_{-1}$,$\log(KK/KMIN)_{-2}$,$\Delta \log KK_{-2}$, $D20201$, $D20202$, $D20203$, $D20204$, $D20211$, $D20212$, $D20213$, $D20214$, $D20214_{-1}$

Table A13: Equation 13
LHS Variable Is $\Delta \log JF$

Equation			χ^2 Tests			
RHS Variable	Coef.	*t*-stat.	Test	χ^2	df	*p*-value
cnst	0.00082	1.17	Lags	14.87	3	0.0019
$\log JF/(JHMIN/HFS)_{-1}$	−0.05320	−4.50	RHO	2.63	1	0.1045
$\Delta \log JF_{-1}$	0.58951	13.72	T	1.81	1	0.1785
$\Delta \log Y$	0.28270	3.57				
*D*593	−0.01810	−5.30				
*D*20201	−0.00564	−1.55				
*D*20202	−0.09792	−12.32				
*D*20203	0.11085	10.20				
*D*20204	−0.02327	−5.87				
*D*20211	−0.00824	−2.48				
*D*20212	0.00014	0.04				
*D*20213	0.00467	1.39				
*D*20214	−0.00254	−0.77				
SE	0.00322					
R^2	0.911					

Lags test adds $\log JF/(JHMIN/HFS)_{-2}$, $\Delta \log JF_{-2}$, and $\Delta \log Y_{-1}$.
Estimation period is 1954.1–2023.2.

First-Stage Regressors

cnst, $\log[JF/(JHMIN/HFS)]_{-1}$, $\Delta \log JF_{-1}$, $\Delta \log Y_{-1}$, *D*593, $\log[(COG + COS)/POP]_{-1}$, $\log[(TRGH + TRSH)/(POP \cdot PH)]_{-1}$, $\log(EX/POP)_{-1}$, *D*20201, *D*20202, *D*20203, *D*20204, *D*20211, *D*20212, *D*20213, *D*20214

Table A14: Equation 14
LHS Variable Is $\Delta \log HF$

Equation			χ^2 Tests			
RHS Variable	Coef.	*t*-stat.	Test	χ^2	df	*p*-value
cnst	−0.00438	−4.92	Lags	6.61	3	0.0854
$\log(HF/HFS)_{-1}$	−0.12962	−4.66	RHO	1.84	1	0.1745
$\log JF/(JHMIN/HFS)_{-1}$	−0.01405	−1.41				
$\Delta \log Y$	0.26874	4.16				
T	0.00001	4.13				
$D20201$	−0.00157	−0.52				
$D20202$	0.01109	1.68				
$D20203$	−0.00852	−1.51				
$D20204$	0.00313	1.11				
$D20211$	−0.00294	−1.01				
$D20212$	−0.00275	−0.95				
$D20213$	−0.00239	−0.85				
$D20214$	−0.00342	−1.19				
SE	0.00273					
R^2	0.398					

Lags test adds $\log(HF/HFS)_{-2}$, $\log JF/(JHMIN/HFS)_{-2}$, and $\Delta \log Y_{-1}$.
Estimation period is 1954.1–2023.2.

First-Stage Regressors

cnst, $\log(HF/HFS)_{-1}$, $\log[JF/(JHMIN/HFS)]_{-1}$, $\Delta \log Y_{-1}$, T, $\log[(COG+COS)/POP]_{-1}$, $\log[(TRGH+TRSH)/(POP \cdot PH)]_{-1}$, $\log(EX/POP)_{-1}$, *D20201*, *D20202*, *D20203*, *D20204*, *D20211*, *D20212*, *D20213*, *D20214*

Table A15: Equation 15

LHS Variable Is log *HO*

Equation			χ^2 Tests			
RHS Variable	Coef.	*t*-stat.	Test	χ^2	df	*p*-value
cnst	3.93658	46.84	Lags	0.07	1	0.7954
HFF	0.01655	8.39	*T*	3.70	1	0.0545
HFF_{-1}	0.00827	4.19				
D20201	0.01431	0.34				
D20202	−0.12866	−2.20				
D20203	0.01712	0.26				
D20204	−0.01540	−0.23				
D20211	−0.03512	−0.53				
D20212	−0.04670	−0.73				
D20213	−0.06485	−1.16				
D20214	−0.05851	−1.38				
RHO1	0.96722	62.71				
SE	0.04425					
R^2	0.961					

Lags test adds HFF_{-2}.

Estimation period is 1956.1–2023.2.

OLS estimation.

Table A16: Equation 16
LHS Variable Is $\log(WF/LAM)$

Equation			χ^2 Tests			
RHS Variable	Coef.	*t*-stat.	Test	χ^2	df	*p*-value
$\log(WF/LAM)_{-1}$	0.93573	54.28	[b]RealWage Res	5.50	1	0.0190
$\log PF$	0.92099	36.68	Lags	0.02	1	0.8784
cnst	−0.04083	−3.77	T	7.41	1	0.0065
*D*20201	0.02788	3.53	RHO	0.03	1	0.8662
*D*20202	0.08456	10.71	$1/UR$	6.29	1	0.0122
*D*20203	−0.01615	−1.96	$1/(GAP+.07)$	2.64	1	0.1041
*D*20204	0.00337	0.41				
*D*20211	−0.01587	−1.95				
*D*20212	0.01336	1.66				
*D*20213	−0.00228	−0.28				
*D*20214	−0.00073	−0.09				
[a] $\log PF_{-1}$	−0.86221	0.00				
SE	0.00785					
R^2	0.947					

[a]Coefficient constrained. See the discussion in the text.
[b]Equation estimated with no restrictions on the coefficients.
Lags test adds $\log(WF/LAM)_{-2}$.
Estimation period is 1954.1–2023.2.

First-Stage Regressors

$cnst$, T, $\log WF_{-1} - \log LAM_{-1} - \log PF_{-1}$, $\log PF_{-1}$, $\log PF_{-2}$, $\log PIM_{-1}$, $\log[(COG+COS)/POP]_{-1}$, $\log[(TRGH+TRSH)/(POP \cdot PH)]_{-1}$, $\log(EX/POP)_{-1}$, $1/UR_{-1}$, UR_{-1}, *D*20201, *D*20202, *D*20203, *D*20204, *D*20211, *D*20212, *D*20213, *D*20214

Table A17: Equation 17
LHS Variable Is $\log(MF/PF)$

Equation			χ^2 Tests			
RHS Variable	Coef.	t-stat.	Test	χ^2	df	p-value
cnst	0.04187	0.87	$\log(MF_{-1}/PF)$	1.22	1	0.2690
$\log(MF/PF)_{-1}$	0.97796	92.20	Lags	6.67	3	0.0830
$\log(X-FA)$	0.01519	2.39	RHO	1.29	1	0.2560
$RS(1-D2G-D2S)$	−0.00502	−3.18	T	8.13	1	0.0044
$D20201$	0.19143	4.21				
$D20202$	0.16598	3.62				
$D20203$	−0.05346	−1.16				
$D20204$	−0.04510	−0.98				
$D20211$	0.01761	0.38				
$D20212$	0.00083	0.02				
$D20213$	0.03357	0.73				
$D20214$	0.03288	0.71				
SE	0.04465					
R^2	0.992					

Lags test adds $\log(MF/PF)_{-2}$, $\log(X-FA)_{-1}$, and $RS(1-D2G-D2S)_{-1}$.
Estimation period is 1954.1–2023.2.

First-Stage Regressors

cnst, $\log(MF/PF)_{-1}$, $\log(X-FA)_{-1}$, $RS(1-D2G-D2S)_{-1}$, $\log[(COG+COS)/POP]_{-1}$, $\log[(TRGH+TRSH)/(POP\cdot PH)]_{-1}$, $\log(EX/POP)_{-1}$, $\log(MF_{-2}/PF_{-1})$, $D20201$, $D20202$, $D20203$, $D20204$, $D20211$, $D20212$, $D20213$, $D20214$

Table A18: Equation 18
LHS Variable Is $\Delta \log DF$

Equation			χ^2 Tests			
RHS Variable	Coef.	*t*-stat.	Test	χ^2	df	*p*-value
[a]	0.02342	3.74	[b]Restriction	0.11	1	0.7427
*D*20201	0.12679	1.56	Lags	0.78	1	0.3762
*D*20202	−0.11292	−1.39	RHO	0.85	1	0.3565
*D*20203	0.12617	1.55	*T*	0.00	1	0.9981
*D*20204	−0.03468	−0.43	cnst	0.14	1	0.7096
*D*20211	0.06341	0.78				
*D*20212	0.07981	0.98				
*D*20213	−0.08404	−1.03				
*D*20214	0.10650	1.31				
SE	0.08114					
R^2	0.062					

[a]Variable is $\log[(PIEF - TFG - TFS - TFR)/DF_{-1}]$
[b]$\log DF_{-1}$ added.
Lags test adds [a] lagged once.
Estimation period is 1954.1–2023.2.

First-Stage Regressors

cnst, $\log[(PIEF{-}TFG{-}TFS)/DF_{-1}]_{-1}$, $\log[(COG{+}COS)/POP]_{-1}$, $\log[(TRGH{+}TRSH)/(POP \cdot PH)]_{-1}$, $\log(EX/POP)_{-1}$ *D*20201, *D*20202, *D*20203, *D*20204, *D*20211, *D*20212, *D*20213, *D*20214

Table A23: Equation 23

LHS Variable Is $RB - RS_{-2}$

Equation			χ^2 Tests			
RHS Variable	Coef.	*t*-stat.	Test	χ^2	df	*p*-value
cnst	0.19660	4.54	[a]Restriction	0.06	1	0.8099
$RB_{-1} - RS_{-2}$	0.91834	57.85	Lags	0.42	2	0.8105
$RS - RS_{-2}$	0.32027	4.93	T	2.50	1	0.1138
$RS_{-1} - RS_{-2}$	−0.26142	−3.51	[b]	0.75	1	0.3854
*D*20201	−0.03960	−0.14	[c]	0.50	1	0.4787
*D*20202	−0.20465	−0.70				
*D*20203	−0.24300	−0.85				
*D*20204	0.05216	0.18				
*D*20211	0.42309	1.49				
*D*20212	0.17777	0.62				
*D*20213	−0.32446	−1.14				
*D*20214	0.00161	0.01				
RHO1	0.20616	3.26				
SE	0.27749					
R^2	0.962					

[a]RS_{-2} added.
[b]$100 \cdot (PD/PD(-4) - 1)$
[c]$100 \cdot [(PD/PD(-8))^{.5} - 1]$
Lags test adds RS_{-3} and RB_{-2}.
Estimation period is 1954.1–2023.2.

First-Stage Regressors

$cnst$, RB_{-1}, RB_{-2}, RS_{-1}, RS_{-2}, RS_{-3}, $100[(PD/PD_{-1})^4 - 1]_{-1}$, UR_{-1}, $\log(PIM/PF)_{-1}$, $\log[(COG + COS)/POP]_{-1}$, $\log[(TRGH + TRSH)/(POP \cdot PH)]_{-1}$, $\log(EX/POP)_{-1}$, T, *D*20201, *D*20202, *D*20203, *D*20204, *D*20211, *D*20212, *D*20213, *D*20214, $D20214_{-1}$

Table A24: Equation 24

LHS Variable Is $RM - RS_{-2}$

Equation			χ^2 Tests			
RHS Variable	Coef.	t-stat.	Test	χ^2	df	p-value
cnst	0.38677	5.54	[a]Restriction	0.12	1	0.7254
$RM_{-1} - RS_{-2}$	0.87750	41.75	Lags	0.60	2	0.7397
$RS - RS_{-2}$	0.37969	3.92	RHO	2.04	1	0.1532
$RS_{-1} - RS_{-2}$	−0.19275	−1.54	T	1.66	1	0.1975
$D20201$	−0.11308	−0.31	[b]	1.34	1	0.2470
$D20202$	0.02473	0.07	[c]	1.09	1	0.2957
$D20203$	−0.21791	−0.59				
$D20204$	−0.21976	−0.60				
$D20211$	0.07430	0.20				
$D20212$	0.09447	0.26				
$D20213$	−0.15864	−0.44				
$D20214$	0.16526	0.45				
SE	0.36338					
R^2	0.899					

[a] RS_{-2} added.

[b] $100 \cdot (PD/PD(-4) - 1)$

[c] $100 \cdot [(PD/PD(-8))^{.5} - 1]$

Lags test adds RS_{-3} and RM_{-2}.

Estimation period is 1954.1–2023.2.

First-Stage Regressors

$cnst$, RM_{-1}, RS_{-1}, $100[(PD/PD_{-1})^4 - 1]_{-1}$, UR_{-1}, $\log(PIM/PF)_{-1}$, $\log[(COG + COS)/POP]_{-1}$, $\log[(TRGH + TRSH)/(POP \cdot PH)]_{-1}$, $\log(EX/POP)_{-1}$, T, $D20201$, $D20202$, $D20203$, $D20204$, $D20211$, $D20212$, $D20213$, $D20214$

Table A26: Equation 26
LHS Variable Is $\log[CUR/(POP \cdot PF)]$

Equation			χ^2 Tests			
RHS Variable	Coef.	*t*-stat.	Test	χ^2	df	*p*-value
cnst	−0.05391	−7.10	$\log(CUR_{-1}/(POP_{-1}PF)$	2.07	1	0.1501
$\log[CUR/(POP \cdot PF)]_{-1}$	0.96732	187.17				
$\log[(X - FA)/POP]$	0.04278	7.66	Lags	10.00	3	0.0186
RSA	−0.00244	−5.90	RHO	0.62	1	0.4317
*D*20201	0.02583	2.48	*T*	10.20	1	0.0014
*D*20202	0.06335	6.07				
*D*20203	0.02217	2.12				
*D*20204	0.00945	0.90				
*D*20211	0.01345	1.29				
*D*20212	0.00673	0.65				
*D*20213	−0.01336	−1.28				
*D*20214	−0.00804	−0.77				
SE	0.01026					
R^2	1.000					

Lags test adds $\log[CUR/(POP \cdot PF)]_{-2}$, $\log[(X - FA)/POP]_{-1}$, and RSA_{-1}.
Estimation period is 1954.1–2023.2.

First-Stage Regressors

cnst, $\log[CUR/(POP \cdot PF)]_{-1}$, $\log[(X - FA)/POP]_{-1}$, RSA_{-1}, $\log[CUR_{-2}/(POP_{-2} \cdot PF_{-1})]$, $\log[(COG + COS)/POP]_{-1}$, $\log[(TRGH + TRSH)/(POP \cdot PH)]_{-1}$, $\log(EX/POP)_{-1}$, *D*20201, *D*20202, *D*20203, *D*20204, *D*20211, *D*20212, *D*20213, *D*20214

Table A27: Equation 27
LHS Variable Is log(IM/POP)

Equation			χ^2 Tests			
RHS Variable	Coef.	*t*-stat.	Test	χ^2	df	*p*-value
cnst	−1.28726	−4.57	Lags	24.69	3	0.0000
$AG1$	0.51852	4.06	RHO	39.22	1	0.0000
$AG2$	0.26326	1.02	logPF	3.46	1	0.0629
$AG3$	−1.12203	−3.79				
log(IM/POP)$_{-1}$	0.77187	21.42				
log(Y/POP)	0.39378	3.48				
log(AA/POP)$_{-1}$	0.00786	0.20				
log(PF/PIM)	0.06400	2.84				
T	0.00098	2.11				
$D691$	−0.12000	−4.43				
$D692$	0.13659	4.99				
$D714$	−0.07140	−2.60				
$D721$	0.11142	4.08				
$D20201$	−0.03674	−1.34				
$D20202$	−0.17503	−5.98				
$D20203$	0.09836	3.40				
$D20204$	0.04561	1.64				
$D20211$	0.00358	0.13				
$D20212$	0.00327	0.12				
$D20213$	0.00353	0.12				
$D20214$	0.02770	0.98				
SE	0.02665					
R^2	0.999					
χ^2 (AGE) = 23.15 (df = 3, *p*-value = 0.0000)						

Lags test adds log(IM/POP)$_{-2}$, log(Y/POP)$_{-1}$, and log(PF/PIM)$_{-1}$.
Estimation period is 1954.1–2023.2.

First-Stage Regressors

cnst, log(IM/POP)$_{-1}$, log(AA/POP)$_{-2}$, log(Y/POP)$_{-1}$, log(PF/PIM)$_{-1}$, $D691$, $D692$, $D714$, $D721$, $AG1$, $AG2$, $AG3$, log[($COG+COS$)/POP]$_{-1}$, log[($TRGH+TRSH$)/($POP\cdot PH$)]$_{-1}$, log(EX/POP)$_{-1}$, T, logPOP, logPOP_{-1}, logPIM_{-1}, log(IM/POP))−2, $D20201$, $D20202$, $D20203$, $D20204$, $D20211$, $D20212$, $D20213$, $D20214$

Table A28: Equation 28
LHS Variable Is log *UB*

Equation			χ^2 Tests			
RHS Variable	Coef.	*t*-stat.	Test	χ^2	df	*p*-value
cnst	0.30996	0.62	Lags	2.21	3	0.5296
$\log UB_{-1}$	0.12976	1.30	*T*	5.60	1	0.0180
$\log U$	1.47623	5.67				
$\log WF$	0.43629	5.50				
RHO1	0.89661	22.08				
SE	0.06393					
R^2	0.996					

Lags test adds $\log UB_{-2}$, $\log U_{-1}$, and $\log WF_{-1}$.
Estimation period is 1954.1–2000.4.

First-Stage Regressors

cnst, $\log UB_{-1}$, $\log U_{-1}$, $\log WF_{-1}$, $\log UB_{-2}$, $\log(PIM/PF)_{-1}$, $100[(PD/PD_{-1})^4 - 1]_{-1}$, $\log[(COG+COS)/POP]_{-1}$, $\log[(TRGH+TRSH)/(POP \cdot PH)]_{-1}$, $\log(EX/POP)_{-1}$, T

Table A29: Equation 29

LHS Variable Is $INTG/(-AG)$

Equation			χ^2 Tests			
RHS Variable	Coef.	*t*-stat.	Test	χ^2	df	*p*-value
cnst	0.00076	7.04	Lags	123.89	2	0.0000
$(INTG/(-AG))_{-1}$	0.83241	48.03	T	3.99	1	0.0457
[a]	0.14741	9.72				
$D20201$	0.00015	0.53				
$D20202$	−0.00077	−2.46				
$D20203$	−0.00035	−1.11				
$D20204$	0.00005	0.14				
$D20211$	0.00033	1.05				
$D20212$	0.00000	−0.01				
$D20213$	0.00022	0.69				
$D20214$	0.00000	−0.01				
RHO1	0.37564	6.21				
SE	0.00029					
R^2	0.997					

[a]Variable is $(.4 \cdot (RS/400) + .75 \cdot .6 \cdot (1/8) \cdot (1/400) \cdot (RB + RB_{-1} + RB_{-2} + RB_{-3} + RB_{-4} + RB_{-5} + RB_{-6} + RB_{-7}))$

Lags test adds $[INTG/(-AG)]_{-1}$ and [a] lagged once.

Estimation period is 1954.1–2023.2.

OLS estimation.

Table A30: Equation 30

LHS Variable Is *RS*

Equation			χ^2 Tests			
RHS Variable	Coef.	*t*-stat.	Test	χ^2	df	*p*-value
cnst	0.69910	4.55	Lags	2.60	3	0.4569
RS_{-1}	0.91555	49.15	RHO	3.14	1	0.0762
$100 \cdot [(PD/PD_{-1})^4 - 1]$	0.07508	3.98	*T*	0.87	1	0.3505
UR	−11.08222	−3.53	[a]	0.28	1	0.5949
ΔUR	−74.03467	−4.85	[b]	1.92	1	0.1655
$D20083 \cdot PCM1_{-1}$	0.01195	2.41				
$D794823 \cdot PCM1_{-1}$	0.21236	9.32				
ΔRS_{-1}	0.23363	4.09				
ΔRS_{-2}	−0.31145	−6.18				
SE	0.48626					
R^2	0.971					

Stability test (1954.1–1979.3 versus 1982.4–2008.3): Wald statistic is 12.521 (8 degrees of freedom, *p*-value = .1294)

[a] $100 \cdot (PD/PD(-4) - 1)$

[b] $100 \cdot [(PD/PD(-8))^{.5} - 1]$

Lags test adds RS_{-4}, $100 \cdot [(PD_{-1}/PD_{-2})^4 - 1]$, and UR_{-2}

Estimation period is 1954.1–2008.3.

First-Stage Regressors

$cnst$, RS_{-1}, $100[(PD/PD_{-1})^4 - 1]_{-1}$, UR_{-1}, ΔUR_{-1}, $D20083 \cdot PCM1_{-1}$, $D794823 \cdot PCM1_{-1}$, ΔRS_{-1}, ΔRS_{-2}, $\log[(COG + COS)/POP]_{-1}$, $\log[(TRGH + TRSH)/(POP \cdot PH)]_{-1}$, $\log(EX/POP)_{-1}$

Table A.5
The Raw Data Variables for the US Model

NIPA Data

No.	Variable	Table	Line	Description
R1	GDPR	1.1.3	1	Real gross domestic product
R2	CD	1.1.3	4	Real personal consumption expenditures, durable goods
R3	CN	1.1.3	5	Real personal consumption expenditures, nondurable goods
R4	CS	1.1.3	6	Real personal consumption expenditures, services
R5	IK	1.1.3	9	Real nonresidential fixed investment
R6	IH	1.1.3	13	Real residential fixed investment
R7	EX	1.1.3	16	Real exports
R8	IM	1.1.3	19	Real imports
R9	PURG	1.1.3	23	Real consumption expenditures and gross investment, federal government
R10	PURS	1.1.3	26	Real consumption expenditures and gross investment, S&L
R11	GDP	1.1.5	1	Gross domestic product
R12	CDZ	1.1.5	4	Personal consumption expenditures, durable goods
R13	CNZ	1.1.5	5	Personal consumption expenditures, nondurable goods
R14	CSZ	1.1.5	6	Personal consumption expenditures, services
R15	IKZ	1.1.5	9	Nonresidential fixed investment
R16	IHZ	1.1.5	13	Residential fixed investment
R17	IVZ	1.1.5	14	Change in private inventories
R18	EXZ	1.1.5	16	Exports
R19	IMZ	1.1.5	19	Imports
R20	PURGZ	1.1.5	23	Consumption expenditures and gross investment, federal government
R21	PURSZ	1.1.5	26	Consumption expenditures and gross investment, S&L
R22	FA	1.3.3	4	Real farm gross domestic product
R23	FAZ	1.3.5	4	Farm gross domestic product
R24	FIUS	1.7.5	2	Income receipts from the rest of the world
R25	FIROW	1.7.5	3	Income payments to the rest of the world
R26	STAT	1.7.5	15	Statistical discrepancy
R27	DC	1.12	16	Net dividends, Total
R28	TRFR	1.12	24	Business current transfer payments to the rest of the world (net)
R29	DCB	1.14	14	Net dividends, corporate business
R30	INTF1	1.14	25	Net interest and miscellaneous payments, nonfinancial corporate business

Table A.5
(continued)

NIPA Data				
No.	Variable	Table	Line	Description
R31	TCBN	1.14	28	Taxes on corporate income, nonfinancial corporate business
R32	DCBN	1.14	30	Net dividends, nonfinancial corporate business
R33	IVA	1.14	35	Inventory valuation adjustment, corporate business
R34	COMPT	2.1	2	Compensation of employees, received
R35	SIT	2.1	8	Employer contributions for government social insurance
R36	PRI	2.1	9	Proprietors' income with inventory valuation and capital consumption adjustments
R37	RNT	2.1	12	Rental income of persons with capital consumption adjustment
R38	PII	2.1	14	Personal interest income
R39	UB	2.1	21	Government unemployment insurance benefits
R40	TRFH	2.1	24	Other current transfer receipts from business (net)
R41	IPP	2.1	30	Personal interest payments
R42	TRHR	2.1	33	Personal current transfer payments to the rest of the world (net)
R43	THG	3.2	3	Personal current taxes, federal government (see below for adjustments)
R44	RECTXG	3.2	4	Taxes on production and imports, federal government
R45	TCG	3.2	8	Taxes on corporate income, federal government
R46	TRG	3.2	9	Taxes from the rest of the world, federal government
R47	SIG	3.2	10	Contributions for government social insurance, federal government, total
R48	TRRG2	3.2	12	Contributions for government social insurance from the rest of the world
R49	RECINTG	3.2	14	Interest receipts, federal government
R50	RECDIVG	3.2	15	Dividends, federal government
R51	RECRRG	3.2	18	Rents and royalties, federal government
R52	TRFG	3.2	20	Current transfer receipts from business, federal government
R53	TRHG	3.2	21	Current transfer receipts from persons, federal government
R54	TRRG1	3.2	22	Current transfer receipts from the rest of the world, federal government
R55	SURPG	3.2	23	Current surplus of government enterprises, federal government
R56	CONGZ	3.2	25	Consumption expenditures, federal government

Table A.5
(continued)

NIPA Data				
No.	Variable	Table	Line	Description
R57	TRGHPAY	3.2	28	Government social benefits to persons, federal government (see below for adjustments)
R58	TRGR1	3.2	29	Government social benefits to the rest of the world, federal government
R59	TRGS	3.2	31	Grants in aid to atate and local governments, federal government
R60	TRGR2	3.2	32	Other current transfer payments to the rest of the world, federal government
R61	PAYINTG	3.2	33	Interest payments, federal government
R62	INTGR	3.2	35	Interest payments, federal government to the rest of the world
R63	SUBSG	3.2	36	Subsidies, federal government
R64	CCG	3.2	48	Consumption of fixed capital, Federal Government
R65	THS	3.3	3	Personal current taxes, S&L
R66	RECTXS	3.3	6	Taxes on production and imports, S&L
R67	TCS	3.3	11	Taxes on corporate income, S&L
R68	SIS	3.3	12	Contributions for government social insurance, S&L
R69	RECINTS	3.3	14	Interest receipts, S&L
R70	RECDIVS	3.3	15	Dividends, S&L
R71	RECRRS	3.3	16	Rents and royalties, S&L
R72	TRFS	3.3	19	Current transfer receipts from business (net), S&L
R73	TRHS	3.3	20	Current transfer receipts from persons, S&L
R74	TRRS	3.3	21	Current transfer receipts from the rest of the world, S&L
R75	SURPS	3.3	22	Current surplus of government enterprises, S&L
R76	CONSZ	3.3	24	Consumption expenditures, S&L
R77	TRRSHPAY	3.3	25	Government social benefit payments to persons, S&L
R78	PAYINTS	3.3	28	Interest payments, S&L
R79	SUBSS	3.3	31	Subsidies, S&L
R80	CCS	3.3	43	Consumption of fixed capital, S&L
R81	PROG	3.10.3	15	Real compensation of general government employees, federal
R82	PROS	3.10.3	50	Real compensation of general government employees, S&L
R83	PROGZ	3.10.5	15	Compensation of general government employees, federal

Table A.5
(continued)

NIPA Data				
No.	Variable	Table	Line	Description
R84	COMPMIL	3.10.5	26	Compensation of general government employees, defense
R85	PROSZ	3.10.5	50	Compensation of general government employees, S&L
R86	TTRRF	4.1	15	Current taxes, contributions for social insurance, and transfer receipts from the rest of the world to business
R87	TTRFR	4.1	32	Current taxes and transfer payments to the rest of the world from business
R88	IV	5.7.6	1	Real change in private inventories
R89	SIHGA	3.14	3	Employee and self-employed contributions for social insurance to the federal government, annual data only
R90	SIQGA	3.14	5	Government employer contributions for social insurance to the federal government, annual data only
R91	SIFGA	3.14	6	Other employer contributions for social insurance to the federal government, annual data only
R92	SIHSA	3.14	18	Employee and self-employed contributions for social insurance to the S&L governments, annual data only
R93	SIQSA	3.14	20	Government employer contributions for social insurance to the S&L governments, annual data only
R94	SIFSA	3.14	21	Other employer contributions for social insurance to the S&L governments, annual data only

- For tables 1.1.3, 1.3.3, and 3.10.3, the respective raw data variable was created by multipling the quantity index for a given quarter by the nominal value of the variable in 2012 and then dividing by 100.
- For table 5.7.6, there is an "A" table and a "B" table. The "A" table is used for data prior to 1998:1, and the "B" table is used for data from 1998:1 on.
- S&L = State and Local Governments.
- R89–R94: Same value for all four quarters of the year. See variables R200–R205 for construction of variables SIHG, SIHS, SIFG, SIGG, SIFS, SISS.

Table A.5
(continued)

Flow of Funds Data			
No.	Variable	Code	Description
R95	CDDCF	103020000	Change in checkable deposits and currency, F1, F.103
R96	NFIF1	105000005	Net lending (+) or net borrowing (−), F1, F.103
R97	IHF1	105012005	Residential investment, F1, F.6
R98	NNF	105420005	Net acquisition of nonproduced nonfinancial assets, F1, F.6
R99	CTF1	105440005	Net capital transfers paid, F1, F.9
R100	PIEFRET	106006065	Foreign earnings retained abroad, F1, F.103
R101	PIEF1X	106060005	Profits before tax, F1, F.103
R102	CCF1	106300015	Capital consumption allowances, F1, F.103
R103	DISF1	107005005	Discrepancy, F1, F.103
R104	CDDCNN	113020005	Change in checkable deposits and currency, NN, F.104
R105	NFINN	115000005	Net lending (+) or net borrowing (−), NN, F.104
R106	IHNN	115012005	Residential Investment, NN, F.6
R107	IKNN	115013005	Nonresidential fixed investment, NN, F.6
R108	IVNN	115020005	Change in inventories, NN, F.104 (only for tesing)
R109	CTNN	115440005	Net capital transfers paid, NN, F.9
R110	GSNN	116300005	Gross saving, NN, F.104
R111	IHBZ	125012063	Residential investment, B, F.6
R112	CDDCH1	153020005	Change in checkable deposits and currency, H, F.101, line 21
R113	MVCE,	154090005	Total financial assets of Households, H, F.101.
R114	CCE		MVCE is the market value of the assets. CCE is the change in assets excluding capital gains and losses
R115	NFIH1	155000005	Net lending (+) or net borrowing (−), H, F.101
R116	REALEST	155035005	Real estate, H, stock variable, table B.101, line 3
R117	CDH	155111003	Capital expenditures, consumer durable goods, H, F.101
R118	NICD	155111005	Net investment in consumer durables, H, F.101
R119	NNH	155420003	Net acquisition of nonproduced nonfinancial assets, H, F.6
R120	CTH	155440005	Net capital transfers paid, H, F.9
R121	CCH	156300005	Consumption of fixed capital, H, F.100
R122	DISH1	157005005	Discrepancy, H, F.101
R123	IKH1	165013005	Nonresidential fixed investment, H, F.6
R124	CDDCS	213020005	Change in checkable deposits and currency, S, F.107

Table A.5
(continued)

Flow of Funds Data			
No.	Variable	Code	Description
R125	NFIS	215000005	Net lending (+) or net borrowing (–), S, F.107
R126	NNS	215420003	Net acquisition of nonproduced nonfinancial assets, S, F.6
R127	CTS	215440005	Net capital transfers paid, S, F.9
R128	DISS1	217005005	Discrepancy, S, F.107
R129	CGLDR	263011005	Change in US official reserve assets, R, F.200
R130	CDDCR	263020005	Change in US checkable deposits and currency, R, F.133
R131	CFXUS	263111005	Change in US official reserve assets, R, F.133
R132	NFIR	265000005	Net lending (+) or net borrowing (–), R, F.133
R133	NNR	265420005	Net acquisition of nonproduced nonfinancial assets, R, F.6
R134	CTR	265440005	Net capital transfers paid, R, F.9
R135	DISR1	267005005	Discrepancy, R, F.133
R136	CGLDFXUS	313011005	Change in US official reserve assets, US, F.106
R137	CDDCUS	313020005	Change in checkable deposits and currency, US, F.106
R138	CSDRUS	313111303	Change in SDR allocations, US, F.106
R139	INS	313154015	Insurance and pension reserves, US, F.106
R140	NFIUS	315000005	Net lending (+) or net borrowing (–), US, F.106
R141	CTGB	315410093	Capital transfers paid by US, financial stabilization payments, F.9
R142	NNG	315420003	Net acquisition of nonproduced nonfinancial assets, US, F.6
R143	CTGMB	315440005	Net capital transfers paid, US, F.106
R144	DISUS	317005005	Discrepancy, US, F.106
R145	CDDCCA	403020005	Change in checkable deposits and currency, CA, F.124
R146	NIACA	404090005	Net acquisition of financial assets, CA, F.124
R147	NILCA	404190005	Net increase in liabilities, CA, F.124
R148	IKCAZ	405013005	Fixed nonresidential investment, CA, F.124
R149	GSCA	406000105	Gross saving, CA, F.124
R150	DISCA	407005005	Discrepancy, CA, F.124
R151	NIDDLZ2	473127003	Net change in liabilities of credit unions of checkable deposits and currency, F.204
R152	CGLDFXMA	713011005	Change in US official reserve assets, MA, F.109
R153	CFRLMA	713068705	Change in federal reserve loans to domestic banks, MA, F.109
R154	NILBRMA	713113003	Change in depository institution reserves, MA, F.109

Table A.5
(continued)

Flow of Funds Data

No.	Variable	Code	Description
R155	CBR	713113003	Change in reserves at Federal Reserve, private depository institutions, F.109
R156	NIDDLRMA	713122605	Net increase in liabilities in the form of checkable deposits and currency of the MA due to the rest of the world, F.109
R157	NIDDLGMA	713123005	Net increase in liabilities in the form of checkable deposits and currency of the MA due to the federal government, F.109
R158	NIDDLCMA	713124005	Net increase in liabilities in the form of checkable deposits and currency of the MA due to government-sponsored enterprises, F.109
R159	NILCMA	713125005	Net increase in liabilities in the form of currency outside banks of the MA, F.109
R160	NIAMA	714090005	Net acquisition of in financial assets, MA, F.109
R161	NILMA	714190005	Net increase in liabilities, MA, F.109
R162	IKMAZ	715013005	Fixed nonresidential investment, MA, F.109
R163	GSMA	716000105	Gross savings, MA, F.109
R164	DISMA	717005005	Discrepancy, MA, F.109
R165	NIDDLCB3	743127003	Net change in liabilities in the form of checkable deposits and currency, banks in U.S.-affiliated Areas, F.113
R166	CBRB1A	753013003	Change in reserves at federal reserve, foreign banking offices in US, F.112
R167	NIDDLCB2	753127005	Net change in liabilities in the form of checkable deposits and currency, foreign banking offices in U.S., F.112
R168	NIDDLCB1	763127005	Net change in liabilities in the form of checkable deposits and currency, US-chartered depository institutions, F.111
R169	CDDCFS	793020005	Net change in assets in the form of checkable deposits and currency of financial sectors, F.108
R170	NFIBB	795000005	Net lending (+) or net borrowing (−), B, F.108
R171	IKBMACA	795013005	Nonresidential fixed investment, B, F.108
R172	CTB	795440005	Net capital transfers paid, B, F.9
R173	GSBBCT	796000105	Gross saving less net capital transfers paid, B, F.108
R174	DISBB	797005005	Discrepancy, B, F.108
R175	MAILFLT1	903023005	Mail Float, US, F.12
R176	MAILFLT3	903028003	Mail Float, S, F.12
R177	MAILFLT2	903029200	Mail Float, private domestic, F.12

Table A.5
(continued)

Interest Rate Data		
No.	Variable	Description
R178	RS	Three-month treasury bill rate (secondary market), percentage points. [BOG. Quarterly average.]
R179	RM	30-year fixed rate mortgage, percentage points. [Quarterly average. Data from BOG up to September 2016. Data from FRED from October 2017 on.]
R180	RB	Moody's Aaa corporate bond rate, percentage points. [Quarterly average. Data from BOG up to September 2016. Data from FRED from October 2017 on.]

Labor Force and Population Data		
No.	Variable	Description
R181	CE	Civilian employment, SA in millions. [BLS. Quarterly average. See the next page for adjustments.]
R182	U	Unemployment, SA in millions. [BLS. Quarterly average. See the next page for adjustments.]
R183	CL1	Civilian labor force of males 25–54, SA in millions. [BLS. Quarterly average. See the next page for adjustments.]
R184	CL2	Civilian labor force of females 25–54, SA in millions. [BLS. Quarterly average. See the next page for adjustments.]
R185	AFT	Total armed forces, millions. [Computed from population data from the US Census Bureau. Quarterly average.]
R186	AF1	Armed forces of males 25–54, millions. [Computed from population data from the US Census Bureau. Quarterly average.]
R187	AF2	Armed forces of females 25–54, millions. [Computed from population data from the US Census Bureau. Quarterly average.]
R188	CPOP	Total civilian noninstitutional population 16 and over, millions. [BLS. Quarterly average. See the next page for adjustments.]
R189	CPOP1	Civilian noninstitutional population of males 25–54, millions. [BLS. Quarterly average. See the next page for adjustments.]
R190	CPOP2	Civilian noninstitutional population of females 25–54, millions. [BLS. Quarterly average. See the next page for adjustments.]
R191	HO	Average weekly overtime hours in manufacturing, SA. [BLS. Quarterly average.]
R192	JT	Employment, total U.S. economy, SA in millions of jobs. [BLS.]
R193	JG	Employment, general government, federal, SA in millions of jobs. [BLS.]
R194	JS	Employment, general government, state & local, SA in millions of jobs. [BLS.]
R195	JM	Employment, armed forces, SA in millions of jobs. [BLS.]
R196	JTH	Hours worked, total U.S. economy, SA in billions. [BLS.]
R197	JGH	Hours worked, general government, federal, SA in billions. [BLS.]
R198	JSH	Hours worked, general government, state & local, SA in billions. [BLS.]
R199	JMH	Hours worked, armed forces, SA in billions. [BLS.]

Table A.5
(continued)

Adjustments to the Raw Data		
No.	Variable	Description
R200	SIHG =	[SIHGA/(SIHGA + SIHSA)](SIG + SIS - SIT) [Employee contributions for social insurance, h to g.]
R201	SIHS =	SIG + SIS - SIT - SIHG [Employee contributions for social insurance, h to s.]
R202	SIFG =	[SIFGA/(SIFGA + SIQGA)](SIG - SIHG) [Employer contributions for social insurance, f to g.]
R203	SIGG =	SIG - SIHG - SIFG [Employer contributions for social insurance, g to g.]
R204	SIFS =	[SIFSA/(SIFSA + SIQSA)](SIS - SIHS) [Employer contributions for social ensurance, f to s.]
R205	SISS =	SIS - SIHS - SIFS [Employer contributions for social insurance, s to s.]
R206	TBG =	[TCG/(TCG + TCS)](TCG + TCS - TCBN) [Corporate profit tax accruals, b to g.]
R207	TBS =	TCG + TCS - TCBN - TBG [Corporate profit tax accruals, b to s.]
	THG =	THG from raw data - TAXADJ
	TRGHPAY =	TRGHPAY from raw data - TAXADJ [TAXADJ (annual rate): 1968:3 = 6.1, 1968:4 = 7.1, 1969:1 = 10.7, 1969:2 = 10.9, 1969:3 = 7.1, 1969:4 = 7.3, 1970:1 = 5.0, 1970:2 = 5.0, 1970:3 = 0.4, 1975:2 = −31.2, 2008.2 = −199.4, 2008.3 = −57.0, 2009.2 = −152.0, 2009.3 = −239.0, 2009.4 = −249.0, 2010.1 = −231.0, 2010.2 = −256.0, 2010.3 = −266.0, 2010.4 = −15.0, 2011.1 = −53.0, 2011.2 = −74.0, 2011.3 = −99.0.]
R208	POP =	CPOP + AFT [Total noninstitutional population 16 and over, millions.]
R209	POP1 =	CPOP1 + AF1 [Total noninstitutional population of males 25–54, millions.]
R210	POP2 =	CPOP2 + AF2 [Total noninstitutional population of females 25–54, millions.]

- BLS = Bureau of Labor Statistics
- BOG = Board of Governors of the Federal Reserve System
- FRED = Federal Reserve Bank of St. Louis
- SA = Seasonally adusted
- For the construction of variables R200, R202, and R204, the annual observation for the year was used for each quarter of the year.

Table A.5
(continued)

Adjustments to Labor Force and Population Data

Variable	1952:1–1971:4	1952:1–1972:4	1973:1	1952:1–1977:4	1970:1–1989:4
POP	1.00547	1.00009	1.00006	-	1.0058886-.0000736075TPOP90
POP1	0.99880	1.00084	1.00056	-	1.0054512-.00006814TPOP90
POP2	1.00251	1.00042	1.00028	-	1.00091654-.000011457TPOP90
(CE+U)	1.00391	1.00069	1.00046	1.00239	1.0107312-.00013414TPOP90
CL1	0.99878	1.00078	1.00052	1.00014	1.00697786-.00008722TPOP90
CL2	1.00297	1.00107	1.00071	1.00123	-
CE	1.00375	1.00069	1.00046	1.00268	1.010617-.00013271TPOP90

• TPOP90 is 79 in 1970:1, 78 in 1970:2, . . . , 1 in 1989:3, 0 in 1989:4.

Variable	1990:1–1998:4
POP	1.0014883-.0000413417TPOP99
POP1	.99681716+.000088412TPOP99
POP2	1.0045032-.00012509TPOP99
(CE+U)	1.00041798-.000011611TPOP99
CL1	.9967564+.0000901TPOP99
CL2	1.004183-.00011619TPOP99
CE	1.00042068-.000011686TPOP99

• TPOP99 is 35 in 1990:1, 34 in 1990:2, . . . , 1 in 1998:3, 0 in 1998:4.

Variable	1990:1–1999:4
POP	1.0165685-.00041421TPOP2000
POP1	1.0188400-.00047100TPOP2000
POP2	1.0195067-.00048767TPOP2000
(CE+U)	1.0156403-.00039101TPOP2000
CL1	1.0208284-.00052071TPOP2000
CL2	1.0151172-.00037793TPOP2000
CE	1.0156827-.00039207TPOP2000

• TPOP2000 is 39 in 1990:1, 38 in 1990:2, . . . , 1 in 1999:3, 0 in 1999:4.

Table A.5
(continued)

Variable	1993:1–2002:4
POP	1.0043019-.00010755TPOP2003
POP1	1.0046539-.00011635TPOP2003
POP2	1.0043621-.00010905TPOP2003
(CE+U)	1.0042240-.00010560TPOP2003
CL1	1.0046137-.00011534TPOP2003
CL2	1.0042307-.00010577TPOP2003
CE	1.0041995-.00010499TPOP2003

• TPOP2003 is 39 in 1993:1, 38 in 1993:2, . . . , 1 in 2002:3, 0 in 2002:4.

Variable	1994:1–2003:4
POP	.9974832+.00006292TPOP2004
POP1	.9982816+.00004296TPOP2004
POP2	.9966202+.00008450TPOP2004
(CE+U)	.9970239+.00007440TPOP2004
CL1	.9977729+.00004454TPOP2004
CL2	.9959602+.00010000TPOP2004
CE	.9970481+.00007380TPOP2004

• TPOP2004 is 39 in 1994:1, 38 in 1994:2, . . . , 1 in 2003:3, 0 in 2003:4.

Variable	1996:1–2005:4
POP	.9997054+.000007365TPOP2006
POP1	.9994935+.000012662TPOP2006
POP2	.9994283+.000014292TPOP2006
(CE+U)	.9991342+.000021645TPOP2006
CL1	.9987934+.000030165TPOP2006
CL2	.9986564+.00003359TPOP2006
CE	.9991385+.000021537TPOP2006

• TPOP2006 is 39 in 1996:1, 38 in 1996:2, . . . , 1 in 2005:3, 0 in 2005:4.

Variable	1997:1–2006:4
POP	1.0013950-.000034875TPOP2007
POP1	1.0009830-.000024575TPOP2007
POP2	1.0016647-.000041617TPOP2007
(CE+U)	1.0010684-.00002671TPOP2007

Table A.5
(continued)

Variable	1997:1–2006:4
CL1	1.0008882-.000022205TPOP2007
CL2	1.0013202-.000033005TPOP2007
CE	1.0010474-.0000261855TPOP2007

• TPOP2007 is 39 in 1997:1, 38 in 1997:2, . . ., 1 in 2006:3, 0 in 2006:4.

Variable	1998:1–2007:4
POP	.9968047+.0000798825TPOP2008
POP1	.9958060+.00010485TPOP2008
POP2	.9976944+.00005764TPOP2008
(CE+U)	.9958557+.0001036075TPOP2008
CL1	.9948031+.0001299225TPOP2008
CL2	.9969464+.00007634TPOP2008
CE	.9959135+.0001021625TPOP2008

• TPOP2008 is 39 in 1998:1, 38 in 1998:2, . . ., 1 in 2007:3, 0 in 2007:4.

Variable	1999:1–2008:4
POP	.9979450+.000051375TPOP2009
POP1	.9973640+.0000659TPOP2009
POP2	.9984844+.00003789TPOP2009
(CE+U)	.9970910+.000072725TPOP2009
CL1	.9964462+.000088845TPOP2009
CL2	.9977695+.0000557625TPOP2009
CE	.9971608+.00007098TPOP2009

• TPOP2009 is 39 in 1999:1, 38 in 1999:2, . . ., 1 in 2008:3, 0 in 2008:4.

Variable	2000:1–2009:4
POP	.9989110+.000027225TPOP2010
POP1	.9978610+.000053475TPOP2010
POP2	.9989019+.0000274525TPOP2010
(CE+U)	.9983693+.0000407675TPOP2010
CL1	.9974105+.0000647375TPOP2010
CL2	.9989507+.0000262325TPOP2010
CE	.9982313+.0000442175TPOP2010

• TPOP2010 is 39 in 2000:1, 38 in 2000:2, . . ., 1 in 2009:3, 0 in 2009:4.

Table A.5
(continued)

Variable	2001:1–2010:4
POP	.9985474+.000036315TPOP2011
POP1	.9989740+.000025650TPOP2011
POP2	.9970233+.000074418TPOP2011
(CE+U)	.9967092+.000082270TPOP2011
CL1	.9956715+.000108213TPOP2011
CL2	.9971304+.000071740TPOP2011
CE	.9966082+.000084795TPOP2011

• TPOP2011 is 39 in 2001:1, 38 in 2001:2, . . . , 1 in 2010:3, 0 in 2010:4.

Variable	2002:1–2011:4
POP	1.0062764-.000156910TPOP2012
POP1	.9899101+.00002522475TPOP2012
POP2	1.0051234-.000128085TPOP2012
(CE+U)	1.0016822-.000042055TPOP2012
CL1	.9889798+.000275505TPOP2012
CL2	1.0041332-.00010333TPOP2012
CE	1.0015354-.000038385TPOP2012

• TPOP2012 is 39 in 2002:1, 38 in 2002:2, . . . , 1 in 2011:3, 0 in 2011:4.

Variable	2003:1–2012:4
POP	1.0005648-.00001412TPOP2013
POP1	1.0003568-.00000892TPOP2013
POP2	1.0007278-.000018195TPOP2013
(CE+U)	1.0008780-.00002195TPOP2013
CL1	1.0006285-.0000157125TPOP2013
CL2	1.0012289-.0000307225TPOP2013
CE	1.0008877-.0000221925TPOP2013

• TPOP2013 is 39 in 2003:1, 38 in 2003:2, . . . , 1 in 2012:3, 0 in 2012:4.

Variable	2005:1–2014:4
POP	1.0021203-.0000530075TPOP2015
POP1	1.0013765-.0000344125TPOP2015
POP2	1.0027041-.0000676025TPOP2015
(CE+U)	1.0022376-.00005594 TPOP2015

Table A.5
(continued)

Variable	2005:1–2014:4
CL1	1.0015986-.000039965TPOP2015
CL2	1.0029975-.0000749375TPOP2015
CE	1.0022012-.00005503TPOP2015

• TPOP2015 is 39 in 2005:1, 38 in 2005:2, ..., 1 in 2014:3, 0 in 2014:4.

Variable	2006:1–2015:4
POP	1.00105185-.00002630TPOP2016
POP1	1.00129812-.00003245TPOP2016
POP2	1.00079462-.00001987TPOP2016
(CE+U)	1.00138637-.00003466TPOP2016
CL1	1.00167363-.00004184TPOP2016
CL2	1.00108367-.00002709TPOP2016
CE	1.00137606-.00003440TPOP2016

• TPOP2016 is 39 in 2006:1, 38 in 2006:2, ..., 1 in 2015:3, 0 in 2015:4.

Variable	2007:1–2016:4
POP	0.99673788+.00008155TPOP2017
POP1	0.99662313+.00008442TPOP2017
POP2	0.99664459+.00008389TPOP2017
(CE+U)	0.99680439+.00007989TPOP2017
CL1	0.99671730+.00008207TPOP2017
CL2	0.99675460+.00008113TPOP2017
CE	0.99679179+.00008021TPOP2017

• TPOP2017 is 39 in 2007:1, 38 in 2007:2, ..., 1 in 2016:3, 0 in 2016:4.

Variable	2008:1–2017:4
POP	1.00190544-.00004764TPOP2018
POP1	1.00246331-.00006158TPOP2018
POP2	1.00144289-.00003607TPOP2018
(CE+U)	1.00208281-.00005207TPOP2018
CL1	1.00273746-.00006844TPOP2018
CL2	1.00141202-.00003530TPOP2018
CE	1.00207029-.00005176TPOP2018

• TPOP2018 is 39 in 2008:1, 38 in 2008:2, ..., 1 in 2017:3, 0 in 2017:4.

Table A.5
(continued)

Variable	2009:1–2018:4
POP	0.99690986+.00007725TPOP2019
POP1	0.99672774+.00008181TPOP2019
POP2	0.99701738+.00007457TPOP2019
(CE+U)	0.99688635+.00007784TPOP2019
CL1	0.99672687+.00008183TPOP2019
CL2	0.99699057+.00007524TPOP2019
CE	0.99688141+.00007796TPOP2019

• TPOP2019 is 39 in 2009:1, 38 in 2009:2, . . . , 1 in 2018:3, 0 in 2018:4.

Variable	2010:1–2019:4
POP	0.99688294+.00007793TPOP2020
POP1	0.99684021+.00007899TPOP2020
POP2	0.99697023+.00007574TPOP2020
(CE+U)	0.99680501+.00007987TPOP2020
CL1	0.99666380+.00008341TPOP2020
CL2	0.99693563+.00007661TPOP2020
CE	0.99680134+.00007997TPOP2020

• TPOP2020 is 39 in 2010:1, 38 in 2010:2, . . . , 1 in 2019:3, 0 in 2019:4.

Variable	2011:1–2020:4
POP	0.99899484+.00004555TPOP2021
POP1	0.99828828+.00004279TPOP2021
POP2	0.99818442+.00002870TPOP2021
(CE+U)	0.99875013+.00003125TPOP2021
CL1	0.99885194+.00002870TPOP2021
CL2	0.99869070+.00003273TPOP2021
CE	0.99879690+.00003008TPOP2021

• TPOP2021 is 39 in 2011:1, 38 in 2011:2, . . . , 1 in 2020:3, 0 in 2020:4.

Variable	2012:1–2021:4
POP	1.00371181-.00009280TPOP2022
POP1	1.00884239-.00022106TPOP2022
POP2	0.99493579+.00012661TPOP2022
(CE+U)	1.00946220-.00023656TPOP2022
CL1	1.01373763-.00034344TPOP2022

Table A.5
(continued)

Variable	2012:1–2021:4
CL2	1.00270579-.00006764TPOP2022
CE	1.00944571-.00023614TPOP2022

• TPOP2022 is 39 in 2012:1, 38 in 2012:2, . . . , 1 in 2021:3, 0 in 2021:4.

Variable	2013:1–2022:4
POP	1.00362121-.00009005TPOP2023
POP1	1.00708707-.00017718TPOP2023
POP2	1.00097373-.00002434TPOP2023
(CE+U)	1.00530373-.00013259TPOP2023
CL1	1.01082533-.00025456TPOP2023
CL2	1.00043254-.00001081TPOP2023
CE	1.00509844-.00012746TPOP2023

• TPOP2023 is 39 in 2013:1, 38 in 2013:2, . . . , 1 in 2022:3, 0 in 2022:4.

The Raw Data Variables in Alphabetical Order Matched to R Numbers Above

Var.	No.	Var.	No.	Var.	No.	Var.	No.
AFT	R185	DISCA	R150	MVCE	R113	RECTXS	R66
AF1	R186	DISF1	R103	NFIBB	R170	RM	R179
AF2	R187	DISH1	R122	NFIF1	R96	RNT	R37
CBR	R155	DISMA	R164	NFIH1	R115	RS	R178
CBRB1A	R166	DISR1	R135	NFINN	R105	SIFG	R202
CCE	R114	DISS1	R128	NFIR	R132	SIFGA	R91
CCF1	R102	DISUS	R144	NFIS	R125	SIFS	R204
CCG	R64	EX	R7	NFIUS	R140	SIFSA	R94
CCH	R121	EXZ	R18	NIACA	R146	SIG	R47
CCS	R80	FA	R22	NIAMA	R160	SIGG	R203
CD	R2	FAZ	R23	NICD	R118	SIHG	R200
CDDCCA	R145	FIROW	R25	NIDDLCB1	R168	SIHGA	R89
CDDCF	R95	FIUS	R24	NIDDLCB2	R167	SIHS	R201
CDDCFS	R169	GDP	R11	NIDDLCB3	R165	SIHSA	R92
CDDCH1	R112	GDPR	R1	NIDDLCMA	R158	SIQGA	R90
CDDCNN	R104	GSBBCT	R173	NIDDLGMA	R157	SIQSA	R93

Table A.5
(continued)

The Raw Data Variables in Alphabetical Order Matched to R Numbers Above

Var.	No.	Var.	No.	Var.	No.	Var.	No.
CDDCR	R130	GSCA	R149	NIDDLRMA	R156	SIS	R68
CDDCS	R124	GSMA	R163	NIDDLZ2	R151	SISS	R205
CDDCUS	R137	GSNN	R110	NILBRMA	R154	SIT	R35
CDH	R117	HO	R191	NILCA	R147	STAT	R26
CDZ	R12	IH	R6	NILCMA	R159	SUBSG	R63
CE	R181	IHBZ	R111	NILMA	R161	SUBSS	R79
CFRLMA	R153	IHF1	R97	NNF	R98	SURPG	R55
CFXUS	R131	IHNN	R106	NNG	R142	SURPS	R75
CGLDFXMA	R152	IHZ	R16	NNH	R119	TBG	R206
CGLDFXUS	R136	IK	R5	NNR	R133	TBS	R207
CGLDR	R129	IKBMACA	R171	NNS	R126	TCBN	R31
CL1	R183	IKCAZ	R148	PAYINTG	R61	TCG	R45
CL2	R184	IKH1	R123	PAYINTS	R78	TCS	R67
CN	R3	IKMAZ	R162	PIEFRET	R100	THG	R43
CNZ	R13	IKNN	R107	PIEF1X	R101	THS	R65
COMPMIL	R84	IKZ	R15	PII	R38	TRFG	R52
COMPT	R34	IM	R8	POP	R208	TRFH	R40
CONGZ	R56	IMZ	R19	POP1	R209	TRFR	R28
CONSZ	R76	INS	R139	POP2	R210	TRFS	R72
CPOP	R188	INTF1	R30	PRI	R36	TRG	R46
CPOP1	R189	INTGR	R62	PROG	R81	TRGHPAY	R57
CPOP2	R190	IPP	R41	PROGZ	R83	TRGR1	R58
CS	R4	IVA	R33	PROS	R82	TRGR2	R60
CSDRUS	R138	IV	R88	PROSZ	R85	TRGS	R59
CSZ	R14	IVNN	R108	PURG	R9	TRHG	R53
CTB	R172	IVZ	R17	PURGZ	R20	TRHR	R42
CTF1	R99	JG	R193	PURS	R10	TRHS	R73
CTGB	R141	JM	R195	PURSZ	R21	TRRG1	R54
CTGMB	R143	JS	R194	RB	R180	TRRG2	R48
CTH	R120	JT	R192	REALEST	R116	TRRS	R74
CTNN	R109	JGH	R197	RECDIVG	R50	TRRSHPAY	R77
CTR	R134	JMH	R199	RECDIVS	R70	TTRFR	R87
CTS	R127	JSH	R198	RECINTG	R49	TTRRF	R86
DC	R27	JTH	R196	RECINTS	R69	U	R182
DCB	R29	MAILFLT1	R175	RECRRG	R51	UB	R39
DCBN	R32	MAILFLT3	R176	RECRRS	R71		
DISBB	R174	MAILFLT2	R177	RECTXG	R44		

Table A.6
Links between the National Income and Product Accounts and the Flow of Funds Accounts

Flow of Funds Data (raw data variables)	
SH =	NFIH1 + DISH1
SF =	NFIF1 + DISF1 + NFINN
SB =	NFIBB + DISBB - NIAMA + NILMA - DISMA - NIACA + NILCA - DISCA
SR =	NFIR + DISR1
SG =	NFIUS + DISUS + NIACA - NILCA + DISCA + NIAMA - NILMA + DISMA
SS =	NFIS + DISS1
Raw Data Variables on the Right-Hand Side	
SHTEST=	COMPT+PRI+RNT+PII-IPP +DC-RECDIVG-RECDIVS+TRGHPAY-TRHG+TRRSHPAY-TRHS+TRFH-TRHG2-SIS-THG-THS-CSZ -CNZ-CDZ-TRHR+INS+NICD+CCH-CTH-(IHZ-IHF1-IHNN-IHBZ)-CDH-IKH1-NNH-TRRG2
PIEFTEST=	CSZ+CNZ+CDZ+IHZ+IKZ+EXZ-IMZ+PURGZ+PURSZ-RECTXG-RECRRG-RECTXS-RECRRS+IVZ+SUBSS-SURPS+SUBSG-SURPG + FIUS-FIROW-(-INTGR+DC-DCB+PIEFRET)-COMPT-PRI-RNT-(PII-IPP-INTF1-(PAYINTG-RECINTG)+INTGR-(PAYINTS -RECINTS))-INTF1-TRFH-NICD-CCH+CDH-TRFS-CCS-(DCB-DCBN)-(TCG+TCS+TTRFR-TCBN)-(GSBBCT+CTB)-CTGB-TRFG -CCG-GSNN-IVA-CCF1-STAT+TTRRF
SFTEST=	PIEFTEST-TCBN-DCBN+IVA+CCF1+PIEFRET-CTF1-(IKZ-IKH1 -IKBMACA)-IHF1-IVZ-NNF+GSNN-CTNN-IHNN
SBTEST=	GSBBCT-GSMA-GSCA-IHBZ-IKBMACA+IKMAZ+IKCAZ
SRTEST=	-EXZ-FIUS+IMZ+FIROW-TTRRF-(TRG+TRRG1+TRRG2+TRRS)+TRHR +TRGR1+TRGR2+TTRFR-CTR-NNR
SGTEST=	GSMA-IKMAZ+GSCA-IKCAZ+THG+RECTXG+RECRRG+TCG+TRHG2 +TRRG2+RECDIVG+TRFG-TRGHPAY+TRHG-TRGR1-TRGR2+TRG+ TRRG-TRGS-PAYINTG+RECINTG-SUBSG+SURPG+CCG-INS-CTGMB-PURGZ-NNG+CTGB
SSTEST=	THS+RECTXS+RECRRS+TCS+SIS+RECDIVS+TRGS+TRFS-TRRSHPAY +TRHS-PAYINTS+RECINTS-SUBSS+SURPS+TRRS+CCS-CTS-PURSZ-NNS
Variables in the Model on the Right-Hand Side	
SHTEST =	YT - SIHG - SIHS + TTRRF - THG - THS - PCS·CS - PCN·CN - PCD·CD + TRGH + TRSH + UB + INS + NICD + CCH - CTH - PIH·IHH - CDH - PIK·IKH - NNH
PIEFTEST=	XX+PIV·IVF+SUBS+SUBG+USOTHER-WF·JF·(HN+1.5·HO)-RNT-INTZ -INTF-TRFH-NICD-CCH+CDH-TBS-TRFS-CCS-TRFR-DB-GSB-CTGB-GSMA-GSCA-TBG-TRFG-CCG-SIFG-SIFS-GSNN-IVA-CCF1-STAT+TTRRF
SFTEST=	PIEFTEST-TF1-DF+IVA+CCF1+PIEFRET-CTF1-PIK·IKF-PIH·IHF-PIV·IVF-NNF+GSNN-CTNN

Table A.6
(continued)

SBTEST =	GSB - CTB - PIH·IHB - PIK·IKB
SRTEST=	-PEX·EX-USROW+PIM·IM+TFR+TRFR+TRHR+TRGR-TRRG2-CTR-NNR-TRRS-TTRRF
SGTEST =	GSMA + GSCA + THG + IBTG + TBG + TFG + SIHG + SIFG - DG + TRFG - PG·COG - WG·JG·HG - WM·JM·HM - TRGH - TRGR - TRGS - INTG - SUBG + CCG - INS - TTRRF - CTGMB - NNG - PIK·IKG + SIGG +CTGB
SSTEST =	THS + IBTS + TBS + TFS + SIHS + SIFS - DS + TRGS + TRFS - PS·COS-WS·JS·HS - TRSH - UB - INTS - SUBS + CCS - CTS - NNS + SISS + TRRS
Tests	
0 =	SH + SF + SB + SR + SG + SS + STAT + TTRG2
0 =	SH - SHTEST
0 =	PIEF1X - PIEFTEST
0 =	SF - SFTEST
0 =	SB - SBTEST
0 =	SR - SRTEST
0 =	SG - SGTEST
0 =	SS - SSTEST
0 =	-NIDDLCB1 - NIDDLCB2 - NIDDLCB3 - NIDDLZ2 + CDDCFS + CDDCF + MAILFLT1 + MAILFLT2 + CDDCUS - NIDDLRMA - NIDDLGMA + CDDCH1 + CDDCNN + CDDCR + CDDCS - NILCMA + MAILFLT3 - NIDDLCMA
0 =	CBR - NILBRMA
0 =	CGLDR - CFXUS + CGLDFXUS + CGLDFXMA - CSDRUS
0 =	CTH + CTB + CTF1 + CTNN + CTGMB + CTR
0 =	NNH + NNF + NNR + NNG + NNS

• See table A.5 for the definitions of the raw data variables.

Table A.7

Variable	Construction (raw data variables on the right-hand side)
AA	Def., Eq. 133.
*AA*1	Def., Eq. 88.
*AA*2	Def., Eq. 89.
AB	Def., Eq. 73. Base Period=1971:4, Value=29.425
AF	Def., Eq. 70. Base Period=1971:4, Value=−303.993
AFT	TL-CE-U
AG	Def., Eq. 77. Base Period=1971:4, Value=−513.731
AH	Def., Eq. 66. Base Period=1971:4, Value=2735.512
AR	Def., Eq. 75. Base Period=1971:4, Value=−18.702
AS	Def., Eq. 79. Base Period=1971:4, Value=−161.8
BO	Sum of CFRLMA. Base Period=1971:4, Value=.039
BR	Sum of CBR. Base Period=1971:4, Value=35.329
*CCF*1	CCF1
CCG	CCG
CCGQ	CCG/*GDPD*
CCH	CCH
CCHQ	CCH/*GDPD*
CCS	CCS
CCSQ	CCS/*GDPD*
CD	CD
CDH	CDH
CG	$MVCE - MVCE_{-1} - CCE$
CN	CN
cnst2cs	Time-varying constant term. See text.
cnst2l2	Time-varying constant term. See text.
cnst2kk	Time-varying constant term. See text.
COG	PURG-PROG
COS	PURS-PROS
CS	CS
CTB	CTB
*CTF*1	CTF1
CTGB	CTGB
CTGMB	CTGMB
CTH	CTH
CTNN	CTNN
CTR	CTR
CTS	CTS
CUR	Sum of NILCMA. Base Period=1971:4, Value=53.521
*D*1*G*	Def., Eq. 47

Table A.7
(continued)

Variable	Construction (raw data variables on the right-hand side)
D1S	Def., Eq. 48
D2G	Def., Eq. 49
D2S	Def., Eq. 50
D3G	Def., Eq. 51
D3S	Def., Eq. 52
D4G	Def., Eq. 53
D5G	Def., Eq. 55
D6G	Def., Eq. 67
DB	DCB-DCBN
DBQ	DB/*GDPD*
DELD	Computed using NIPA asset data
DELH	Computed using NIPA asset data
DELK	Computed using NIPA asset data
DF	DCBN
DG	-RECDIVG
DISB	DISBB-DISMA-DISCA
DISF	DISF1
DISG	DISUS+DISCA+DISMA
DISH	DISH1
DISR	DISR1
DISS	DISS1
DR	DC-DCB
DRQ	DR/*GDPD*
DS	-RECDIVS
E	TL-U
EX	EX
EXPG	Def., Eq. 106
EXPS	Def., Eq. 113
FA	FA
GDP	Def., Eq. 82, or GDP
GDPD	Def., Eq. 84
GDPR	GDPR
GNP	Def., Eq. 129
GNPD	Def., Eq. 131
GSB	GSBBCT+CTB-GSMA-GSCA
GSBQ	GSB/*GDPD*
GSCA	GSCA
GSMA	GSMA

Table A.7
(continued)

Variable	Construction (raw data variables on the right-hand side)
GSNN	GSNN
GSNNQ	GSNN/*GDPD*
GNPR	Def., Eq. 130
HF	((JTH-JGH-JSH-JMH)/(JT-JG-JS-JM))·(1000/4)
HFF	Def., Eq. 100
HFS	Peak-to-peak interpolation of *HF*. The peaks are 1952:4, 1960.3, 1966:1, 1977:2, 1990:1, 2000:1, 2001:4, 2004:2, and 2018.3. Flat end.
HG	(JGH/JG)·(1000/4)
HM	(JMH/JM)·(1000/4)
HN	Def., Eq. 62
HO	13·HO. Constructed values for 1952:1–1955:4.
HS	(JSH/JS)·(1000/4)
IBTG	RECTXG+RECRRG
IBTS	RECTXS+RECRRS
IGZ	PURGZ-CONGZ
IGZQ	IGZ/*GDPD*
IHB	IHBZ/(IHZ/IH)
IHF	(IHF1+IHNN)/(IHZ/IH)
IHH	(IHZ-IHF1-IHBZ-IHNN)/(IHZ/IH)
IKB	(IKBMACA-IKMAZ-IKCAZ)/(IKZ/IK)
IKF	(IKZ-IKH1-IKBMACA)/(IKZ/IK)
IKG	((IKCAZ+IKMAZ)/(IKZ/IK)
IKH	IKH1/(IKZ/IK)
IM	IM
INS	INS
INTF	INTF1
INTG	PAYINTG-RECINTG
INTGR	INTGR
INTS	PAYINTS-RECINTS
INTZ	PII-IPP-INTF1-(PAYINTG-RECINTG)+INTGR-(PAYINTS-RECINTS)
INTZQ	INTZ/*GDPD*
ISZ	PURSZ-CONSZ
ISZQ	ISZ/*GDPD*
IVA	IVA
IVF	IV
JF	JT-JG-JS-JM
JG	JG
JHMIN	Def., Eq. 94
JM	JM

Table A.7
(continued)

Variable	Construction (raw data variables on the right-hand side)
JS	JS
KD	Def., Eq. 58. Base Period=1952:1, Value=278.7, Fixed Assets table 1.2, line 15. Dep. Rate = DELD
KH	Def., Eq. 59. Base Period=1952:1, Value=2598.6, Fixed Assets table 1.2, line 8. Dep. Rate=DELH
KK	Def., Eq. 92. Base Period=1952:1, Value=2619.7, Fixed Asset table 1.2, line 4. Dep. Rate=DELK
KKMIN	Def., Eq. 93
L1	CL1+AF1
L2	CL2+AF2
L3	Def., Eq. 86
LAM	Computed from peak-to-peak interpolation of $\log[Y/(JF \cdot HF)]$. Peak quarters are 1955:2, 1963:3, 1966:1, 1973:1, 1992.4, 2010.4, and 2023.2.
LM	Def., Eq. 85
M1	Def., Eq. 81. Base Period=1971:4, Value=240.964
MB	Def., Eq. 71. Also sum of -NIDDLCB1-NIDDLCB2-NIDDLCB3-NIDDLZ2+CDDCFS-CDDCCA. Base Period=1971:4, Value=-197.969
MDIF	CDDCFS-MAILFLT1
MF	Sum of CDDCF+MAILFLT1+MAILFLT2+CDDCNN+MAILFLT3, Base Period=1971:4, Value=84.075
MG	Sum of CDDCUS+CDDCCA-NIDDLRMA-NIDDLGMA-NIDDLCMA, Base Period=1971:4, Value=10.526
MGQ	MG/*GDPD*
MH	Sum of CDDCH1. Base Period = 1971:4, Value = 132.050
MHQ	MH/*GDPD*
MR	Sum of CDDCR. Base Period = 1971:4, Value = 12.725
MRQ	MR/*GDPD*
MS	Sum of CDDCS. Base Period = 1971:4, Value = 12.114
MSQ	MS/*GDPD*
MUH	Peak-to-peak interpolation of Y/KK. Peak quarters are 1953:2, 1955:3, 1959:2, 1962:3, 1965:4, 1969:1, 1973:1, 1977:3, 1981:1, 1984:2, 1988:4, 1993:4, 1998:1, 2006:1, 2019:1. Flat beginning.
NICD	NICD
NNF	NNF
NNG	NNG
NNH	NNH
NNR	NNR
NNS	NNS
PCD	CDZ/CD
PCGDPD	Def., Eq. 122

Table A.7
(continued)

Variable	Construction (raw data variables on the right-hand side)
PCGDPR	Def., Eq. 123
*PCM*1	Def., Eq. 124
PCN	CNZ/CN
PCS	CSZ/CS
PD	Def., Eq. 33
PEX	EXZ/EX
PF	Def., Eq. 31
PFA	FAZ/FA
PG	(PURGZ-PROGZ)/(PURG-PROG)
PH	Def., Eq. 34
PIEF	Def., Eq. 67, or PIEF1X
PIEFRET	PIEFRET
PIH	IHZ/IH
PIK	IKZ/IK
PIM	IMZ/IM
PIV	IVZ/IV, with the following adjustments: 1954:4 = .2382, 1959:3 = .2084, 1970:1 = .2399, 1971:4 = .2386, 1975:3 = .3634, 1975:4 = .3634, 1983:2 = .6142, 1983:3 = .6142, 1986:4 = .5842, 1987:3 = .6306, 1992:1 = .7708, 1993:3 = .7399, 1995:3 = .7867, 1995:4 = .7867, 1996:1 = .7867, 1997:1 = .6830, 2001:2 = .6578, 2002:1 = .6629, 2003:3 = .7461, 2005:2 = .8539, 2005:3 = .8539, 2008:1 = .8290, 2010:1 = 1.0097, 2011.3 = .9457, 2016.3 =1.0832, 2017.1 = 1.0653, 2018.2 = .7584, 2019.4 = 1.0255, 2020.1 =1.0255, 2020.4 = 1.1146, 2022.3 = 1.22524, 2023.1 = 1.1853, 2023.2 = 1.1853
PKH	REALEST/KH
POP	POP
*POP*1	POP1
*POP*2	POP2
*POP*3	POP-POP1-POP2
PROD	Def., Eq. 118
PS	(PURSZ-PROSZ)/(PURS-PROS)
*PSI*1	Def., Eq. 32
*PSI*2	Def., Eq. 35
*PSI*3	Def., Eq. 36
*PSI*4	Def., Eq. 37
*PSI*5	Def., Eq. 38
*PSI*6	Def., Eq. 39
*PSI*7	Def., Eq. 40
*PSI*8	Def., Eq. 41
*PSI*9	Def., Eq. 42

Table A.7
(continued)

Variable	Construction (raw data variables on the right-hand side)
*PSI*10	Def., Eq. 44
*PSI*11	Def., Eq. 45
*PSI*12	Def., Eq. 46
*PSI*13	(PROG+PROS)/(250(JGH+JSH+JMH))
*PSI*14	Def., Eq. 55
*PSI*15	Def., Eq. 56
PUG	Def., Eq. 104 or PURGZ
PUS	Def., Eq. 110 or PURSZ
PX	(CDZ+CNZ+CSZ+IHZ+IKZ+PURGZ-PROGZ+PURSZ-PROSZ+EXZ-IMZ-IBTG-IBTS)/ (CD+CN+CS+IH+IK+PURG-PROG+PURS-PROS+EX-IM)
Q	Sum of CGLDFXUS+CGLDFXMA-CSDRUS. Base Period=1971:4, Value=13.985
QQ	Q/*GDPD*
RB	RB
RECG	Def., Eq. 105
RECS	Def., Eq. 112
RM	RM
RMA	Def., Eq. 128
RNT	RNT
RNTQ	RNT/*GDPD*
RS	RS
RSA	Def., Eq. 127
SB	Def., Eq. 72
SF	Def., Eq. 69
SG	Def., Eq. 76
SGP	Def., Eq. 107
SH	Def., Eq. 65
SHRPIE	Def., Eq. 121
SIFG	SIFG
SIFS	SIFS
SIG	SIG
SIGG	SIGG
SIHG	SIHG
SIHS	SIHS
SIS	SIS
SISS	SISS
SR	Def., Eq. 74
SRZ	Def., Eq. 116
SS	Def., Eq. 78

Table A.7
(continued)

Variable	Construction (raw data variables on the right-hand side)
SSP	Def., Eq. 114
STAT	STAT
STATP	Def., Eq. 83
SUBG	SUBSG - SURPG
SUBS	SUBSS - SURPS
T	1 in 1952:1, 2 in 1952:2, etc.
TBL2	Time-varying time trend. See text.
TBG	TBG
TBGQ	TBG/*GDPD*
TBS	TBS
TCG	TCG
TCS	TCS
TFG	Def., Eq. 102
TFR	TTRFR - TRFR
TFS	Def., Eq. 108
*TF*1	TCBN
*THETA*1	PFA/*GDPD*
*THETA*2	CDH/(PCD·CD)
*THETA*3	NICD/(PCD·CD)
*THETA*4	PIEFRET/PIEF
THG	THG
THS	THS
TRFG	TRFG
TRFH	TRFH
TRFR	TRFR
TRFS	TRFS
TRG	TRG
TRGH	TRGHPAY - TRHG - UB
TRGHQ	TRGH/*GDPD*
TRGR	TRGR1 + TRGR2 - TRG - TRRG1
TRGS	TRGS
TRGSQ	TRGS/*GDPD*
TRHR	TRHR
TRRS	TRRS
TRSH	TRRSHPAY-TRHS
TRSHQ	TRSH/*GDPD*
TTRRF	TTRRF
U	(CE+U)-CE

Table A.7
(continued)

Variable	Construction (raw data variables on the right-hand side)
UB	UB
UR	Def., Eq. 87
USOTHER	Def., Eq. 57
USROW	FIUS-FIROW
V	Def., Eq. 117. Base Period = 1996:4, Value = 1781.1, table 5.8.6A
WA	Def., Eq. 126
WF	WF=[COMPT-PROGZ-PROSZ-(SIT-SIGG-SISS) +PRI]/[(JT-JG-JS-JM)(((JTH-JGH-JSH-JMH)/(JT-JG-JS-JM))·(1000/4)+.5HO)]
WG	(PROGZ-COMPMIL)/(250(JGH))
WH	Def., Eq. 43
WM	COMPMIL/(250(JMH))
WR	Def., Eq. 119
WS	PROSZ/(250(JSH))
X	Def., Eq. 60
XX	Def., Eq. 61
Y	Def., Eq. 63
YD	Def., Eq. 115
YS	Computed from peak-to-peak interpolation of log *Y*. Peak quarters are 1953:2, 1966:1, 1973:2, 1999:4, 2006:4, and 2023.2.
YT	Def., Eq. 64

• The variables in the first column are the variables in the model. They are defined by the identities in table A.3 or by the raw data variables in table A.5. A right-hand side variable in this table is a raw data variable unless it is in italics, in which case it is a variable in the model. Sometimes the same letters are used for both a variable in the model and a raw data variable.

Notes

1 Why This Book?

1. See Fair and Taylor (1983, 1990).

2 Macro Data

1. See Fair (2020) for more details.

3 The Econometrics

1. This rule of thumb is discussed in Fisher (1965).

2. See, for example, Stock and Watson (1998).

3. The original discussion is in Fair and Dominguez (1991).

4 Specification and Estimation of the US Model

1. Some specifications take u^* to be time varying.

2. "Price level" will be used to describe p even though p is actually the log of the price level.

3. Note that if u^* follows a linear time trend, this will be picked up by the inclusion of t in the equation.

4. Note that there is a large change in the estimate of the coefficient of the time trend when π_{t-1} and p_{t-1} are added. The time trend is serving a similar role in this equation as the constant term is in equation (4.6).

5. Because the equations are linear, it does not matter what values are used for *PIM* and t as long as the same values for each are used for both simulations. Similarly, it does not matter what values are used for *UR* as long as each value for the second simulation is one percentage point higher than the corresponding value for the base simulation. Also, unless *UR* is exactly at the NAIRU, the base simulation for equation

(4.6) will either have an accelerating or decelerating inflation and price path. The computed differences in this case are differences from the accelerating or decelerating path. For equation (4.6) with π_{t-1} added, the base simulation will have an accelerating or decelerating price path. For this reason results are presented in table 4.5 only out 120 quarters.

6. These weights were chosen after some experimentation. The results are not sensitive to slightly different choices.

7. Paul Volcker was chair of the Fed between 1979.3 and 1987.2, but the period in question is only 1979.4–1982.3.

8. I can remember when William Miller was chair of the Fed in 1978 and he visited Yale. There was a lunch at Mory's with Jim Tobin, William Brainard, me, and a number of others. I had recently finished my estimated Fed rule, and I gave Miller an envelope that I said predicted what he would do in the next year! Unfortunately, I don't have any records of how accurate this was.

7 Exogenous Variables

1. Each year, I give one of my classes an assignment to explain the quarterly log change in the S&P 500 index since 1954 using any set of macro variables they want. Nothing sensible is ever found. There may be some explanatory power in predicting future stock prices or stock returns at long horizons. See, for example, Greenwood and Shleifer (2014) and references therein. The lack of explanatory power at quarterly frequencies is what is relevant for a model like the US model.

9 Size of Wealth Effects

1. No attempt was made in the present study to estimate asymmetrical effects. It is unlikely using aggregate data that any such effects could be estimated even if they exist.

11 Changes in Fed's Behavior Since 2008

1. Part of the low inflation during subperiod E can be explained by *PIM*. Between the fourth quarter of 2012 and the fourth quarter of 2017, *PIM* fell by 9.9 percent, an annual rate of −2.1 percent. (Note that *PIM* is an important variable in equation 10.) In other words, there were favorable cost shocks during this period.

12 Effects of Inflation Shocks

1. Note that this is a shock to the price equation, not to the wage equation. If the shock were instead to the wage equation, there would be an initial rise in the real wage, which would have much different effects.

2. Private correspondence with Andrew Levin and David Reifschneider.

13 Size of Government Spending Multipliers

1. These draws are actually unnecessary. One can instead use the originally drawn errors for the 2016.1–2019.4 period.

2. Commercial forecasting models like the ones used by the CBO (2010) and Romer and Bernstein (2009) are not in the academic literature, and so it is hard to evaluate them. It does not appear, however, that the structural equations in these models are consistently estimated.

3. Barro and Redlick (2011) also estimate a tax multiplier.

15 Explaining Contractions and Expansions

1. The coefficient estimates, however, are the ones estimated through 2023.2, the ones in Tables A1 through A30.

2. The actual percentage change in the GDP deflator over the 5 quarters is 7.1 percent, and the predicted change is 7.9 percent.

16 Models with Rational Expectations

1. The material in this subsection is taken from Fair (1993).

2. There is a possibly confusing statement in Cumby, Huizinga, and Obstfeld (1983), p. 341, regarding the movement of the instrument set backward in time. The instrument set must be moved backward in time as the order of the autoregressive process increases. It need not be moved backward as the order of the moving average process increases due to an increase in j.

3. The estimator that is based on the minimization of (16.19) is also the 2S2SLS estimator of Cumby, Huizinga, and Obstfeld (1983).

4. Some of the discussion in this subsection is taken from Fair and Taylor (1990).

5. Guessed values are usually taken to be the actual values if the solution is within the period for which data exist. Otherwise, the last observed value of a variable can be used for the future values or the variable can be extrapolated in some simple way. Sometimes, information on the steady-state solution (if there is one) can be used to help form the guesses.

6. The material in Fair and Taylor (1983) is also presented in Fair (1984), chapter 11, and so the corrections discussed in this subsection pertain to both sources.

7. These are again estimates of the structural error terms, not the reduced-form error terms. Step (iii) on page 1176 in Fair and Taylor (1983) is in error in this respect. The errors computed in step (iii) should be the structural error terms.

8. Some of the discussion in this subsection is also taken from Fair and Taylor (1990).

9. Note that these solutions of the error term ϵ_{it} are only approximations when f_i is nonlinear. Hence, the method gives an approximation of the likelihood function.

10. In the notation presented in Subsection 2.3.1, k rather than K is used to denote the dimension of α. K, however, is used in this subsection for the dimension of α since k has already been used in the description of the EP method.

11. Derivatives computed this way are "one sided." "Two-sided" derivatives would require extra K solutions, where each coefficient would be both increased and decreased by the given percentage. For the work here, two-sided derivatives seemed unnecessary. For the results below, each coefficient was increased by five percent from its base value when computing the derivatives. Five percent seemed to give slightly better results than one percent, although no systematic procedure of trying to find the optimal percentage size was undertaken.

12. Some of the discussion in this subsection is also taken from Fair and Taylor (1990).

13. In principle, one could reestimate the model to get coefficients rather than draw from $N(\hat{\alpha}, \hat{V}_4)$, as discussed in section 8.2, but in practice this is unlikely to be computationally feasible.

14. It may also be that the actual value of x_s differs from what the agent expected it to be at the end of $s-1$.

Appendix

1. See Young (1992) and Triplett (1992) for good discussions of the chain-type weights.

References

Amemiya, T. (1977). The maximum likelihood and the nonlinear three-stage least squares estimator in the general nonlinear simultaneous equations model. *Econometrica, 45*, 955–968.

Andrews, D. W. K. (2003). End-of-sample instability tests. *Econometrica, 71*, 1661–1694.

Andrews, D. W. K., & Fair, R. C. (1988). Inference in nonlinear econometric models with structural change. *Review of Economic Studies, 55*(4), 615–640.

Angeletos, G-M., Collard, F., & Dellas, H. (2020). Business-cycle anatomy. *American Economic Review, 110*, 3030–3070.

Auerbach, A. J., & Gorodnichenko, Y. (2012). Measuring the output responses to fiscal policy. *American Economic Review: Economic Policy, 4*, 1–27.

Barro, R. J., & Redlick, C. J. (2011). Macroeconomic effects from government purchases and taxes. *Quarterly Journal of Economics, 126*, 51–102.

Blanchard, O. (2019). Public debt and low interest rates. *American Economic Review, 109*, 1197–1229.

Blinder, A. S. (1981). "Retail inventory behavior and business fluctuations." Brookings Papers on Economic Activity, no. 2, 443–505.

Brumm, J., Feng, X., Kotlikoff, L. J., & Kubler, F. (2021). "When interest rates go low, should public debt go high?" NBER Working Paper, no. 28951, June.

Caballero, R. J., Farhi, E., & Gourinchas, P-O. (2017). Rents, technical change, and risk premia: Accounting for secular trends in interest rates, returns on capital, earning yields, and factor shares. *American Economic Review: Papers and Proceedings, 107*, 614–620.

Candia, B., Coibion, O., & Goroodnichenko, Y. (2021). "The inflation expectations of U.S. firms: Evidence from a new survey." NBER Working Paper, no. 28836, May.

Carroll, C., Slacalek, J., & Sommer, M. (2013). "Dissecting saving dynamics: Measuring wealth, precautionary and credit effects." CFS Working Paper Series 2012/10.

Case, K. E., Quigley, J. M., & Shiller, R. J. (2012). "Wealth effects revisited 1975–2012." Cowles Foundation Discussion Paper no. 1884, December.

Christian, J. W. (1968). A further analysis of the objectives of American monetary policy. *Journal of Finance, 23*, 465–477.

Clarida, R., Galí, J., & Gertler, M. (1999). The science of monetary policy: A new Keynesian perspective. *Journal of Economic Literature, 37*, 1661–1707.

Clarida, R., Galí, J., & Gertler, M. (2000). Monetary policy rules and macroeconomic stability: Evidence and some theory. *Quarterly Journal of Economics, 115*, 147–180.

Coenen, G., Erceg, C. J., Freedman, C., et al. (2012). Effects of fiscal stimulus in structural models. *American Economic Journal: Macroeconomics, 4*, 22–68.

Coibion, O., Goroodnichenko, Y., Kumar, S., & Pedemonte, M. (2020). Inflation expectations—a policy tool? *Journal of International Economics, 124*(Issue C).

Congressional Budget Office. (2010). "Estimated impact of the American Recovery and Reinvestment Act on employment and economic output from October 2009 through December (2009)." February.

Cumby, R. E., Huizinga, J., & Obstfeld, M. (1983). Two-step two-stage least squares estimation in models with rational expectations. *Journal of Econometrics, 21*, 333–355.

D'Acunto, F., Malmendier, U., & Weber, M. (2022). "What do the data tell us about inflation expectations?" CESifo Working Paper, no. 9602.

DeLong, J. B., & Summers, L. H. (1988). Is increased price flexibility stabilizing? *The American Economic Review, 78*, 1031–1043.

DeLong, J. B., & Summers, L. H. (2012). "Fiscal policy in a depressed economy." Brookings Papers on Economic Activity, March 20.

Dewald, W. G., & Johnson, H. G. (1963). "An objective analysis of the objectives of American monetary policy, 1952–61." In D. Carson (Ed.), *Banking and monetary studies* (pp. 171–189). Richard D. Irwin.

Fair, R. C. (1969). *The short-run demand for workers and hours*. North-Holland Publishing Co.

Fair, R. C. (1978). The sensitivity of fiscal policy effects to assumptions about the behavior of the Federal Reserve. *Econometrica, 46*, 1165–1179.

Fair, R. C. (1979). An analysis of a macro-econometric model with rational expectations in the bond and stock markets. *American Economic Review, 69*(4), 539–552.

Fair, R. C. (1984). *Specification, estimation and analysis of macroeconometric models.* Harvard University Press.

Fair, R. C. (1985). Excess labor and the business cycle. *American Economic Review, 75,* 239–245.

Fair, R. C. (1989). The production smoothing model is alive and well. *Journal of Monetary Economics, 23,* 353–370.

Fair, R. C. (1993). Testing the rational expectations hypothesis in macroeconometric models. *Oxford Economic Papers, 45,* 169–190.

Fair, R. C. (2004). Testing for a new economy in the 1990s. *Business Economics,* 43–53.

Fair, R. C. (2010). Estimated macroeconomic effects of the U.S. Stimulus Bill. *Contemporary Economic Policy, 28,* 439–452.

Fair, R. C. (2012). Analyzing macroeconomic forecastability. *Journal of Forecasting, 31*(2), 99–108.

Fair, R. C. (2017). Household wealth and macroeconomic activity: 2008–2013. *Journal of Money, Credit and Banking, 49,* 495–523.

Fair, R. C. (2018a). Explaining the slow U.S. recovery: 2010–2017. *Business Economics,* 184–194.

Fair, R. C. (2018b). Macroeconometric Modeling: 2018. fairmodel.econ.yale.edu /mmm2/mm2018.pdf.

Fair, R. C. (2020). Variable mismeasurement in a class of DSGE models: Comment. *Journal of Macroeconomics,* 66, December.

Fair, R. C., & Parke, W. R. (1980). Full-information estimates of a nonlinear macroeconometric model. *Journal of Econometrics, 13,* 269–291.

Fair, R. C., & Dominguez, K. M. (1991). Effects of the Changing U.S. Age Distribution on Macroeconomic Equations. *American Economic Review, 81,* 1276–1294.

Fair, R. C., & Taylor, J. B. (1983). Solution and maximum likelihood estimation of dynamic rational expectations models. *Econometrica, 51,* 1169–1185.

Fair, R. C., & Taylor, J. B. (1990). Full information estimation and stochastic simulation of models with rational expectations. *Journal of Applied Econometrics, 5,* 381–392.

Fay, J. A., & Medoff, J. L. (1985). Labor and output over the business cycle: Some direct evidence. *American Economic Review, 75,* 638–655.

Federal Reserve Board. (2000). "FRB/US equation documentation for the VAR-based expectations version of the model."

Fisher, F. M. (1965). "Dynamic structure and estimation in economy-wide econometric models." In J. S. Duesenberry, G. Fromm, L. R. Klein, & E. Kuh (Eds.). *The Brookings Quarterly econometric model of the United States*. North-Holland.

Fuhrer, J. C. (1997). The (un)importance of forward-looking behavior in price specifications. *Journal of Money, Credit and Banking, 29*, 338–350.

Gilchrist, S., & Zakrajšek, E. (2012). Credit spreads and business cycle fluctuations. *American Economic Review, 102*, 1692–1720.

Gourinchas, P-O. (2017). Discussion of "Are low real interest rates here to stay?" *International Journal of Central Banking, 13*, 43–53.

Greenwood, R., & Shiefer, A. (2014). Expectations of returns and expected returns. *Review of Financial Studies, 27*, 714–746.

Haavelmo, T. (1944). The probability approach in econometrics. *Econometrica, 12*, (Suppl), 1–118.

Hall, R. E. (2009). "By how much does GDP rise if the government buys more output?" *Brookings Papers on Economic Activity*, Fall, 183–231.

Hamilton, J. D. (1983). Oil and the macroeconomy since World War II. *Journal of Political Economy, 91*, 228–248.

Hamilton, J. D. (2009). "Causes and consequences of the oil shock of 2007–08." *Brookings Papers on Economic Activity*, Spring, 215–261.

Hansen, L. P. (1982). Large sample properties of generalized method of moments estimators. *Econometrica, 50*, 1029–1054.

Heckman, J. J. (2000). Causal parameters and policy analysis in economics: A twentieth century retrospective. *Quarterly Journal of Economics, 115*, 45–97.

Hendry, D. F., Pagan, A. R., & Sargan, J. D. (1984). "Dynamic specifications." In Z. Griliches & M. D. Intriligator (Eds.). *Handbook of econometrics* (pp. 1023–1100). North-Holland.

Jorgenson, D. W., & Laffont, J-J. (1974). Efficient estimation of nonlinear systems of simultaneous equations with additive disturbances. *Annals of Economic and Social Measurement, 3*, 615–640.

Judd, J. P., & Rudebusch, G. D. (1998). Taylor's Rule and the Fed: 1970–1997. *FRBSF Economic Review, 3*, 3–16.

Kehoe, P. J., Lopez, P. Midrigan, V., & Pastorino, E. (2020). "Credit frictions in the Great Recession." NBER Working Paper 28201, December, National Bureau of Economic Research.

Khoury, S. S. (1990). "The Federal Reserve reaction function: A specification search." In T. Mayer (Ed.). *The Political Economy of American Monetary Policy* (pp. 27–490). Cambridge University Press.

King, S. K. (1988). Is increased price flexibility stabilizing? *American Economic Review, 78*, 267–272.

Kydland, F. E., & Prescott, E. C. (1982). Time to build and aggregate fluctuations. *Econometrica, 50*, 1342–1370.

Laubach, T., & Williams, J. C. (2003). Measuring the natural rate of interest. *Review of Economics and Statistics, 85*, 1063–1070.

Lucas, R. E., Jr. (1976). "Econometric policy evaluation: A critique." In K. Brunner & A. H. Meltzer (Eds.). *The Phillips curve and labor markets*. North-Holland.

Ludvigson, S., & Steindel, C. (1999). How important is the stock market effect on consumption. *Economic Policy Review, 5*, 29–51.

Mankiw, N. G. (2022). "Government debt and capital accumulation in an era of low interest rates." NBER Working Paper, no. 3024, May.

Marschak, J. (1953). "Economic measurement for policy and prediction." In W. Hood & T. Koopmans (Eds.), *Studies in econometric method* (pp. 1–26). John Wiley.

McCallum, B. T. (1976). Rational expectations and the natural rate hypothesis: Some consistent results. *Econometrica, 44*, 43–52.

McKay, A., & Reis, R. (2008). The brevity and violence of contractions and expansions. *Journal of Monetary Economics, 55*, 738–751.

McNees, S. K. (1986). Modeling the Fed: A forward-looking monetary policy reaction function. *New England Economic Review*, November/December, 3–8.

McNees, S. K. (1992). A forward-looking monetary policy reaction function: Continuity and change. *New England Economic Review*, November/December, 3–13.

Mian, A., Rao, K., & Sufi, A. (2013). Household balance sheets, consumption and the economic slump. *Quarterly Journal of Economics, 128*(4), 1687–1726.

Mian, A., & Sufi, A. (2015). House of debt: *How they (and you) caused the Great Recession and how we can prevent it from happening again*. University of Chicago Press.

Mitchell, W. C. (1927). *Business cycles: The problem and its setting*. National Bureau of Economic Research.

Okun, A. M. (1971). "The personal tax surcharge and consumer demand, 1968–70." Brookings Papers on Economic Activity, *1*, 167–204.

Parke, W. R. (1982). An algorithm for FIML and 3SLS estimation of large nonlinear models. *Econometrica, 50*, 81–96.

Poole, W. (1976). "Rational expectations in the macro model." Brookings Papers on Economic Activity, *2*, 463–505.

Rachel, L., & Smith, T. D. (2017). Are low real interest rates here to stay? *International Journal of Central Banking, 13*, 1–42.

Ramey, V. A. (2011). Can government purchases stimulate the economy? *Journal of Economic Literature, 49*, 673–685.

Reifschneider, D., Tetlow, R., & Williams, J. (1999). "Aggregate disturbances, monetary policy, and the macroeconomy: The FRB/US perspective." *Federal Reserve Bulletin*, January, 1–19.

Romer, C. D., & Bernstein, J. (2009). "The job impact of the American Recovery and Reinvestment Plan." Council of Economic Advisers, January 10.

Romer, C. D., & Romer, D. H. (2010). The Macroeconomic effects of tax changes: Estimates based on a new measure of fiscal shocks. *American Economic Review, 100*, 763–801.

Romer, D. (2000). Keynesian macroeconomics without the LM curve. *Journal of Economic Perspectives, 14*, 149–169.

Rossi, B. (2021). Forecasting in the presence of instabilities: How we know whether models predict well and how to improve them. *Journal of Economic Literature, 59*, 1138–1190.

Savignac, F., Gautier, E., Gorodnichenko, Y., & Coibion, O. (2021). "Firms' inflation expectations: New evidence from France." NBER Working Paper, no. 29376, October.

Smets, F., & Wouters, R. (2007). Shocks and frictions in US business cycles: A Bayesian DSGE approach. *American Economic Review, 97*, 586–606.

Starr-McCluer, M. (1998). "Stock market wealth and consumer spending." Board of Governors of the Federal Reserve System.

Stock, J. H., & Watson, M. W. (1998). Median unbiased estimation of coefficient variance in a time-varying parameter model. *Journal of the American Statistical Association, 93*, 349–358.

Svensson, L. E. O. (2003). What is wrong with Taylor rules? Using judgement in monetary policy through targeting rules. *Journal of Economic Literature, 41*, 426–477.

Summers, L. H. (2020). Accepting the reality of secular stagnation. *Finance and Development, 57*(1), 17–19.

Taylor, J. B. (1993). Discretion versus policy rules in practice. *Carnegie Rochester Series on Public Policy, 39*, 195–214.

Taylor, J. B. (1999a). "A historical analysis of monetary policy rules." In J. B. Taylor (Ed.), *Monetary policy rules* (319–341). University of Chicago Press.

Taylor, J. B. (1999b). "Introduction." In J. B. Taylor (Ed.), *Monetary policy rules* (1–14). University of Chicago Press.

Taylor, J. B. (1999c). *Monetary policy rules*. University of Chicago Press.

Taylor, J. B., & Uhlig H. (1990). Solving nonlinear stochastic growth models: A comparison of alternative solution methods. *Journal of Business and Economic Statistics, 8*, 1–21.

Tinbergen, J. (1939). *Statistical testing of business-cycle theories. Part II: Business cycles in the United States of America*, 1919–1932. League of Nations.

Triplett, J. E. (1992). Economic theory and BEA's alternative quantity and price indexes. *Survey of Current Business, 72*, 49–52.

Wicksell, K. (1936). *Interest and prices*. Macmillian.

Young, A. H. (1992). Alternative measures of change in real output and prices. *Survey of Current Business, 72*, 32–48.

Zhou, X., & Carroll, C. D. (2012). Dynamics of wealth and consumption: New and improved measures for U.S. states. *The B.E. Journal of Macroeconomics, 12*(2), (Advances), Article 4.

Index

Note: Page numbers followed by f indicate figures, and page numbers followed by t indicate tables.